POLLING AND PUBLIC OPINI
A CANADIAN PERSPECTIVE

The importance of public opinion polls is widely recognized today. Indeed, in addition to their primary purpose of collecting and disseminating data about public opinion on issues and events, polls have also become a poweful medium for communicating ideas and beliefs, especially in light of declining public participation in community organizations and interest groups.

In *Polling and Public Opinion* Peter M. Butler examines the impact that polls have on the thoughts and behaviour of the public. He considers the power of public opinion polls as an element of mass persuasion in media stories, advertising, and government policy. Using such controversial issues such as free trade, health care, same-sex marriage, and national security, Butler argues that popular opinion on such hot-button topics as these can be guided and changed according to how polls are interpreted for and presented to the public. As well as analysing the impact of polls on the public, Butler is concerned with demystifying the methods by which opinions are collected, showing that the techniques used to determine public opinion can be just as selective as those by which the results are disseminated.

Focusing on many of the vital issues of our time, *Polling and Public Opinion* is an in-depth look at the rise of one of the most important but least understood methods by which politicians and governments gauge the popular will.

PETER M. BUTLER is an associate professor in the Department of Sociology and Social Anthropology at Dalhousie University, and has worked as a research consultant with national public opinion research firms.

PETER M. BUTLER

# Polling and Public Opinion

## A Canadian Perspective

Foreword by Michael Adams

UNIVERSITY OF TORONTO PRESS
Toronto Buffalo London

© University of Toronto Press Incorporated 2007
Toronto Buffalo London
Printed in Canada

ISBN 978-0-8020-3899-9 (cloth)
ISBN 978-0-8020-3819-7 (paper)

Printed on acid-free paper

**Library and Archives Canada Cataloguing in Publication**

Butler, Peter Marshall
  Polling and public opinion : a Canadian perspective / Peter M. Butler.

  Includes bibliographical references and index.
  ISBN 978-0-8020-3899-9 (bound)
  ISBN 978-0-8020-3819-7 (pbk.)

  1. Public opinion – Canada – Textbooks.   2. Public opinion polls –
Textbooks.   I. Title.

HN103.5.B88 2007      303.3'80971      C2006-906664-7

University of Toronto Press acknowledges the financial assistance
to its publishing program of the Canada Council for the Arts and the
Ontario Arts Council.


University of Toronto Press acknowledges the financial support for
its publishing activities of the Government of Canada through the
Book Publishing Industry Development Program (BPIDP).

*Dedicated to the memory of my parents*

# Contents

# Foreword

MICHAEL ADAMS

Canadians read about polls in the news media almost every day. Hearing about the aggregated opinions of our fellow citizens has become as familiar to us as reading the views of our favourite columnists or skimming over advertisements to get to the news stories that interest us. In our information-saturated world, the availability of public opinion data seems altogether unremarkable. Some even complain of poll fatigue, fretting that we know too much about what our fellow citizens think – perhaps to the detriment of the coherence and resolve of our own opinions. Although polling is ubiquitous today, the art and science of public opinion research were much less familiar in Canada a generation ago and all but unheard of in the decades before that. The ideas, methods, approaches, and findings Peter Butler describes in this book evolved largely over the latter two-thirds of the twentieth century. For students of our evolving democracy, the development of public opinion research as an increasingly important medium in our political culture has been fascinating to watch. I first became interested in public opinion polling while reading Theodore White's *The Making of the President*. In that book, White wrote in glowing terms of pollster Louis Harris's role in Kennedy's campaign. A pollster at the round table of John F. Kennedy's Camelot: how romantic.

I read the book in 1962, about the time that I, a high school student in Toronto's Rexdale, became interested in Canadian history and government. Although American politics seemed much more exciting than the shenanigans being perpetrated by a bunch of old men in Ottawa, Canada nevertheless was an object of fascination to me. The Russians were attempting to arm Cuba with nuclear missiles while we were debating whether or not to live up to an agreement to arm our Bomarcs. What the

Americans were doing seemed consequential; what Canadian politicians were debating seemed in comparison almost comical.

Even so, I got hooked on Canadian politics and the art, science, and romance of public opinion polling. When it came time to choose a university, I picked Queen's partly because the political studies department there was led by a professor named John Meisel who believed that public opinion research had something to contribute to the science of politics. This was rather revolutionary as political studies in Canada at the time seemed, to me at least, more a branch of the study of history or jurisprudence. The notion that the views of average citizens were relevant was novel because Canadian politics was generally characterized as an exercise in accommodation among Canada's various elites.

Canada's rulers were male, white, middle class, and very often lawyers. Their ancestors came from Europe. The tradition of brokering regional, linguistic, and ethnic interests was what brought Canada East (Quebec/formerly Lower Canada) and Canada West (Ontario/formerly Upper Canada) together in the 1840s and that imperative was also what enticed two other British colonies (Nova Scotia and New Brunswick) into confederation in 1867.

That existential political necessity, elites cutting deals, was what continued to keep the country together. 'Muddling through' was a less polite description of how Canada's leaders kept the federation intact. This muddling gave rise to a certain spirit of compromise and equivocation, and so we find Canada's longest serving prime minister, William Lyon Mackenzie King, faced with a classic Canadian political dilemma during World War II, saying, 'Conscription if necessary, but not necessarily conscription.' This little Canadian chiasmus falls somewhat short of American revolutionary Patrick Henry's clarion declaration 'Give me liberty or give me death.'

The story of Canada, throughout its history of elite accommodation, was that of a shy, unassuming anti-revolutionary people ever deferential to their political masters. Canadians, it was known, voted for the party of their fathers and grandfathers, hoping someone in the family would receive a patronage job as a reward for party loyalty. Consequently, students of political studies spent as much time poring over the decisions of the Judicial Committee of the Privy Council (JCPC) in London and comparative federal systems of government as they did studying the reasons French Canadians and Catholics voted Liberal and English-speaking Canadians and Protestants voted Conservative. We read textbooks with titles like *How We Are Governed* (not *How We Govern!*).

But all this seemed to change in the 1950s when prairie firebrand John Diefenbaker stormed into office, even capturing 50 of Quebec's 75 seats in his 1958 election sweep, which gave his Progressive Conservative Party its first majority since 1930. Canadian voters were proving to be interesting – even, to use a word that has become a cliché in modern political analysis, 'volatile!'

The country's history since 1960 has proven anything but boring. After Diefenbaker's sweep and subsequent implosion we were treated to bursts of nationalism and then separatism in Quebec. We saw the patriation of the constitution in 1982, enshrining in our new basic law a charter of rights and freedoms. In one of the country's most exciting and important elections, we witnessed an historic free trade agreement negotiated by a party (the Conservatives) that had previously fought (and won) elections opposing trade agreements with the United States.

A constitutional agreement (the Meech Lake Accord), negotiated in the old elite accommodation/brokerage style among the prime minister and the premiers, failed for lack of support among the provinces in 1990. This was followed in 1992 by the defeat of the Charlotte-town Agreement, Canada's first and so far only national referendum on a constitutional proposal – a referendum granted the public because then prime minister Brian Mulroney understood that Canadians had evolved from their status as *de facto* subjects and had become grown-up citizens.

What was remarkable about both Meech and Charlottetown was that they were negotiated and drafted, as was the case with the patriation process in 1981–82, entirely by middle-class males of European descent who by the late 1980s represented maybe one in five eligible voters. No girls allowed, as the clubhouse doors used to say – let alone people whose ancestors may have hailed from other continents.

So how did the other eight in ten have their say? In two ways. First, pollsters told Canadians what they and their fellow citizens thought about Meech and Charlottetown. Those polls included random samples of women, who were then 50.7 per cent of the population, Canada's silent or silenced majority. They also included other minorities not represented at the constitutional tables. Not surprisingly to those of us who believe in random samples, the constitutional referendum on Charlottetown reflected more or less what pollsters had been saying about Canadians' stance on the agreement. Charlottetown went down in flames. From the perspective of the eight in ten who comprised Canada's 'minorities,' the failure of Meech and Charlottetown signalled the death of political elitism in Canada. It was everyone's country now and, in the perfectly apt words of journalist Peter C. Newman, Canadians had evolved from deference to defiance.

This climate of socio-political change became the petri dish for the new science of public opinion polling in this country. Pollsters measured the increasing and much heralded volatility of the Canadian electorate, as well as its declining party loyalty and deference to elites. In newspapers and broadcast media, pollsters gave voice to ordinary people. They let Canadians know what other Canadians, including those eight in ten heretofore silent 'minorities' thought. I believe the pollsters and their surveys became a new medium for political expression in this country, assuming some of the sway once held by MPs who had traditionally been the ones bringing constituents' views, gathered in barber shops and at barbecues, to the nation's capitals. To some extent, polling results also displaced the wisdom of editorialists, columnists, and other pundits once charged with telling the nation what it thought; this is one reason why pollsters are both so respected and so resented in this country.

Following John Meisel's lead, academics began applying for and receiving substantial funding from the Social Sciences and Humanities Research Council to study elections not by reading campaign platforms and sifting through newspaper clippings but by analysing scientific surveys of public opinion. York University established the Institute for Survey Research so the academic community could avail itself of first-class survey research methodologies. Political parties imported the likes of the aforementioned Louis Harris and Republican pollster Robert Teeter to help them understand Canadian voters. Liberal strategists even smuggled Louis Harris into Canada in the early 1960s (under a pseudonym) to help the then-opposition Liberals unseat the incumbent Conservatives led by John Diefenbaker, whom President Kennedy loathed. (In 2006, the idea of the Liberal party importing a U.S. pollster to help unseat an anti-American Conservative prime minister sounds like a scenario for the *Air Farce*.)

After Louis Harris left town, indigenous polling talent emerged in this country. First, political anthropologist Martin Goldfarb polled for the Liberals. By 1984, Goldfarb was heralded on the cover of *Saturday Night* magazine as the most influential private citizen in Canada; in that article, Jeffrey Simpson accused the Trudeau government of 'leadership by Goldfarb.' Then a young Carleton university student, Allan Gregg, founded Decima Research with the help of Ronald Reagan's pollster Richard Wirthlin (the Canadian version of Wirthlin's firm, Decision

Making Information, DMI). Decima helped first Joe Clark and then more successfully Brian Mulroney win elections in the late 1970s and 80s. Goldfarb and Gregg were Canada's first 'pollstars,' to use Peter Butler's cute neologism.

With the parties committed to Messrs Goldfarb and Gregg, I found myself turning to the only high-profile outlet for my research left available to me, the media. My firm, Environics, persuaded the *Globe and Mail*'s managing editor, Geoffrey Stevens, to embrace public opinion polling. Thus for the first time in the history of Canada's national newspaper, the *Globe* had a formal relationship with a professional polling firm. Prior to this development and the relationship Winnipeg pollster Angus Reid had forged with the Southam chain of newspapers, the only regular polling to which ordinary Canadians had been exposed was that of the Gallup organization, known in this country as the Canadian Institute for Public Opinion (CIPO). CIPO's early days in Canada are recounted with great flare in Claire Hoy's 1989 book *Margin of Error*.

Hoy tells a wonderful story about Saul Rae (renowned diplomat and father of former Ontario premier Bob Rae). In 1940 as a graduate student at the London School of Economics, Saul Rae had co-authored *The Pulse of Democracy: Public Opinion and How It Works* with polling pioneer George Gallup. Rae later brought Gallup to Canada and, under a code of strict secrecy, helped Mackenzie King's government understand public opinion. Of particular interest were opinions on the explosive issue of conscription during World War II. In those elitist times, politicians would rather admit to visiting a bordello than consulting a public opinion pollster. 'Where are your convictions, man?' the pundits would have screamed. And the opposition would have had a field day grilling the government over wasting the voters' money on polling when reflecting voter opinion was the job of members of parliament.

For nearly four decades, from the mid 1940s to the mid 1980s, the Gallup Poll had been Canada's poll. Their releases were regularly reported in a syndicate of newspapers across the country, which paid a small annual fee of only a few hundred dollars. Gallup made its money by doing omnibus polling for advocacy groups and standard consumer marketing research for commercial clients. In Quebec, the polling firm CROP began doing regular polling for the media, starting in the mid-1960s when nationalism surged and volatility became the norm in Quebec politics. Canadian politics was becoming more interesting too as voters became more unpredictable. At the same time, newspapers' competition for readers' attention was heating up. Managing editors found they could no longer afford to ignore the views of average Canadians, even if the columnists in their employ complained that the man and woman on the street were dull and ill-informed.

So the modern era of public opinion polling really dates from the 1970s and 1980s when political parties, academics, and the media became hooked on polling. And it hasn't changed very much since then, although some of the players have changed places, moving back and forth from partisan polling to media punditry.

Polls, in my view, are a mirror of society. Properly conducted and insightfully interpreted, they do for our country what Dr Freud did for individuals a century ago. They allow for introspection and empathy. Who am I and where do my beliefs and world view fit within the larger context? Knowing which opinions exist in a society and in what proportions is a new sort of information in our evolution as a species. We now have scientific data on what people we will never meet are thinking and feeling, and can take that information into account in making our own decisions. And Canadians have quickly proved adept at using information about their fellow citizens' opinions in adjusting their own opinions and behaviour.

Canadian voters are barraged with polling data during election campaigns and at least some of them use the polls to vote 'strategically' – that is, they vote for their second choice in the hope of stopping another party from winning. Polls showing a possible Conservative government in 2004 and a possible Conservative majority in 2006 convinced some voters to vote for the party best able to stop the Conservatives in those electoral contests. And why not? Some complain about an excess of polling during election campaigns, but why would less information be better than more when we are doing our best to make thoughtful and informed choices as citizens? The idea that Canadians do not know what to do with all the public opinion data generated in advance of election day – that they must be protected from the confusion that might arise from an excess of information or be tempted to jump on a bandwagon or vote strategically – strikes me as condescending, harkening back to the days when Canadians were treated like children by political leaders who thought they knew better than their constituents. The Niagara of numbers pollsters produce, like the figures marshalled by economists and census-takers, reveals empirical realities that inform the workings of democratic societies. Polling makes democratic decision making more rational, more legitimate, more efficient, and ulti-mately more effective.

When we see how people respond to an awareness of the other, we begin to understand the human narrative and how different societies (like species) adapt or fail to adapt, and consequently thrive or fail to thrive. The relatively new science of polling the general public, so often derided by dictators and even democratic elitists like Winston Churchill (quoted amusingly in this book) provides the positive and negative feedback that intelligent systems need if they are to adapt and survive. If we are an intelligent species, one that becomes more democratic and more egalitarian, then we will continue to value the science of polling. Survey techniques will surely change as technology evolves, but what will not change, I hope, is our desire to hear from and understand one another as we negotiate our life together on this small planet.

# Acknowledgments

Many people have made it possible for me to write this book. I wish to acknowledge the unfailing support I have received from the members of the faculty and staff of the Department of Sociology and Social Anthropology at Dalhousie University, especially Emma Whalen who first discussed the idea of polling and moral panic with me, and Mary Morash-Watts and Lori Vaughan who have both seen me through the warm summer days of writing. A grant from the Research Development Fund for the Humanities and Social Sciences at Dalhousie University helped to defray the costs of researching this book and in particular allowed me to retain the services of my graduate assistant, Sandra McRae, who made an invaluable contribution to the final preparation of the manuscript. Thanks also go to the University of Toronto Press, especially to Virgil Duff for his encouragement at all stages of this project but most importantly when I first proposed to undertake it, and to Richard Ratzlaff who ably copy-edited the manuscript and responded enthusiastically to the ideas that I presented.

I wish to thank my friend and distinguished colleague Michael Adams for generously agreeing to lend his name to this book. His work on values communities continues to provide seminal insights for understanding diversity in both Canadian and American societies.

The book has been inspired by the dedication of all the soldiers in all the political wars that I have been part of; I thank them all for the things they have taught me about public opinion.

Lastly, special thanks go to my family, to my wife, Mary, and my sons Marshall and Gregory; each has contributed enormously to my research. Their advice, encouragement, and love have allowed me to finish this book.

# POLLING AND PUBLIC OPINION

# Introduction

Our opinions do not really blossom into fruition until we have expressed them to someone else.

– Mark Twain

Polling and public opinion have occupied a central place in presentations I have made on Canadian society to students at Dalhousie University and when serving as a consultant to political clients. Those who have found some value in the presentations often request that I direct them to literature which would explain the nature of public opinion polling and perhaps show how opinions collected from individuals may be interpreted to reflect the collective thinking of large numbers of people. There are, of course, a variety of good books about public opinion. They are usually focused on the United States and deal with controversial issues that have concerned and sometimes tormented the American people. Many start out by defining what the term 'public opinion' means and are then concerned to show the dynamics of opinion formation and change relative to the political orientations of Americans. There are fewer books which are concerned with the opinions of Canadians; many of these are primarily aimed at explaining voting behaviour. Only recently have books been published which provide in-depth analyses of opinions in Canada, or explore the divergence between opinions expressed by residents of this country and those of our neighbours to the south. There are also several texts on research methods available which explain techniques for conducting polls and surveys. Many of these have a Canadian orientation, but they do not always deal with the problems and challenges of collecting public opinion data, or provide sufficient direction on how to reliably interpret the meaning of that data relative to the issues and events being studied.

Today the importance of polling opinions, particularly on controversial topics, is well recognized. It is sometimes argued that polling has become an important medium for communicating ideas and beliefs in mass societies, especially since many people have become less involved in community organizations and interest groups like churches or trade associations, which have usually provided a focal point for shaping opinions. As already noted, these studies are often identified with politics, involving assessments of the performance of candidates and governments, or are studies of current voting preferences used in election campaigns. However, tracking opinion is by no means limited to politics, since corporations, public servants, and the media also use opinion data to make decisions. In fact, the public as consumers are regularly consulted on matters such as brand preferences, ratings of television shows and films, and impressions of corporations. The power of public opinion even on something as speculative as stockholders' decisions is well illustrated by the behaviour of investors a few years ago. Canadians have not been overly involved in investing in stocks, but the demand for technology brought surprising gains for many investors, which unfortunately did not last. Nevertheless, during the buying frenzy which took place, it was alarming for many to learn that the value of their shares was as likely to be attributed to public opinion, or in this case shareholder confidence, as it was to the business performance of the technology companies whose shares were being traded. Indeed, changing perceptions about the value of investing, and expectations about the opportunity for increasing net worth by holding shares in the technology sector, had much to do with the day-to-day performance of the market.

My purpose in writing this book is to take some of the mystery out of public opinion polling and to provide students of social science as well as other readers a perspective on its influence in determining what we think and how we act. A second objective is to explain, as simply and straightforwardly as possible to those who are untrained in the methods of social science research, the techniques for gathering opinions by conducting polls. I will discuss not only the way opinions are collected, but also how they are measured and interpreted. A third aim of the book is to explore areas other than politics where public opinion research has had noticeable effects on Canadian society. In particular, the discussion will be centred on both *communications* and *social issues* research. The former includes the use of polls by the media and advertisers; the latter describes ways public opinion polls are used to assess the immediacy of problems confronting decision makers.

Chapter 1 considers the social basis of opinion formation and change, arguing that what we think is a product of group life. The first part of the chapter reviews theoretical perspectives on public opinion, surveying some of the best-known social science thinking on the subject. It also introduces a sociological orientation to the study of opinions, proposing the concept of *moral panic* to explain the formation of opinion on several controversial issues in Canadian society. The chapters which follow show that there may be no consistent relationship between a controversial issue and moral panic and yet the publication of polls about an issue and their use by the media may be a cause of moral panic. Chapter 1 also describes the early years of public opinion research and considers the evolution of polling from the first straw polls, which were used to predict election outcomes, to the variety of sophisticated quantitative studies being done today. It concludes by examining the emergence of polling as an industry in Canada.

In Chapter 2 methods of collecting opinions are explained. The kinds of problems public opinion researchers encounter in doing their work are discussed in the context of the choices which are made in adopting one research strategy or another. I also examine the impact of conclusions which are drawn when the numbers from polls are presented. Numbers do not necessarily speak for themselves and pollsters are often responsible for providing direction for decision making; the advice pollsters give is usually presumed to have been drawn from the information produced by their research.

Chapter 3 looks at the relationship between the mass media and public opinion, both in terms of reporting about issues and events as well as providing the basis for a news story. The chapter also explores the use of polling results as political entertainment. Polling results are often featured during election campaigns and are also a prominent element of public affairs programming on radio and television. I consider the power of public opinion polling as an element of mass persuasion, as a means of convincing people to adopt dominant values. I also explore how the use of polling in the advertising industry may alter or reinforce the way we experience life in Canada.

Chapter 4 considers the way public opinion polls are used to shape public policy. Some researchers maintain that public reaction to government policy decisions is a product of the most recently published poll.

This topic is pursued by analysing Canadians' opinions about the controversial public issues of free trade and health care. I explore reactions to these issues in terms of the concept of *moral panic*. I conclude with a consideration of the role of political ideology in identifying the priority given to these public issues, and how they became the symbols of Canadian unity which in turn influenced the outcome of national election campaigns.

Chapter 5 focuses on understanding stability and change in opinions. The chapter begins by looking at how demography, values, and technology have been sources of opinion change. It then examines two 'hot button' issues – same-sex marriage and national security – and provides data to show how the opinions of Canadians on these issues have changed during the past five years. The chapter concludes with a presentation of postmodern theory relative to the conduct of polling and addresses criticisms from postmodernists in regard to the quantification of social experience. I also speculate on the future of polling, as alternatives to the standard research design in place today are under intense scrutiny by critics.

The book concludes with a synopsis of the social determinants of public opinion, focusing on the impact of opinion polling and the emergence of moral panic. In addition, the meaning of polls is considered in a global context, thus addressing the issue of 'world opinion,' a notion often raised today. Clearly there will continue to be significant challenges for pollsters and the importance given to their work by society in the years to come.

# 1 Polling and Understanding Public Opinion

In the final stretch of an election campaign which is garnering elevated levels of voter attention, a new EKOS Research poll conducted for the *Toronto Star* and *La Presse* points to an electorate which may well produce a national stalemate with no party able to secure a clear moral or legal mandate to govern ... These data are based on telephone interviews conducted June 16 and 17, 2004 with a sample of 895 Canadians aged 18 and over.

EKOS Research (2004)

## The Social Basis of Public Opinion

*The Individual and Collective Thinking*

Assessments of public opinion have become everyday events in Canadian society, helping to determine what we will buy, how we will spend our tax dollars, and, especially, how we will vote in elections. A question frequently asked of pollsters, pundits, and professors who study public opinion is how, in a country as diverse as Canada, can a few scant observations provided by a selected number of individual respondents be taken as an expression of the beliefs of entire communities or indeed of the whole nation? This question is at the root of any presentation which claims to explain what the public thinks. Essentially the question is twofold: 'How can the diversity of individual opinions actually represent all of Canadians?' and if so, 'How many individual opinions is it necessary to have in order to represent those opinions accurately?'

While the political poll has become synonymous with public opinion, there are other public affairs studies about a variety of issues, and market research that is concerned with the reactions of segments of the public to products or advertising. The principal difference is the kinds of attitudes and opinions that are being measured in each approach. The problem of explaining collective assessments in terms of individual preferences remains the same for each.

The issues related to the gathering of opinions will be considered in the chapter that follows. However, as we begin to look at public opinion, its formation and change, we must explain how the thinking of individual respondents can be reconciled with collective views. Sociology has been at the forefront of this problem because of its ability to offer a meaningful interpretation of the connections among everyday events, rendering them less subjective and more predictable than they would otherwise appear to be.

Understanding public opinion begins by recognizing that views held by individuals are always to some degree an expression of collective thinking. By this we mean that the formation of attitudes and opinions, as well as the values they usually reflect, are influenced by what we see and hear from others as we participate in group life. While this principle is generally accepted by social science, it has not always been taken into account in the analysis of public opinion data. Converse (1987) observes that in the early years, public opinion was more likely to be seen as simply a collection of the views of community leaders, newspaper editors, or other elites who were perceived to be most knowledgeable about the issues of the day. Clearly, public opinion was understood to be a group product, but the opinions of only some 'publics' were relevant. Ordinary individuals were not perceived as being well informed about important issues and therefore their opinions did not count.

This convention was challenged during the evolution of quantitative public opinion polling in the twentieth century, when more scientific techniques were applied to gathering responses both to increase accuracy and to account for the diversity of society. According to observers of those early years of polling in the United States, however, these approaches tended to simply equate public opinion with the sum of unrelated individual responses to pollsters' questions. Little consideration was given to how the ideas and opinions of individuals are derived from the groups or cultures in which they were embedded. Of course, sociologists had long argued that the actions, ideas, and beliefs of individuals are derived from organized social life. Public opinion was not simply the aggregation of individual actions, ideas, or beliefs; it should take into account the values and beliefs that give shape to the actions of individuals (see Parsons, 1951).[1] Indeed, in a well known critique of public opinion polling during that era, American sociologist Herbert Blumer left no doubt that public opinion was a reflection of social processes: 'public opinion gets its form from the social framework in which it moves and from the social processes in play in that framework; also that the function and role of public opinion is determined by the part it plays in the operation of the society' (Blumer, 1948, p. 543).

From Blumer's perspective, respondents' answers to opinion polls should not be taken as isolated, unconnected views; rather, they are rooted in group experiences. Moreover, in the analysis of public opinion data, social and demographic variables such as age, gender, ethnicity, and socio-economic status, or other categories of group belonging should have considerable power to explain individual attitudes. When the relevant group has been identified, a summation of collected responses may be seen to be merely 'dipping deeper' into the same pool. In other words, summated responses of individuals can indeed be assumed to represent what entire communities think, particularly if effective procedures have been applied to obtain them.

Incidentally, the argument presented by Blumer was also a criticism of the propensity of opinion researchers to give equal weighting to any and all individual responses. In his view, it was clear that the contexts which shape opinions were not being recognized in polling methods and that random replies to pollsters' questions deserved less consideration than the opinions presented in formal discussions of issues by relevant groups. In any case, his argument has been largely ignored as public opinion researchers have emphasized precision in quantitative sampling techniques and have been less focused on the views of opinion leaders (Converse, 1987).

---

1 In their attempts to develop a theory of personality, social psychologists of that era actively pursued the adjustment of the individual's behaviour to group memberships as well. Lewin (1947) argued that personality was directly affected by 'background' or, in other words, belonging to groups like families and ethnic communities. Indeed he suggested that those who were unsure about the nature of their belonging to groups would exhibit unstable personalities. Lewin's studies of experimentally created primary groups were designed to investigate how interaction in autocratic or democratic groups could produce outcomes like cooperative or egotistical personalities among their members.

Blumer's orientation to the relationship between individual and collective opinion can also be thought of as considering the behaviour of groups most closely identified with key issues of the day. The term *issue public* is sometimes used to refer to interest groups that regard themselves as having a common concern about some event or activity; their members speak with one voice. The degree to which any issue is able to attract general interest is likely to be dependent on the social significance of the issue. For example, in the period 2000–1, the Nova Scotia government embarked on a 'Campaign for Fairness' to attract public support for its negotiations with the federal government over keeping a greater share of its off-shore oil revenues. (It is customary for about 80 per cent to be retained by Ottawa in revenue-sharing agreements with the provinces.) In Canada, provincial revenues are governed by equalization whereby the federal government ensures that provinces maintain national standards for the delivery of social services. Nova Scotia argued that as a 'have not' province which receives substantial payments under equalization, it was unfair for the federal government to subtract oil revenue from the payments. It also maintained that it should be allowed to keep more of this windfall revenue and have a gradual reduction of the transfer over time to allow it to ultimately lessen its dependence on Ottawa. Despite the best efforts of the province to mobilize popular support for the idea, the campaign completely fizzled – largely because Nova Scotians and other Canadians were not persuaded that it was a significant issue. There was in other words, no issue public among industry or the community which expressed strong views on the matter. Indeed, the premier of Ontario said it was 'like winning the lotto and asking to remain on welfare.' More recently a happy outcome has been achieved as both Newfoundland and Nova Scotia have reached an agreement with Ottawa to retain a larger share of their oil and gas royalties.

At any rate, issue publics or interest groups are not quite the same as other social groups who are identified by their demographic characteristics, since they have focused opinions which they actively seek to advance by influencing others in society. The important thing to remember about interest groups, however, is that they attempt to shape public opinion by an emotional appeal to those who are identified in some way with a controversial topic. Thousands of interest groups operate in Canada to promote business, ethnic, and professional objectives and obviously they have an influence on the way their members think about everyday events. For example, the opinions of members of the Canadian Nurses Association regarding the importance of increased taxation to sustain spending on public health care are very likely to be different from the opinions of those who are members of the Canadian Federation of Independent Business (whose mandate is to lobby governments on behalf of small and medium-sized business on issues such as costs and prices). The thinking of members from each group on public issues is very likely to be in line with the objectives of their respective associations. More broadly, the members' opinions of the ability of politicians and governments to solve societal problems will usually reflect the relative priority the members perceive is being given by decision makers to their own top issue. In fact, some have argued that most citizens become aware of the key issues of the day only because opposing viewpoints are put forward by competing issue publics and are made known by the media (Blumer, 1960).

It should also be noted that when studies of public issues are done, they usually specify that the data has been collected from individuals who are 18 years of age and older. This is not to suggest that those who are younger do not have important opinions, but it means that the studies have been designed to gather information from respondents who are potentially part of the electorate; these studies are more relevant to decision makers in government, as well as to politicians and the media. The opinions of specific sub-groups in society, including adolescents, seniors, and minorities, frequently form the basis for market opinion research or even policy-oriented studies that are aimed at gaining knowledge about the way expectations and attitudes vary among different groups within a community. Thus sub-groups are not usually ignored, but it is more likely that mainstream studies of public opinion will focus on 'adult populations' (see Bardes & Oldendick, 2003).

Finally, in considering ways of reconciling individual and public opinion, it is important to draw a distinction between opinion and attitude. These are often used interchangeably, but over the years there has been an attempt, at least among social scientists, to distinguish between them. In an early inquiry into the effects of communication on opinion change by social psychologists, Hovland et al. make an important distinction between opinions and attitudes: 'opinions are considered to be verbalizable, while attitudes are sometimes "unconscious"' (1953, p. 7). It is also generally understood that attitudes are relatively long-term orientations towards events and issues (see Berelson and Janowitz, 1966; Katz, 1972). That is to say, they reflect predispositions toward something, such as persons, ideas or events, which are rooted in the significant social experiences of individuals over relatively long periods of time. Hovland's research on the basis for opinion change tested the ability of individuals to resist persuasive communications which were contrary to group attitudes. He hypothesized that the ability to resist was a function of the degree of belongingness to these groups. The amount of opinion change in the direction of the persuasive communication was found to correlate with the degree of perceived importance respondents placed on their membership in the group. Less importance placed on membership resulted in less resistance to communications containing opinions contrary to group norms (Hovland et al., 1953, p. 141).

For this reason, group involvements, from families to circles of friends, maintain attitudes. Even the combination of social class, ethnic background, or region can influence attitudes on topical issues. For example, the residents of Alberta apparently hold quite different views on the appropriate model for the delivery of public and private health care from those held by the residents of eastern Canada. Albertans tend to be more accepting of the idea of choice in the delivery of private or public health care services, whereas eastern Canadians are much less accepting of policies that diminish the role of governments in health care (Hawaleshka, 2002).

Attitudes also convey emotions; people become bound to ideas and their commitment to those ideas is expressed in the intensity of the responses they provide. Individuals respond favourably or unfavourably when alternatives are being considered; they either agree or disagree strongly or they are very satisfied or very dissatisfied when questioned about things that matter to them. On the issue of a public and private delivery system for health care, Canadians hold very strong views one way or the other. This is because their attitudes are most likely derived from what has come to be called their *core values*. These are general ideas and standards for behaviour shared by members of our society about what is desirable and undesirable. How we as Canadians react to ideas relating to health care, immigration, sex, or even consumer products is a result of the interrelationship of shared values such as honesty, tolerance, success, and individualism. We shall consider this more fully in the next sections, but it is important to recognize that the intensity with which attitudes are conveyed in studies of social priorities like health care is an indication of the values by which we have defined ourselves as Canadians. We see ourselves as altruistic people who are concerned with the collective good of society and the burden of publicly funded social services like health care is generally accepted as a worthwhile thing for our society to support.

When attitudes cluster to form coordinated beliefs about the way a society should be, they are usually referred to as *ideologies*. These are shared perspectives that provide the justification for the outlook on life that we adopt. In particular, political opinions are often described in terms of ideologies; these are broadly perceived as 'left wing' or liberal views in contrast to 'right wing' or conservative views. Surveys have shown that these perspectives can be differentiated from one another by attitudes toward the immediacy of social change and the extent that governments should be involved in the economy (McClosky and Zaller, 1984). Political ideologies in Canada, for example, have been described as being organized around two contrasts; the values of individualism versus collectivism on the one hand, and equality versus elitism on the other (Marchak, 1988). According to Marchak, over the years Canadians have supported liberal values of collectivism and egalitarianism as part of the dominant ideology we share. However, this dichotomy is the subject of a continuing debate among social scientists in this country and describing national identity has been problematic. Given the cultural and structural diversity which impacts upon notions of national identity, it may well be that no one Canadian identity is predominant (see Hiller, 2000). The connections between the attitudes expressed by Canadians and core values will be reviewed again in Chapter 5.

In contrast to attitudes, opinions refer to relatively more transitory judgments about issues or events and are more likely to be the outcome of a mood current in society (Nimmo and Bonjean, 1972). It has been argued that opinions are often specific, provisional responses to questions and the manner in which they are asked at the time; they do not necessarily reflect any underlying connection between ideas in the way that systems of belief and attitudes are assumed to have formed (Converse, 1964). Nevertheless, over the years social scientists have attempted to describe public opinion in terms of attitude similarities and have argued that it is not enough to seek answers to questions which provide only superficial indicators of opinions that are often independent of each other. In order to estimate public opinion accurately, methods are usually applied which are aimed at discovering consistencies among statements; this can then be taken to indicate a real belief about an issue. Indeed, as we shall see in the chapters to come, real beliefs have been amenable to measurement by means of aggregating responses to a series of attitude questions on various subjects relating to the issue.

Finally, we should realize that opinions are a consequence of the attitudes which are held by individuals over time. For example, opinions derived from the value of tolerance may lead individuals to approve strongly of increased government expenditures on multiculturalism. On the other hand, a belief that increased immigration may lead to greater social instability in Canadian society may bring other opinions into play, such as the need for greater consensus in our country. Opinions may reflect an acceptance of multiculturalism but with reservations about immigration policy. When opinions are a product of competing, contradictory views held by an individual and are not meaningfully connected; they may be held weakly and are subject to change when social priorities shift.

In conclusion, we should recognize that attitudes and opinions are part of a continuum of beliefs. It is the basis of the beliefs which is important in explaining why members of a public think the way they do. The differences we have considered here are really analytical and, in practice, public opinion studies rarely report whether their respondents' answers have been collected to measure beliefs or simply provide opinions on events under study. Before we can deal with this effectively, we need to consider how various sources of information we encounter in day to day relationships may have an influence on the opinions we form.

*Sources of Information and Opinion*

In the preceding section we discussed the social basis of opinions and explained that views that are expressed by the public are influenced both directly and indirectly by many groups. In a pluralistic society like Canada, the variety and sometimes conflicting nature of alternate information sources can pull people in different directions and have varying effects upon what they think. Clearly, we are not susceptible to all the influences we encounter each day, and some groups have much more persuasive power over us than others. Therefore, it is important that we consider how reference groups and opinion leaders play a part in forming the attitudes and beliefs which we are likely to hold.

Usually, we think of a reference group as those people who provide a point of comparison for our own behaviour. Studies of social process have shown that all groups promote conformity; members are strongly controlled by fear of rejection and carefully avoid being seen to be at odds with prevailing group standards and opinions. Reference groups may include family, co-workers, and neighbours and the idea is that opinions held by an individual are very likely to be based on a perception of what the current consensus on various issues is within these groups. For example, agreement on political issues is most likely to occur among those who share a common social characteristic, such as being a university student or belonging to the Chamber of Commerce; in other words, there is agreement among peers. Political socialization, the learning process by which individuals acquire political values and attitudes, is also considered by social science writers as being attributable to the influence of family, school, and peer groups at all stages of our lives (Dyck, 2004). The social experiences shared among group members provide a basis for deciding what are 'politically correct' and 'politically incorrect' attitudes. Moreover, it is a matter not simply of sharing information, but of mutually reinforcing attitudes among group members about what is 'morally right' (Berelson and Steiner, 1967). University students in Canada are likely to find that there is a good deal of agreement among their peers about the need for increased government expenditures on university education, but they are also likely to find that there is considerably less agreement with their views among the members of the Chamber of Commerce. The prevailing view there may be that more government expenditures should be directed at small business; even though many members of the Chamber of Commerce may only recently have ceased to be university students themselves! The assessment of the urgency of various issues is a reflection of the values of the respective groups relative to government priorities.

Social science also offers a rich literature on the dangers of excessive group identification, notably about the potential for self-inflicted violence related to demands made by leaders on cult members (see Dawson, 1998). Émile Durkheim's early explorations into the power of peer groups to affect various forms of suicide are a well-known example of this. Durkheim identified a kind of suicide called *altruistic* suicide which is characteristic of people who are so tightly bound to group beliefs they seem unable to see themselves apart from the goals of the group. Suicide bombings in Iraq and Afghanistan illustrate Durkheim's theory, showing the devastating consequences brought about by excessive immersion in group opinion.

Raymond Breton's (1990) research on the social integration of immigrants to Canada during the 1960s examines another dimension of group opinion; the power of an ethnic community to retain an immigrant within its social boundaries, apart from the mainstream community. Breton uses the concept of *institutional completeness*, which describes the extent to which an ethnic group maintains its own churches, schools, media, banks, and shops, offering services in its own language and culture; these are pivotal for the formation of an 'ethnic public.' In other words, if immigrants are able to meet all of their daily needs within the boundaries of the ethnic culture, they have more restricted involvement with the institutions of the wider community. The degree of institutional completeness is therefore predictive of the degree to which immigrants may identify themselves with Canadian society.

Canadians recently came face to face with the potential for a home-grown terrorist attack and the possibility of jihadist martyrs operating in our country. To many people it was unthinkable that our own citizens could contemplate actions which were so incompatible with Canadian core values and beliefs. On the other hand, a *Maclean's* magazine story suggested that the alleged terrorists arrested were not unlike those who had been exposed as terrorists in several European cities. They were identified as being part of a 'small, *self-radicalizing* autonomous cell with good operational security,' by an expert quoted in the story (Friscolanti, Gatehouse, and Gillis, 2006, p. 23). In other words, these were described as individuals who had become so immersed in extremist views and so isolated from mainstream opinions, that the ability to accept an alternative way of thinking was likely to be perceived by them as compromising loyalty to the expectations of their cell.

Studies of collective decision-making have shown another dimension of the power of group opinion. When insider groups of government officials permit only one view to prevail, the result may be a kind of information paralysis, called *groupthink* (Janis, 1972). Absolute conviction about the appropriateness of a course of action is the basis of groupthink, implying that alternative positions are evidence of disloyalty. The decision of presidential advisors in the United States to push ahead with the invasion of Iraq, despite the absence of evidence for the existence of weapons of mass destruction, is frequently cited by the media as an example of this. It is often argued that advisors around President George W. Bush were unwilling to accept any opposing opinions that would contradict their certainty that invading Iraq was morally correct, in view of the threat of continued terrorist attacks. In other words, these officials are being accused of groupthink. The point is that mutually supported attitudes reinforce the power of others to determine whether an individual may entertain views that are disconnected from the group.

In Canada, the Meech Lake and Charlottetown Accords are some-times cited as examples of problems arising from groupthink. At a national conference between the provincial premiers and the prime minister in 1987, an agreement was reached (the Meech Lake Accord) that was intended to address the concerns about the place of Quebec in confederation.[2] The agreement proposed to recognize Quebec as a dis-tinct society in Canada, provide for an elected Senate, guarantee ab-original self-government, and reorganize the division of federal and provincial powers. The most controversial of these concerns, in terms of public opinion at least, was the official recognition of Quebec as a 'distinct society' with powers not enjoyed by other provinces. The view of the place of Quebec in Canada held by the drafters of the Accord was not widely shared by the electorate and objections to the agreement resulted in legislators in both Manitoba and Newfoundland refusing to give the legislative approval mandatory from all provinces. The New-foundland legislature withheld its support for the agreement despite the fact that its own premier had originally supported it.

In an effort at damage control and in the belief that the end of the Accord would result in a victory for sovereigntists in Quebec, the pre-miers and the prime minister agreed to a second arrangement which became known as the Charlottetown Accord. This time a national refer-endum was held, in 1992, to ensure that provincial legislators would have the benefit of their electorate's opinion. But again, the referendum showed that the opinions of the political leaders were not in sync with those of the public, as a majority (55 per cent) of Canadians voted against the Accord. This happened despite sustained support in the media from intellectuals and the political elite, including then prime minister Brian Mulroney, and despite the fact that local community leaders had joined together and campaigned in favour of accepting the agreement.

Analysts have since maintained that public opinion had turned against the agreement because of a declining confidence in political leadership which had begun during the 1980s. There was also a sense that the agreement might create too much division among Canadians. How-ever, it can also be argued that the political leaders of the country had

---

2 The province had refused to sign the *Constitution Act* in 1982 because its demands for special powers in areas of social policy, based on its cultural distinctiveness, had not been recognized in the negotiations leading up to the *Act* (for a full discussion, see Dyck, 2004, pp. 395–405).

engaged in a form of groupthink based on a shared sense of urgency about needing to meet the demands of the government of Quebec. Even a majority of those who were residents of Quebec (57 per cent) voted against the Charlottetown Accord. In this case, a majority of the public believed they were being pressured by the elite to vote for a change when it had not fully explained to them why it was necessary to do so.

It is also important to recognize that groups to which we do not belong can be a source of our opinions. For example, in everyday life many of us follow the lifestyles of celebrities; we use the phrases we hear spoken by actors in television programs or in movies and dress in the clothing styles preferred by those whom we admire. Moreover, when a reference group is selected as a model, individuals do not choose just any group; they usually refer to groups whose approval they seek, or they pattern their behaviour to imitate members of groups to which they would like to belong. Imitating the lifestyles of the wealthy is an ancient custom of the less well off who endeavour to keep up appearances. Subjectively, these individuals recognize that they are not members of the groups they imitate, but perhaps because most individuals do not have the first-hand experience of membership which might allow for more critical judgments to be made, these reference groups become powerful agents of socialization. They influence attitudes and opinions because aspirants perceive them to be appropriate.

One of the reasons reference groups have this hold over what we think is that in complex societies, groups to which individuals do not belong also assume an important role in providing information about events which take place outside of the experience of most individuals. That is to say, to a very large extent, people depend on those whom they do not know and are never likely to meet – journalists, politicians, entertainers, and others who are considered to be knowledgeable – to interpret events which are 'out of reach' to the uninformed public. In turn, ordinary people are more likely to follow the positions put forward by these experts because they do not take the time to understand the complexities of public affairs or they simply are not engaged by current issues apart from a momentary look at the evening news on television.[3] Thus, the views that many people hold about issues and

---

3 Stuart Soroka (2002) has explored the formation of public opinion around major policy issues. He argues that issues which have become important to the public in Canada are part of the process of agenda setting by the media or government. Soroka has categorized issues as being either prominent issues – those which have a direct

events are often those that they have absorbed from experts and have not come up with for themselves. Moreover, Zaller notes that when the public relies on experts for information, it often receives only a selective record of events, since experts may simplify or reconstruct facts to allow them to be more easily understood by the average person. Experts frequently present advice on what the public *should* think about issues; it is unlikely to be the result of a forthright assessment of what is happening. 'In consequence, the public opinion that exists on a given issue can rarely be considered a straightforward response to "the facts" of a situation. Even topics that are within the direct experience of some citizens such as poverty, homosexuality and racial inequality are susceptible to widely different understandings, depending on how the facts about them are framed or stereotyped, and on which partisan elites are associated with which positions' (Zaller, 1992, pp. 13–14).

We will discuss the role of elites in opinion formation in chapter 3, but we should nevertheless recognize that reference groups are often composed of people who have never engaged in a conversation. Indeed, if we consider that many Canadians who identify with the ideology of the Liberal Party of Canada may never have had any contact with those who have prepared its policy positions, we can understand why the party plays a powerful role in situating the ideals of those who profess to hold liberal beliefs and values.

Individuals who help to determine what the public thinks are described as *opinion leaders*. The term usually refers to people who are seen to have extensive knowledge and awareness of public issues because of their active involvement in them. Opinion leaders are likely to be individuals such as community activists, politicians, academics, or religious leaders who are highly visible to the public. The key thing to remember about

---

impact on people's lives – such as inflation and unemployment; sensational issues – those which are based on dramatic events – such as crime or environmental concerns; or governmental issues – those which are defined as important public policy – such as taxation or the national debt. Understanding the formation of public opinion around an issue involves an exploration of how it becomes identified as important to the media, or to the government's agenda. According to this theory, sensational-type issues like same-sex marriage, which does not directly affect the majority of citizens, become public opinion items primarily because of their potential for dramatic stories in the media. By contrast, national unity, a policy issue that has a broader impact on citizens, has been an item on the public agenda for a number of years because it has been kept prominent by politicians and bureaucrats. Issues are more likely to become salient to the public when the agenda of the media and policymakers come together.

opinion leaders is that these are the individuals who have the power to affect how we think, especially about complex or controversial issues, since, as we have said above, most members of the community are likely to have only a general grasp of them. Usually, journalists will seek out well-known community members whenever a difficult decision is required on an issue. McClosky and Zaller (1984) have portrayed these people as an 'opinion elite' who interpret the norms and values of society and present attitudes that are regarded as being 'politically respectable' because they are in line with the prevailing norms and values. Their research shows that when there is considerable agreement among opinion elites, their views are likely to receive popular support. The implication of this is that the agenda for public policy decisions on controversial issues is far more likely to be an outcome of the sense of urgency about them expressed by respected public personalities rather than by ordinary members of Canadian society. In a similar vein, Justin Lewis (2001) maintains that public opinion should be seen largely as a construction of elite interests which are selectively reproduced by conducting public opinion polls about them. He condemns polls which restrict the amount of thinking interviewees can give to their responses and whose results are then reported by media representatives who are primarily interested in findings that are most relevant to elite concerns. Thus, he concludes that polls rarely reflect actual public knowledge about issues or even popular will. They reflect opinions which are constructed around the concerns of elites. He concludes that this contributes to a widespread suspicion that political decisions are manufactured from polling results: 'The notion of a poll-driven body politic is plausible only because the media coverage of polls reflects the political agendas of elites ... The media thus produce a form of public opinion that is largely compatible with the elites who claim, most of the time, to represent the popular will and it is from this narrow space that assumptions can be made about politicians drifting with the ebb and flow of the polls' (Lewis, 2001, pp. 200–1).

On the other hand, elites do not always have the power to influence public opinion they are presumed to have. This is clearly demonstrated by Canadians' rejection of the 1992 Charlottetown Accord (see Dyck, 2004).

One further point which deserves mention at this juncture, because an important role in opinion formation is attributed to it, is the role of the media and the public opinion research industry on the dissemination of polling results. It is often maintained that political polls and other public issue studies increase sensitivity to political attitudes and events because the research findings are regularly made available to the public and thereby influence their opinions. Moreover, market research findings are sometimes used to promote the attractiveness of one product relative to another, encouraging consumers to buy products based on the putative popularity of such products among them. It has been argued that the publication of political polls (as well as media interpretations of the findings), particularly during elections, may distort the democratic process (Hoy, 1989; Fox, 1991). During elections, voters and the media make up their minds about eventual winners and losers on the basis of the election outcomes predicted by published polling results. The critics claim that voters who otherwise pay little attention to politics will be more likely to cast their votes for parties or candidates who are perceived to be ahead in the polls or for those whom the media has projected as winners rather than on the basis of any reflection about policies. Pollsters on the other hand believe that polls create more involvement in politics since the release of poll results not only builds up interest in politics and public issues, but allows people to assess how they relate to attitudes and opinions being reported upon. 'Polls provide an instant means for the individual to identify himself on the scale of public opinion. Polling belongs to the world of universal democracy. The process enables citizens to understand where their opinions and values fit in the range of attitudes about issues that affect their lives and their country' (Goldfarb and Axworthy, 1988, p. 11).

Others have argued that the variety of information which flows from publication of polling research has rendered campaigns much more unpredictable (Frizzell, 1991). When campaigns are portrayed primarily in terms of their entertainment value and much less on comparisons of policies, it may indeed mean that voter opinions become more volatile. For example, opinion polls which are used to measure voter reaction to leadership debates and to the potential impact of controversial statements made by leaders seem to shift attention to candidates as competitors in a race. The consequence is that the opinions of voters may become shallow, as the data are derived not from questions about platforms but from reactions to performance and are likely to reveal views that are changed by the next piece of sensational news.

Volatility of opinion may also be an outcome of the constant bombardment of different ideas, whether derived from opinions about products, people, or issues. However, the uneasiness about the power of survey information to determine who wins elections has at various times generated a call for a ban on the publication of polls during campaigns.[4] This has not yet happened, but the debate has over the years focused attention on the accuracy of polls and the methods used by pollsters. In fact, the *Canada Elections Act* was amended in 2000 to require survey results on voting intentions which are published during an election period to include, along with the results of the poll and the name of the polling organization, the methodology that was used. For example, published polls are required to report the size of the sample, the response rates during the data collection, the time the survey was completed, as well as any adjustments made by the pollsters to account for problems with expected response rates. Durand (2005) has examined the inclusion of information referred to in the *Act* in a selected number of national polls published in the 2004 federal election. She finds that most of the required information is being reported by the various polling firms. However, the reporting of response rates is uneven, which makes it more difficult to assess the accuracy of the sample size used to represent populations. If, for example, 1000 contacts yield only 100 completes, there would be grounds for concern about the sample's accuracy. We will address this subject more fully in our next chapter.

Voting choice has been the subject of much study by political scientists in Canada. A dominant theme of this research is how the connection between *long-term* influences such as socio-demographic characteristics like region, ethnicity, gender, age and social class and the importance of *short-term* issues like the performances of candidates and leaders, is associated with the decision to vote for one of the three main political parties (see Jackson and Jackson, 2006, p. 448). Elections Canada, the body set up by Parliament as a non-partisan agency to monitor elections and referenda, participates in the Canadian Election Study, providing independent scholarly analysis of voting patterns after each general election.[5] One theme for research on the 2004 general election was the level of interest expressed by young Canadians in the campaign and whether or not they had chosen to vote. This data showed considerable apathy about the political process among young Canadians, that is,

---

4  Chapter 3 will explore the role of journalists and the media in creating a 'bandwagon effect' by reporting opinion polls on voting choices. For a discussion of the influence of polls on voters during elections and an analysis of the issues around regulating the publication of polling data by the media during elections, see Lachapelle (1991).

5  See Elections Canada at www.elections.ca.

those in the 18 to 29 age cohort. The percentage of voter turnout among younger and first-time voters was 15 points lower than among those who were 30 years and older (Gidengil et al., 2005). Many reported they had very little interest in politics; on the other hand, of all the age groups, they had expressed the least negative feelings about parties and leaders. Low voter turnout among the young has been attributed to a difference of opinion between generations on the most important issues (Turcotte, 2005). Younger voters paid less attention to the personalities of candidates and leaders and more to their approach to the issues that concerned younger voters the most. It is also interesting that recent analysis of voter behaviour in a number of Canadian elections shows overall that all voters are giving increasing importance to important policy issues as the prime determinants of their voting choices rather than party loyalty or past voting patterns (Pammett and Dornan, 2004).

Comparative studies of voting behaviour between the United States and Canada and other developed countries have also emphasized the process of *cultural modernization*, or societal development to a post-industrial, knowledge-based economy, as having changed the way citizens relate to politics and the electoral process (see Inglehart, 1997). We will explore this in more detail in Chapter 5; however it is important at this point to note that the theory argues that economic security, increasing levels of education, and liberal democratic policies in post-industrial societies have led to greater citizen participation in politics. But political activism in these societies is likely to take on an altered quality described as *protest politics*, as the interests of the general public are mobilized away from traditional political parties to interest groups and grassroots associations. In particular, it is argued that voter turnout will increase for all age cohorts in post-industrial society. However, comparative cross-national research on the effect of gender on political activism shows that, on measures of both traditional and modern political activism, women have, overall, lower levels of participation. Interest in politics, levels of voter turnout, party membership, and union membership, all tend to be lower among women than among men. And they persist despite post-industrial development, where protest politics involving community activism like boycotts are used as measures of political interest (Inglehart and Norris, 2005, pp. 114–17). Indeed, significant gender gaps for all forms of political participation are most strongly evident in industrial and agrarian societies.

Finally, we should take note that in a situation where there is extreme uncertainty about a controversial public issue, and where public discussion about that issue is also accompanied by data from public opinion polls and the coverage given to the polls by the media, *moral panic* may occur. The notion comes from the study of British youth culture in the 1960s, where changing attitudes about sexuality, the use of drugs, and an attachment to rock and roll music as the basis for in-group identity were regarded as a threat to social values (Cohen, 1972). Angst about the lifestyle of the youth was turned into a moral question about the threat to established order, generating moral panic. However, a crucial element in the notion of a panic is that the extent of the threat is frequently quite disproportionate to the problem that it actually poses to the public. Nevertheless, the concept of moral panic also offers a useful way to explain the roots of group opinion which may be stimulated by the release of polling data. In chapters 4 and 5 we will consider this concept again and show how Canadian opinion on some key national issues has been constructed by polling in ways that are disproportionate to the facts relating to those issues.

## Sincerity of Opinions

The volatility of opinions relating to voting behaviour or even to consumer preferences raises concern about the sincerity of the attitudes and preferences collected in public opinion research. Critics dispute whether respondents actually give honest responses to researchers' questions and, perhaps more importantly, whether they have sufficient knowledge about the issues being investigated to be able to provide genuine answers to questions. Some have raised doubts about whether lengthy interviews, usually on the telephone and often initiated at a time when it is least convenient for interviews, actually engage people in the topics being investigated or simply discourage them from giving their real opinions (Hoy, 1989). One area this has been dealt with is in research on voters. For some time, political scientists have shown that respondents show considerable confusion about their beliefs when asked about political issues. Views expressed in opinion polls about central issues in American life have often been described as unconnected and contradictory because the attitudes being measured are not clustered together enough to indicate real political orientations (see Converse, 1964). It is alleged that because political awareness is so low, ordinary American voters do not really comprehend political questions before they offer their answers. As a result, political opinions are neither well thought through nor based on organized political ideas. Thus, while the media may trumpet 'left' or 'right' leaning views with respect to such issues as the role of private and public participation in the economy or beliefs about the need to have public health care in a compassionate society, there is little evidence to suggest that people grasp the ideologies implied in the use of these terms well enough to describe their own attitudes in these terms (Converse, 1987).

According to this thesis, political polls are often based on *pseudo-opinions*, which are simply a reaction to an interview situation (Neuman, 1986). That is to say, when being interviewed, many people feel obliged to give answers either to help the interviewer or in order to avoid appearing to be ignorant. They may not deliberately falsify their answers but they offer only top-of-mind views. Indeed, some data collection procedures may even contribute to this outcome. In conducting public opinion surveys, many studies rely on the use of 'forced choice' as a basis for questionnaires rather than providing respondents with opportunities to give answers in their own words. As we shall discuss in the next chapter, there are legitimate reasons to use this approach; it offers a common frame of reference for questions and allows for a more precise comparison of responses obtained. Yet, the approach lends itself to the criticism that if people are forced to choose an answer, many will, but with little thought given to the answers they provide.

To compensate for the problem of pseudo-opinions, political surveys use multiple measures. Respondents are often asked several supplementary questions which are designed to contribute to the overall reliability of the information supplied by respondents. For example, when voting intentions are assessed, people are asked several questions about how they will vote, including current preferences, past voting preferences, and which candidate they may be currently leaning toward. However, while voting intentions may often be derived from combining the answers from several questions, they are reported as if they were expressed as an opinion. They may reflect a general orientation rather than an attitude. Other data collection techniques can help to reduce these kinds of problems but these examples call attention to the fact that measuring opinion is not simply a matter of straightforwardly reporting what people say, even when clear and unambiguous questions are asked. Reporting on opinions is thus also a matter of considering the nature of the interview process which may itself lead to generating inaccurate information.

Are respondents actually faking it when they are interviewed? A useful way of considering sincerity in public opinion is to reflect on it as a matter of *impression management*. Goffman (1967) describes social behaviour in terms of performances; individuals attempt to present the most favourable impressions of themselves in their interactions with others. Goffman maintains that impression management presupposes sincerity rather than deception. In order to establish a perception we want others to have, we must believe in our own performances. Individuals rarely set out to engage in misrepresentation but they do attempt to sustain favourable impressions and not communicate any ideas that are at odds with the way they wish to present themselves. In so doing, they may actually engage in deception but come to consider it as representing truth, as a way of managing the impression they wish to convey.

Performance is also a matter of not 'losing face.' Thus, when respondents to public opinion surveys who are unfamiliar with issues and events under study give answers that are based on very little knowledge, they may not set out to deliberately deceive interviewers. Goffman describes this as 'being taken in by our own act' (Goffman, 1967). They give the answers they do because they wish to provide a good performance and avoid 'losing face.' Consider this example: during the 2004 federal election in Canada the published polls indicated that many Canadians expressed disgust with the scandals that plagued the Liberal government during its term of office. Yet the Liberals won at least enough seats to form the government again. Did voters cynically attempt to misrepresent their views about the scandal and deceive the pollsters? Did they change their minds over the course of the 2004 election campaign? Or did they simply attempt to manage impressions by providing responses on the issue that were in line with what they believed to be majority opinions?

Most likely, all three factors explain the events surrounding the 2004 election campaign. But this way of looking at the interview process raises a concern for the quality of information yielded by polls given the present proliferation of polls. Most respondents perhaps do not knowingly attempt to misrepresent their opinions, but we need to recognize that respondents may interpret an interview in an opinion poll as being exactly like any other social interaction setting in which they participate. That is, individuals may see it as a matter of role playing which involves anticipating how others may react to their views and taking that perception into account as they give their responses. Perhaps Canadians found it easier to provide their opinions when secluded in the voting booth.

## The Role of Values in Opinion Formation

*How We See Ourselves*

Polling on the mood of Canadians conducted by Decima Research Limited, a national public opinion research firm, revealed that throughout the 1980s a process of reassessment of value orientations had taken place in the country (Gregg and Posner, 1990). The data led to the conclusion that Canadians had for some time been questioning the values which had always defined who they were and how they behaved. The most interesting finding concerned a widespread loss of confidence in institutions such as political parties, banks, and schools. More importantly, the elites who represented these institutions were trusted much less than at any time before. For example, there was an eight point drop (70 per cent to 62 per cent) from 1987 to 1989 in the number of respondents who agreed with the statement that 'our system of government is one of the things that makes Canada the best place in the world to live.' Moreover, the customary role of government in economic and social affairs was not seen to have worked as it had in the past and many decided that it should be changed.

> As we entered the 1980s, our post-war values were challenged by changing experience. Inflation was eroding real income. Our dollar, no longer pegged to the American buck, had fallen to 84 cents U.S. And for the first time in Canadian history, home ownership in major urban centres eluded the grasp of the middle class. But rather than abandon traditional values, Canadians choose to reassess the traditional means of realizing them. Rather than abandon the belief that education was the key to success, they concluded that something must be wrong with the educational system. Rather than abandon the belief that government could solve all problems, they concluded that government was badly run and the nation's political leaders to blame. (Gregg and Posner, 1990, pp. 10–11)

Changing attitudes in the 1980s showed that our cultural patterns were being critically examined and many saw old ways of meeting expectations as no longer appropriate to changing social and economic circumstances. For one thing, government and political leaders could no longer command the unquestioned respect they had enjoyed during previous decades. The public preferred that governments protect health care, provide public services, and enable entrepreneurial activity, but they were no longer willing to accept that elite groups far away could be trusted to look out for their happiness and personal well-being.

Some other observers of this value transformation have interpreted it to mean that Canadians had become less deferential to authority over the decade. That is, they had become much less willing to trust without question the views of those who occupy positions of authority in key societal institutions. Baer, Grabb, and Johnson (1990) address the issue of trust in government as an historical character trait in their comparative analysis of beliefs and attitudes among Americans and Canadians. Their research shows that twice as many Americans as Canadians are likely to provide favourable opinions about their national government. Canadians were much more likely to indicate agreement with statements indicating alienation from government. Similarly, Grabb and Curtis (2005) conduct a value comparison between Canada and the United States by identifying four regional 'societies' within the two countries: English Canada, Quebec, the northern United States, and the southern United States. A comparison of the four societies on attitudes indicating political trust and confidence in government shows that residents of the southern region of the United States express the highest levels of political confidence (Grabb and Curtis, 2005, p. 227).

Peter C. Newman considers the extent to which discontent with traditional institutional arrangements has come to shape our outlook as a nation to be a kind of revolution from the standpoint of public opinion; the quality emerging among Canadians has been one of defiance rather than our customary attitude of deference (Newman, 1995). Defiance in this case refers to alienation or even crankiness, caused by the knowledge that many of the things that were taken for granted in Canada, such as protective government, a competent business community, a peacekeeping military, a compassionate clergy, and even domination of professional ice hockey, have proven to be untenable. In Newman's view, the revolution has been about changing attitudes towards self-reliance, the pursuit of self-interest, and mistrust of others rather than common interests. It has also been about declining respect for others in day-to-day social interaction, a far cry from the tolerance and moderation which are traditionally seen as core values in this country. He argues that people are much less polite and even indifferent towards each other now. They got above all the message that the social contract was no longer valid and that everyone was on their own (Newman, 1995, pp. 80–1).

On the other hand, changes in patterns of culture are not at all unique to Canada. They have also emerged in a number of advanced industrial-ized countries.[6] Similar value transformations which have been measured in North America and western Europe during the last decades of the twentieth century are conceptualized as reflecting 'post-material-ism' (Nevitte, 1996). According to this theory, individuals whose formative years took place during the prolonged period of prosperity and economic security following the end of World War II experience the world in a different way than do earlier generations. Nevitte's research shows that their sense of public priorities has shifted away from the materialist preoccupation with consumption and acquisitiveness. A post-materialist orientation is more likely to emphasize quality-of-life values such as job satisfaction, social justice, moral permissiveness, tolerance, and understanding, while materialist orientations where economic is-sues matter are more likely to be evident among older generations.

   Overall, Nevitte's study contends that deferential attitudes have been rejected in the advanced industrial nations included in the analysis, particularly by the young and more educated members of society. More-over, in a comparison of contemporary Canadian and American differ-ences, Nevitte concludes that Canadians are more likely than Americans to be postmaterialists with respect to social values. In fact, the findings relative to political behaviour provide further support for the notion that Canadians have become less deferential to authority. Political pro-test, as a measure of postmaterial attitudes, has increased in almost all of the countries studied; increasing numbers of respondents in every country say they would engage in political actions such as boycotts, unlawful demonstrations, unofficial strikes, and the occupation of build-ings. Canadians turn out to be significantly more likely to be willing to engage in protest behaviour than Americans (Nevitte, 1996, pp. 79–80).

   The point is that public attitudes are likely to be transformed by major societal events such as international migration, economic up-heavals, or civil unrest. As social conditions change, values that have sustained them may be revised. Thus, beliefs about our national institu-tions and their importance are best understood as an adaptation to our current social and economic realities. For example, it might be argued that historically Canadians were respectful and passive relative to gov-ernment influence in their lives. However, the changing beliefs about

---

6  Ronald Inglehart's (1997) work provides the most thorough cross-cultural examination of changing values and belief systems associated with social and economic
   development in national societies.

individualism and self-reliance identified above, which emerged out of extensive demographic change in this country as the twentieth century drew to a close, changed the attitude of Canadians towards their governments. There had been an enormous growth in urban centres and a corresponding decline in rural living; the knowledge economy expanded the requirement for a more mobile highly skilled and educated population. Moreover, internal migration as well as immigration has created a more heterogeneous society composed of new kinds of Canadians who think about the country in different ways. These conditions have surely generated highly varied views about ourselves.

A recent approach to gaining a more specific understanding of the diversity of contemporary Canadian values has explored the way they tend to cluster together to form the basis for different lifestyles (Adams, 1997). This model proposes that there are distinct differences among Canadians *within* broad value orientations. To develop the argument, Adams classifies patterns of attitudes and beliefs using a two dimensional model. One axis of differentiation tests whether respondents exhibit a *traditional* or *modern* view and contrasts the importance of traditional gender roles and religious identification, and a rejection of conformity with flexible gender identity and secularism. The other axis of differentiation identifies a social or an individualistic orientation, an orientation to 'others' as opposed to a need for personal autonomy and self fulfillment (Adams, 1997, pp. 46–7). Individuals are placed on the resulting matrix according to the degree to which their attitudes reflect aspects of the four quadrants. Respondents who share similar beliefs are grouped into twelve 'social values tribes.' The matrix should help to provide a better explanation of the way values have changed among Canadians.[7] In a later analysis Adams (2003) looked at the values in American quadrants.

Understanding communities of values further enhances our ability to predict evolving social trends. A segmentation approach like this goes beyond the idea that value differences can be explained by demography alone. For example, one can no longer confidently assume that

---

7 Through a cross-classification of these differences, four broad values orientations among Canadians and Americans are identified which are related in each society to age group, region, gender, and socio-economic status (Adams, 2003). In Adams' model, age and generational variables are added to the four-category scheme we have discussed above. Adams refers to them as the *elders*, *boomers*, and *generation X*. This produces the twelve 'social values tribes,' who are quite different from each other in attitudes and behaviour.

older people will exhibit traditional values or that Canadians are less self-reliant than Americans. In Adams' model this depends very much on the 'values tribe' to which one belongs. Moreover, the model helps to explain why social policies often receive mixed receptions from the electorate, since policies cannot be designed on a 'one size fits all' basis. The current debates about refining definitions of gender and about policies advocating flexibility with respect to marriage and the family may be explained more fully in terms of the numbers of people within values tribes who support or oppose change. A values segmentation approach also allows for a more complete understanding of evolving consumer behaviour, since brand managers now tailor messages about their products to the kinds of people who are most likely to be receptive to them.

In summary, the information presented in this section underscores the conclusion that the principles which shape opinions evolve over time. Attitudes are clearly not simply a product of demographic differences; they are also connected to social experience in many different ways. The extent of diversity among Canadians is clear but the boundaries between value communities may not always be visible. As we shall see, there continue to be many opinions which are not widely shared on either a national or regional basis.

## Understanding Variations in Opinions

In view of the diversity of values among Canadians, one might well wonder if there is national consensus on any issue and in particular whether political polls or market research can actually claim to offer national perspectives. Indeed, on most issues of public importance, regional and cultural differences make complete uniformity of opinions unlikely. Leaving aside until the next chapter questions about whose opinions are to be studied and the size of the public that needs to be included to make the case, we need to review the basis for reporting on a Canadian viewpoint, considering that opinions may vary considerably among the different regions of the country.

### The Mood of the Country

The goal of public opinion research is usually to describe, as accurately as possible, the way a *population* of individuals such as consumers, voters, or students perceive an issue or event. However, public opinion polls rarely collect information from a total population, unlike a national *census* of Canadians that would aim to report on all the residents of Canada. Consider the time, effort, and cost of making contact with a population like all the residents of Canada and you will understand why a census is a demanding method for collecting information. Instead, opinion studies rely on a sample of opinions to approximate the views of larger groups. Thus, a study of the opinions of the residents of Ontario (the population) would be based on the views of a smaller group (the sample) of people from that province. National studies usually split the country into geographic divisions or regions: British Columbia, the Prairies, Ontario, Quebec, and the Atlantic provinces – although sometimes Ontario is subdivided into Metropolitan Toronto and the balance of Ontario. Samples are drawn from the populations of these regions in proportion to the number of people who live there. Similarly, province-wide studies segment the population into more homogeneous areas to assess regional similarities and differences in opinions. The results are then projected onto the entire population. Clearly, however, different opinions can occur even within these homogeneous populations.

National public opinion studies aim to assess the general mood of the nation and how it changes. While regional and other variations are provided, the typical national study – such as those which are conducted by major national public opinion polling organizations like Ipsos Reid, Leger Marketing, Environics Research, and Ekos Research – focuses on attitudes towards the issues that are perceived by Canadians to be the most important ones facing the country. Research on the national mood, for example, may focus specifically on the performance of the national economy and how it is perceived over a given time period. This information is presented relative to an assessment of the public's level of satisfaction with the state of well-being in the country – both the public's own well-being and the nation's as a whole. Pollsters may also collect comprehensive data on the salient issues of the day, such as the debt, unemployment, the environment, taxes, or crime. In their assessments, respondents may be asked to evaluate the importance of one issue relative to another.

Pollsters attempting to assess the mood of the nation also collect information on consumer confidence issues. This involves measuring the number of individuals who consider it a good time to make a major purchase or investment. The premise is that those who consider it a good time to spend have a positive outlook on the social and economic prospects of the country. Perceptions about prospects for the long term, or confidence in the future of the country, are predominant factors in purchase behaviour and in the level of public trust in institutions such as governments, banks, and political leaders. Therefore they are an expression of the public's mood about the state of the nation. Altogether, measures of public opinion and consumer confidence emphasize the stability or instability of populations, giving indications of change to come.

*Accounting for Differences and Opinion Shifts*

Apart from predicting trends among large populations, public opinion studies set out to explain differences *within* groups as well. This means that a sample is subdivided into a number of categories based on culture or demography, in order to assess the stability of views among majority and minority opinion groups. Surveys and polls are designed to collect information on the background characteristics of respondents which impact on their attitudes and opinions. For example, political pollsters might find that there are interesting differences in voting choices between males and females; they may be interested in examining whether gender differences hold in all circumstances – in all regions of the country, for example – or whether political preferences vary when the age of each gender group is taken into account.

The other thing to remember about variations in public opinion is that attitudes change; they vary over time because people are exposed to new information and to competing ideas. People may alter their views in response to how opinion leaders define issues, or how news stories present them. Even the measurement process can influence opinions, for example, by the way questions on opinion surveys are phrased. 'The notion that citizens have "just one" attitude on typical issues is made to look foolish every time multiple polling agencies become involved in trying to measure opinion on some issue. What they find is not evidence of the public's "true attitude" but of many different attitudes. In the build-up to the Persian Gulf War, for example, support for a war against Iraq fluctuated greatly – not over time but across the different questions used by different polling organizations trying to measure the same attitude' (Zaller, 1992, p. 93).

On the other hand, opinions which are rooted in values will not change significantly despite fluctuations due to unexpected events. The issue of immigration and multiculturalism and the attacks on the World Trade Center in New York City illustrates the way fluctuations in opinions occur. Canada has always been dependent upon immigration to meet the demand for a skilled labour force and, indeed, for the development of its industrial economy; however, the number and types of immigrants Canada should permit to enter has always been subject to controversy (see Palmer, 1993). Throughout much of the early twentieth century, immigration policy was driven by the desire to attract people who were culturally similar to those who were already residents of this country. However, immigration during the past 60 years has greatly diversified the country and institutionalized the development of Canada as a multicultural society.

On the other hand, the attacks on the World Trade Center on 11 September 2001 created uncertainty in the minds of some people about the level of openness which has been characteristic of Canada as a democratic and multicultural society and raised questions about our increased vulnerability to international terrorism. Many Canadians expected the attacks to have some impact on attitudes to immigration policy and, in particular, to strengthen the belief that new Canadians should be encouraged to abandon their traditions and distinctiveness, in order to become 'more Canadian.'

Environics Research Group has conducted public opinion research on attitudes towards immigrants for the federal Department of Canadian Heritage, Citizenship and Immigration. It is interesting to note that the attitudes of Canadians to the number of immigrants admitted to this country were remarkably unaffected by the events of 11 September 2001. In a survey that was completed in October 2001, only a month after the attacks, 50 per cent of Canadians interviewed said that the right number of immigrants was coming into the country. Moreover, the proportion who expressed attitudes which were somewhat more negative, that is, they indicated there were too many immigrants coming to Canada, remained remarkably consistent both before and immediately after the attacks. Indeed, these attitudes are consistent with the attitudes expressed in data collected in both March and June of 2001 (see Table 1.1). Moreover, Environics also reported that on a national basis, a majority (55 per cent) of Canadians disagreed that minorities should give up parts of their religion and culture to be fully accepted into Canadian society (Environics, 2001).

While dramatic events may be expected to shake our confidence and alter the way we think about life, these events are situational. In this example, fears about terrorism and national security, if they existed to any great extent, were weakly held; they were transitory and dependent on the unfolding of events. In other words, the fears did not lead to the exaggerated response typical of moral panic. Indeed, the Environics

Table 1.1 Attitude of Canadians to immigrants

| | Number of immigrants coming to Canada (%) | | | | | | | |
|---|---|---|---|---|---|---|---|---|
| | Jan 96 | Jan 98 | Jan 99 | Jan 00 | Mar 01 | Jun 01 | Sept 01 | Oct 01 |
| Too many | 46 | 41 | 38 | 37 | 33 | 34 | 36 | 36 |
| About the right number | 42 | 47 | 47 | 50 | 51 | 49 | 47 | 50 |
| Too few | 6 | 8 | 9 | 12 | 13 | 12 | 11 | 7 |

Q.4 In your opinion, do you feel there are too many, too few, or about the right number of immigrants coming to Canada? N = 2003
Source: *Canada after September 11th: A Public Opinion Perspective.* Environics Research Group, 2001.

data suggest that while many may have expected fears about terrorism to be expressed by a rejection of newcomers to the country, these expectations did not take into account deeply held beliefs about the kind of society Canadians wish to have.

## Polls and 'Pollstars'

*Early Polling and the American Public Opinion Industry*

Institutionalized public opinion research as we know it in Canada today has its origins in the application of scientific survey techniques to American politics. George Gallup is usually credited with pioneering efforts at systematic polling of voting preferences during the 1936 presidential elections, but polls go back a long way before that. Gray and Guppy (1999) refer to the use of a survey by Karl Marx late in the nineteenth century to assess perceptions of exploitation among French factory workers. However, these authors also point out that his approach to sampling and questionnaire construction would probably receive short shrift by current scientific standards. For example, he did not employ a sampling method that ensured that the workers interviewed were typical of all French factory workers. We will discuss the idea of representativeness in Chapter 2.

In 1824, an American newspaper, the *Harrisburg Pennsylvanian*, conducted a public opinion survey on the popularity of the presidential candidates and published the results as an election forecast (Hennessy, 1970). This was an early attempt to measure voting preferences on a large scale using a survey method called a *straw poll*. Little effort was made to ensure that people who gave opinions were in any way typical of those who were on the list of registered voters; in that sense they used an unscientific approach to data collection. In fact, they were very much like contemporary 'hamburger polls' which determine the popularity of various candidates by the number of hamburgers bearing a candidate's name consumed during a campaign. No attempt is made to account for who buys and more than one purchase is always possible!

Nevertheless, political prediction by straw polls of those available to answer has long been associated with 'objective' newspaper journalism. They were conducted throughout the nineteenth century to capitalize on the excitement of presidential elections. Journalists of that era were attempting to provide a more nonpartisan assessment of the likely outcome of the election than was available from newspapers that were often openly identified with one party or another. Straw polls to assess voting choice provided neither systematic nor error-free measurement, yet they should be seen as a legitimate attempt to assess voting preferences using a value-free compilation of opinions. 'Nonpartisan newspapers with objective news stories could appeal to a larger number of readers than the parties. Straw polling fit into the framework of this [sic] independence movement, for by their very nature straw polls were nonpartisan. And, thus, as the country worked its way into the 20th century, more and more newspapers began conducting straw polls for their inherent news interest and for the attraction they had for readers' (Moore, 1995, p. 34).

The best-known straw polling was associated with the *Literary Digest Magazine*, which dominated political polling in the United States from 1916 to 1936. The approach of the *Literary Digest* was to deal with issues of accuracy and scientific data-gathering by sending out a large number of 'ballots' to those who were on its lists of subscribers, sometimes supplemented by names listed in telephone books and in automobile registration. Measurement precision was premised on the *size of the poll*; in the case of the presidential poll of 1928, 18 million were consulted and in the case of a prohibition poll 20 million (Hennessy, 1970). Of course precision was premised also on its *impartiality*, interested respondents simply mailed in their preferences. The *Literary Digest* was confident that these conditions would guarantee accurate prediction by its polls and, indeed, for a number of elections it did. Until the presidential campaign of 1936, that is. During a time of profound economic depression, when incumbent Democratic President Franklin D. Roosevelt, a liberal reformer, was being opposed by Republican conservative candidate Alfred Landon, there was a good deal of attention given to the best method to use to obtain an accurate measurement of voter preferences. A few weeks before the election, based on the ballots returned by mail, the *Literary Digest* confidently forecast a defeat for President Roosevelt with Landon expected to receive about 57 per cent of the vote. This turned out to be completely inaccurate as President Roosevelt was elected by a landslide, with 61 per cent of the vote.

The significance of this event for the evolution of public opinion polling is that it called attention to the consequences of the measurement error associated with the procedures employed the *Literary Digest* to generate ballots by. A poorly selected sample was to blame for the misleading results, since the *Literary Digest* identified potential respondents from lists of its own subscribers, from telephone books, and from lists of those registering automobiles. The lists tended to over-represent Republicans and were a key source of error. In other words, those polled were more likely to be middle- and high-income individuals who were educated, owned automobiles and telephones, and who were much more likely to have a vested interest in opposing the social reforms of President Roosevelt, rather than the mass of American voters who were dealing with the difficulties of the Depression. The *Literary Digest* also paid little attention to measurement error caused by the numbers of ballots which were never returned. They made no effort to profile those who did not bother to send in a ballot and compare them with those who did. At any rate, it was not merely the size of the straw poll which undid the credibility of the *Literary Digest*, but a poor sampling strategy that neglected to deal adequately with impartiality; in this case the sample did not take social class bias into account.

It is interesting that for some time the magazine had been subject to criticism for its method for selecting respondents. The best-known critic was George Gallup, a market researcher and journalism professor, who predicted that the method employed by the *Literary Digest* poll would show a win for Landon because lower-income respondents were less likely to be on their lists of potential respondents. He argued for a more scientific approach, using a polling procedure where individuals were selected based on their actual past voting patterns. This procedure is called *quota sampling* (see Chapter 2). In defining the quotas, Gallup attempted to estimate the factors that had segmented the vote in the past, including relevant demographics and previous election preferences, and selected Democratic, Republican, and third-party voters in proportion to voting history (Hennessy, 1970). Gallup identified the quotas in proportion to the population and maintained they would reflect how Americans were likely to vote. Gallup confidently predicted a big victory for Roosevelt. Moreover, Gallup rejected the idea of a mailed ballot in favour of personal interviews with respondents.

Essentially, pollsters like Gallup had employed the principle of 'knowing your market,' accounting not only for the demographic and economic characteristics of consumers but also for their attitudes and motivations. During the early years of the twentieth century, business research had helped to position products to meet consumer preferences by determining who wanted to buy what. This required a good cross section of the population; quota samples were far better at providing this than straw polls.

In the wake of the polls done by George Gallup, Elmo Roper, and others during the 1936 presidential campaign, quota samples became synonymous with polling and political research. However, critics pointed out that the difficulty of determining quotas that would allow for accurate predictability was a significant limitation to the method; not surprisingly, some also argued that individual behaviour was much too complex to be boiled down to a few questions in a pollster's interview. One critic wrote that 'polling is most suited to understanding those situations where the sum of individual preferences is relevant ... such as in voting or consumer preferences. And that's why polling was successful in market research and voting forecasts. But what the public thinks on policy issues is much more complex and cannot be adequately addressed by public opinion polling' (Moore, 1995, p. 58).

During and after World War II, scientific polling was conducted extensively by American academics and departments of government to contribute to communications programs for morale boosting and to gather information on how Americans were experiencing the war. A series of opinion studies was even conducted with individuals serving in the military that were designed to show the armed services how to get soldiers to fight more effectively (Stouffer et al., 1949).

In fact, the method employed by Gallup and others to gather opinions selectively was seen to be less scientific than a method based on probability. This involves selecting a sample randomly from a list of everyone in a given population (see Chapter 2). The assumption is that, unlike in a quota sample, everyone has an equal chance of being selected for inclusion in the sample. It is believed that random sampling is effective in reducing the kind of sampling error introduced by having to decide which quotas are necessary to accurate prediction. Indeed, in the 1940s, probability sampling methods were preferred by academic and government-based researchers because they were believed to be more accurate (Jackson, 1999). Yet, commercial researchers and pollsters refused to adopt the probability approach because it was too complicated and more expensive (Bardes and Oldendick, 2003).

Public opinion research suffered a major setback in 1948 because of the so-called scientific methodology of quotas. Well-known pollsters including George Gallup and Elmo Roper, who were most closely identified with this procedure, failed to predict the outcome of the presidential election between Harry Truman and Thomas Dewey. Both expected that President Truman would be easily defeated by Dewey since Truman's policies had made him unpopular in the country and even disliked in his own party. They both had predicted that the campaign would have little impact on the mood for change. Roper even suggested that polling was unnecessary because the mood of the country was so strongly negative towards the president (Moore, 1995). Once again the incumbent defeated the challenger; this time the polls were wrong despite the use of a more scientific polling method. Poor sampling was identified as the culprit; so too the assumption that voting preferences are controlled by group membership and determined far in advance of election day. Pollsters defend their performance in the 1948 election, however, by arguing that they did not poll close enough to election day when a conflicted electorate finally made up its mind to vote for Truman. The method of selecting quotas to form samples came into question.

One result of the controversy was to initiate the academic study of voting behaviour. *The People's Choice* (Lazarsfeld, Berelson, and Gaudet, 1948) was the first such study. It interviewed the same sample of respondents on a number of occasions to determine which factors correlated with changing voter preferences over time. This is referred to as a *panel study*. The study showed that when people made up their minds about how they would vote, they paid far less attention to the actual campaigning by candidates than they did to the views of others. Lazarsfeld, Berelson, and Gaudet referred to these variables as 'cross pressures,' or sources of political persuasion which range from groups of friends, union members, and clubs to political commentators. Voting studies became less concerned with predicting election outcomes than with explaining factors associated with different political preferences.

*Polls and Market Research in Canada*

It should be noted that the driving force behind the emergence of polling for elections was newspaper and magazine sales. Systematic national public-opinion polling in Canada also began owing to efforts to have newspapers in Canada publish the research produced by George Gallup's polling organization.[8] Hoy (1989) points out that the Gallup organization had come to Canada in the 1940s in search of new markets because many American newspapers had unsubscribed from his syndicated polling reports. He had signed up a number of Canadian newspapers to carry the results of his studies on national issues and, to do so, founded the Canadian Institute of Public Opinion in Toronto. Gallup's first national survey was to be about attitudes towards conscription. The idea of a conscript army being sent overseas had created an uproar in the country, especially in Quebec. In fact, an unpublished poll conducted by Gallup's company had shown that conscription was perceived by a majority of Canadians to be the top issue facing the country and that one in every three opposed the idea of conscription for overseas service, with even higher numbers in Quebec. Realizing the sensitivity of the subject, the Liberal government of the day, which had planned a plebiscite on the issue, believed that the publication of a poll showing profoundly different attitudes between French and English Canadians on conscription could be quite divisive for the country and might undermine the war effort. 'It wasn't that the Liberal government didn't want to know public opinion on conscription. Rather, they didn't want the public to be reminded how badly French and English opinion was split on the issue, and they especially didn't want newspapers publishing results of a conscription poll before the April 27, 1942 plebiscite' (Hoy, 1989, p. 14).

The government retained the Canadian Institute of Public Opinion to conduct a poll on conscription in Quebec, but in secret, to develop a strategy for dealing with widespread opposition to conscription (Emery, 1994). It was a good thing for the country that the government did keep the results secret; apparently almost half of the respondents in the survey perceived that conscription was being introduced because Ottawa held such a negative view of French-Canadian support for the war. The decision was delayed almost to the end of the war; perhaps opinion polling on the issue may be credited for the prime minister's skill at keeping the country together during a critical time.

Marketing research began in this country in 1932 when Canadian Facts was founded in Toronto as Canada's first survey firm (Blankenship,

---

8 For an interesting discussion of the first Gallup polls in Canada, see Claire Hoy (1989).

Chakrapani, and Poole, 1985).[9] Prior to that time there was a group of economists in Montreal who informally provided statistical analysis to the advertising business (King, 1968). In contrast to the industry in the United States, the market research industry in Canada did not serve as a springboard for the development of its sibling, public opinion polling. The focus remained on consumer behaviour and the best use of advertising techniques, but its method was survey research. Evidently the research companies of that period had little interest in probing public issues or assessing public satisfaction with politicians, although one company, Elliott-Haynes, did conduct a series of public-attitude studies during the years of the Second World War on awareness of corporations, wartime pricing, and private versus public ownership (Blankenship, Chakrapani, and Poole, 1985). The Gallup polls were the most authoritative measure of Canadian attitudes until the 1960s when the use of public opinion polling really came into its own. Not surprisingly, it was associated with political research. Prior to the 1960 election in Quebec, which set the stage for the political modernization of the Quiet Revolution, the Liberal Party conducted polling to assist in the development of a campaign strategy (Emery, 1994). Social scientists in Quebec also conducted extensive opinion polling on social and economic issues immediately prior to the vote (Pinard, Breton, and Breton, 1960), but their interest was to understand the parameters of change in Quebec society and not to influence voting. At any rate, strategic campaigning with the use of opinion polling to direct party communications was used so extensively during the 1962 federal election that one political commentator declared, 'Ad-Men and Scientists Run This Election.' The 'new men of power' in political campaigns were pollsters and communications experts; they had become as relevant to electoral success as back-room organizers (Gwyn, 1962). Pollsters today have a national presence often shared with professional political organizers.[10]

---

9 Canadian Facts is now TNS-Canadian Facts, part of the multinational market information group Taylor, Nelson, Sofres of London in the UK. It describes itself as the world's largest provider of Internet-based custom marketing research.

10 John Laschinger is arguably Canada's best-known professional campaign manager. He has managed leadership bids and election campaigns coast to coast in this country since 1973. In the book *Leaders and Lesser Mortals*, Laschinger makes a number of significant points about the development of a successful political campaign. His 'Ten Commandments' for using polls to sustain a successful strategy begins with the suggestion that campaigns need a pollster who will give the campaign manager advice!

*Political Research in Canada*

Public opinion research has become a significant industry in Canada today.[11] There are now several well-known polling firms including Millward Brown Goldfarb, Ipsos-Reid, Environics, Pollara, CROP, Ekos, and the Strategic Counsel. Almost all are located in Toronto and all are regular contributors of data on politics and public issues to private clients and to the national media in a manner that is not too dissimilar to the dissemination of polling data by Roper and Gallup in an earlier era. While the number of national firms has expanded to meet increased demands of business, since the 1980s regional polling organizations such as Western Opinion Research, now NRG Research Group in Winnipeg and Vancouver, Corporate Research Associates in Halifax, and Omnifacts in St John's have become credible research companies who may also poll nationally. Linkages between Canadian and American organizations have continued; many of the national firms named above are now part of international polling organizations.

Political research has also been central to the development of the polling industry. Elections at the national, provincial, and municipal levels rarely take place without the use of polls. However, it is important to note that these are completed not just to predict who is going to win an election, but to determine how voters identify the factors which are likely to be important to winning. Campaign polls are used to position candidates and parties on the key issues, which are likely to be emphasized in speeches and campaign literature. Not only are such studies conducted by political parties for this purpose, they are regularly used by government departments to plan and assess how their policy goals relate to the public mood. For example, it is not unusual for a government department to assess reactions to educational priorities, job creation efforts, or levels of taxation prior to a Throne Speech in the legislature. When a health department believes it necessary to gauge perceptions of progress on health care delivery programs, it will undertake a 'public consult,' often using public opinion polls to do so. Other public and private institutions, like the Canadian Medical Association, the provincial Hydro Corporations, or the Chambers of Commerce, frequently retain professional polling organizations to help them re-

---

11 The *Research Buyer's Guide 2003*, published by the Professional Marketing Research Society of Canada, provides a comprehensive list of 137 consulting companies who specialize in qualitative and quantitative marketing and public opinion research.

spond to the public's perception of a controversial issue. This has become one of the most important functions of public opinion research today. Few organizations would dare to develop a work plan without consulting those who are most affected by it. Like the market researchers who determine who will buy which products, opinion pollsters have become important advisors on how to adapt the needs of organizations to the social environments in which they exist.

Much of the credit for this goes to the work of political party pollsters. Two polling firms have been particularly influential in the systematic use of issues surveys and polls by both parties and governments: Decima Research and Pollara Strategic Polling and Market Research. Decima was founded in 1979 by its chief pollster Allan Gregg; in the 1980s and in 1990s it became what one writer has referred to as the 'General Motors of public affairs polling in Canada' (Sawatsky, 1987, p. 165). This is mainly because it was the firm of choice for the federal Progressive Conservative governments of the 1980s and a succession of Tory provincial governments across Canada. After the defeat of the federal Progressive Conservatives in 1993, Gregg left Decima and the firm underwent a management change.

Pollara was founded in 1985 by Michael Marzolini who worked as the chief pollster for the Liberal Party of Canada. Like Gregg, he became a political advisor to the prime minister. Also like Decima, Pollara has expanded well beyond its political base to become a major supplier of research to other non-political organizations, including the pharmaceutical and heath care industry, financial institutions, as well as the entertainment industry.

*Pollsters and Punditry*

Collecting opinions, whether done by professional polling consultants or marketing research firms, may involve the use of methods similar to those used in other data gathering. While some firms do both political polling and marketing research, the latter is conducted with a view to enhancing the sales of goods and services. However, it is also the different expectations of reporting that differentiates the two opinion research streams most clearly. Public opinion polling, particularly when derived from attitudinal data on current issues, lifestyles, and political behaviour, places a good deal of emphasis on interpretation and analysis. In the past fifty years, pollsters have often had to go back to their social scientific roots to produce their insights, using the explanatory power of disciplines like sociology and political science to make sense of their information. It is now the quality of *interpretations* of the data and not the data collection itself that sets the good pollster apart from the ordinary one who is talented. 'Deciphering the nuances of attitudes, opinions and behaviours in a context of cultural complexity is a difficult task. It requires intellectual instinct, intuition and an immense amount of experience' (Goldfarb and Axworthy, 1988, p. 12).

The emergence of pollsters as seers has also raised questions about what they do and the legitimacy of the methods which they have used. There is no doubt that polling can be a very expensive undertaking. A large national survey can cost more than $100,000 to complete. During elections, the costs of professional political polling can be prohibitive for all but well-funded campaigns, since 'polling to win' is conducted well in advance of the writ period. Few provincial governments do not have public opinion research allocations in their annual budgets. Some have argued, in fact, that opinion polls involve the expenditure of too much money and allow pollsters to wield too much power, particularly when their clients are governments. Criticism of polling has been directed at the influence pollsters can have on policy decisions. The pollster's take on an issue can often generate an entirely new course of action as their conclusions can affect perceptions of government and of politicians' performances. Indeed, measurement error, which can make predictions and interpretations invalid, can be overlooked when influential pollsters report their findings to clients (see Sabato, 1981; Hoy, 1989).

Some national pollsters have also become media figures. Allan Gregg, for example, now with the Strategic Counsel, a Toronto-based public opinion firm, provides interpretations of issues for the *Globe and Mail* and CTV. Michael Adams of Environics Research is a much-sought-after media analyst on Canadian lifestyles. Angus Reid, another national figure in the polling industry and founder of the Angus Reid Group, which is now known internationally as Ipsos-Reid, began his career as a professor of Sociology at the University of Manitoba.

Finally, the role of analyst may unfortunately position the pollster as an opinion leader who can bias opinions simply by reporting on them as an expert. In fact, this is the basis for the argument in favour of a publication ban on political polls during the course of an election campaign. However, it is doubtful that pollsters or even the publication of their findings ever have that much influence on voters. Even more importantly, it is equally unlikely that electors would ever accept such an extraordinary restriction on their right to know as much information as they can as they make up their minds on how to vote (see Dyck, 2004).

## Summary

In this chapter we explored the formation of public opinion. In particular we reviewed ways in which individual opinions may be understood to be a product of group experience; this is relevant both to the theoretical foundations of public opinion research as well as to the methods used in the study of public opinion. We also considered whether answers that are given by respondents in opinion polls are actually an expression of real opinions and indeed whether respondents are informed about the issues about which they are being questioned. Having looked at opinion formation and change, we moved on to think about the overall impact on society when public opinion is mobilized on any issue that becomes the subject of a pervasive controversy. We contend that in such cases public opinion may best be seen in terms of moral panic and we will develop this argument in the following chapters.

We also noted that the origins of polling in Canada date back to market research on consumer behaviour, but we have shown that it has grown in importance because of its relevance to politics and public policy. We have noted and in subsequent chapters will expand upon the argument that public opinion research has contributed to our ability to manage national crises in Canada. Beginning with the conscription crisis during the later years of World War II, the polling which set the agenda for political change during the Quiet Revolution in Quebec society in the 1960s, as well as current fears about continentalism, public opinion polls have played a leading role in putting issues and concerns into a perspective which is more meaningful to the average Canadian. Public opinion research has become widely recognized as an important factor in decision making in both the public and private sectors. While this has raised questions about its use by the media, and the undue influence of polling and of pollsters on social policy decisions and on the way voters behave during election campaigns, both polling and pollsters have become a familiar part of the dynamics of contemporary communications.

# 2 Methods of Collecting Opinions

Polls are really only good to dogs to urinate on.

– John G. Diefenbaker

## Turning Opinions into Numbers

Despite a growing use of opinion polls, there are many misconceptions about how they are done. To convey the 'facts' about what people think, the trick has always been to turn the opinions of individuals into a reliable representation of the public mood. As we have noted above, problems have often been attributed to poor research techniques. Therefore, to solve problems with measurement, pollsters usually apply the basic methods of social science research to their data gathering. This begins with systematic and verifiable observation, involving both quantitative and qualitative data-collection techniques. Qualitative techniques account for categorical differences, the difference between males and females, for example, or the different political party preferences of voters. More specifically, the term describes research which looks for similarities and dissimilarities among social phenomena. The emphasis is on description rather than explanation. On the other hand, quantitative techniques in social science research aim to account for the magnitude of differences between two or more objects or events, such as the average years of education found among most members of a protest group, or the intensity of opposition to and support for a social issue. The emphasis is on turning findings about opinions and behaviour into computable numbers which may be manipulated in some manner to explain relationships between them.

Public opinion studies may be conducted using either method and sometimes involve both at the same time. However, in order to make meaningful statements about the attitudes and opinions of the public, researchers need either to classify information into categories or to measure quantitatively. Moreover, in both methods, the sources of opinions and attitudes are explored by relating them to other aspects of the social life of the individuals and groups being studied. Quantitative procedures which are applied to public opinion research will occupy our attention first.[1]

*Polling and Social Science*

Like other social scientists, pollsters must take abstract information and link it to observable indicators of attitudes and behaviour. To illustrate this, consider students' evaluations of their professors' teaching skills. Students may hold positive or negative views about a professor's teaching, but how would one be able to tell anything about these views without some indicators of the way students think? In other words, we need to be able to account for the views in an observable way. We first need to decide what would be an appropriate indicator of their opinions, that is, a proxy for something we are unable to observe directly. We might consider using indirect indicators such as levels of attendance at class, since irregular attendance could denote a negative view of the professor. Or we could look at the atmosphere in class such as infrequent laughter and smiles that might indicate the professor did not really engage the students. On the other hand, if we wanted to account for their opinions more directly, we could ask the students to provide us with statements about their evaluations of the professor in a number of performance areas. In each example, we have been using indicators which allow us to create a measure for assessing performance. This process is referred to as *operationalism* and involves decisions about both the accuracy of the procedures and the collection and analysis of data. The last technique, which involves asking questions about the students' attitudes, is the approach taken most often in public opinion studies. The questions which are asked of respondents are intended to create indicators for underlying beliefs, attitudes, and opinions.

Since the goal is to provide researchers with precise measurements of the phenomena under investigation, one of the key challenges with

---

1 For a full discussion of levels of quantitative research see Jackson (1999).

using indicators is that numeric representations should be accurate, causing the least number of *measurement errors*. We have already seen how straw polls and data collection based on quota samples contributed to considerable measurement error during the early days of political-opinion research in the United States, but poor indicators also diminish the value of the measurement process. Numerical representations of opinions are therefore subject to assessments of their *validity* and *reliability*.

Validity, in this case, refers to the correspondence between the indicator and what it claims to measure. In public opinion research this refers to whether the respondent's real opinion is being revealed by the indicator(s) being used. In other words, are the right questions being asked during the interview to yield the respondent's true opinions? In a practical sense the pollster is concerned that there be some correspondence between an individual's answers and his/her beliefs and attitudes. For example, views on individual responsibility (belief) and support for direct government involvement in job creation (attitude) may be related. It is important to note, moreover, that measurement error is also a product of failing to account for degrees of opinion, that is, how strongly we believe in what we say. Simple, categorical yes or no answers are rarely precise enough to yield this kind of information, so sometimes opinions are collected by asking respondents about how strongly they agree or disagree with an issue or idea.[2] Another way of showing intensity of opinions and attitudes is to combine the responses on more than one question together in a summative manner in order to create an overall score. This is termed *index construction* or *scaling*; validity is clearly more likely to be enhanced when the intensity and flexibility of opinion relative to different issues is considered. More discussion of scaling techniques will be presented later in this chapter.

Measurement error may also be attributed to problems with reliability. Some measures of opinion are more reliable than others. In our previous example, we suggested three methods by which perceptions of a professor's performance could be obtained. In this case, directly asking students for a written assessment would yield a more reliable measure than using their class attendance, since low attendance might

---

2 Simple yes or no answers are considered to be categorical measures and do not allow statements about intensity or degree of difference. This distinction is best understood by reading about 'levels of measurement' (see Jackson, 1999).

be attributable to conflicts with jobs or the demands of other classes rather than to a poor performance by the professor.

A concern of pollsters is that their data will not actually reflect changes in the way the public thinks as much as the instability of the measures they have employed. A measure must be able to represent the same quantity in repeated applications. Thus, an indicator should not score inconsistently like a rubber ruler which produces different measures of length each time it is used. Attitude measurement depends on being able to differentiate those who are in support of a course of action from those who oppose it each time the questions are asked. Moreover, public opinion is dynamic; it can change over time and even as it is being measured. As a result of the methods of measurement available in social research, unreliability will always be a problem; errors may be built into the instruments we use. Instruments like questionnaires and interviews are plagued by obscure wordings, inattentive respondents, bored interviewers, and even technical difficulties that impede our ability to provide error-free measurement. Achieving the most reliable and valid measurement possible is essential to scientific opinion polling.

*Types of Public Opinion Polls*

The scientific accuracy of public opinion research also depends on the kind of studies we design. Any research that is correctly designed and executed is more likely to be accurate than research that is not. Moreover, the association of public opinion research with a simple compilation of numeric information enhances the potential for results to be misleading. Discussing criticism of polls as valid indicators of public opinion, Crespi observed that 'one reason opinion polls are so misunderstood is that conducting them seems so deceptively simple. Most anyone can draw up a list of questions, ask them of a number of people, and then tally the answers. But conducting, analysing and interpreting a valid poll are technically demanding skills' (Crespi, 1989, p. 47). Thus, the scientific rigor of public opinion research is in part determined by the approach taken to collecting and presenting information. There is a misconception that a poll is a poll, when in fact there are a many types of public opinion studies which are designed for different purposes and which are likely to produce quite different findings. We need, therefore, to review the types of studies currently in use.

The opinion studies conducted by political campaigns, the media, government departments, and even university researchers almost al-

ways use survey research to collect their data. Hence polls are synonymous with quantitative measurement techniques. However, despite
similarities in methods when polls are conducted by each of the institutions identified above, they are likely to be very dissimilar because they
have been designed to achieve different objectives. A useful way of
thinking about this is to consider them as being either action-oriented
or judgement-oriented studies. Action-oriented opinion polls are usually conducted to measure behaviour or the likelihood of a course of
action. For example, the political polling conducted on Canadian voting
intentions prior to and during the winter election campaign of 2005 is
this kind of research. The goal was to collect data on how voters intended to act. For that reason these polls demanded more of the respondents intellectually because they had to come to conclusions about their
voting choices. Moreover, these polls required pollsters to use the more
precise kind of intensity measurement we have mentioned above.

On the other hand, polling on Canadians' perceptions of key issues
facing the nation in 2004, such as the state of health care or the implications of the Gomery inquiry, was mainly judgment-oriented. It can be
distinguished from the former polling objective by the fact that it attempted simply to measure attitudes and beliefs rather than expected
behaviour (see Oskamp, 1977). While respondents in judgement-oriented
polls are asked to state a preference or sometimes even to make an
evaluation, the research usually does not probe respondents to assess the
outcomes of their attitudes. In any case, the distinction is fairly arbitrary,
especially since action-oriented polls may also include many issues questions and because judgment-oriented polls presume that respondents'
behaviour will reflect their knowledge of the issues. Yet this provides a
simple way of recognizing differences between the types of polls.

The earliest polls on political opinion were of the action-oriented type
but they did not use scientific methods. As we noted earlier, the straw
polls conducted by various media aimed at predicting voting behaviour.
The key characteristic of this polling method was the ability of any
voter to be included in the poll if they cared to be; voters just had to
respond to the questions. Of course, straw polls make no attempt to
ensure that everyone had the chance to be included in the poll, and, as
we have seen, they were dismissed for this reason in favour of more
representative surveys. Nevertheless, we should be aware that straw
polls are still being used by the media as a method of measuring voting
intentions. In fact, 'call-in' polls are regularly used as part of news
programming in the United States and Canada. Radio listeners were

frequently encouraged to call and express their views about the policies and promises of the party leaders during the 2005 federal election in Canada. These calls tended to be portrayed as indicators of what Canadians in one part of the country or the other thought about the election. The media rarely made any attempt to explain that listeners who have strongly held views are the most likely to wish to have their views recorded. Erikson and Tedin (2001) have described this as an example of the entertainment quality of television journalism. They argue that in the United States the major television networks regularly use call-in opinion polling to illustrate probable voting behaviour. While television hosts may provide a disclaimer about the unscientific nature of the practice, they do not inform viewers that call-in data offers a meaningless picture of how voters are likely to decide.

Another type of unscientific polling that is action-oriented is the *push poll*, which aims to influence political orientations and behaviour. These opinion surveys attempt to persuade respondents to give their support to a party or a candidate. They are polls which are intentionally designed to 'influence and mislead' (Chakrapani, 2000, p. 447). The idea is not to assess opinion but to masquerade at polling in order to provide information which intends to 'push' the respondent toward a point of view or a candidate. To accomplish this, questions are worded to lead to desired answers. Alternatively, information may be provided in a question which aims to skew the choice of response; the following is an example of this: 'would you vote for Conservative leader, Stephen Harper, knowing that he intends to cap the amount of federal money available for health care?' Indeed, Humphrey Taylor notes a common abuse is to show the public as having opinions because the respondents answered the question, although they had never heard about or addressed the issue before they were asked about it (Taylor, 2000).

To measure political opinion in a more scientific manner, contemporary election campaigns usually begin with judgement-oriented studies designed to yield information on performance and move on to action-oriented studies of voting behaviour. When a decision to participate in a campaign is made, a *benchmark poll* is used to:

- assess the general mood of the electorate;
- evaluate perceptions and attitudes regarding political parties and their leaders; and
- identify key issues on the public agenda and determine perceptions of the way these have been handled.

These polls are really 'environment scans,' designed to provide snap-shots of opinion on a variety of issues and help specify which groups are most identified with them. The data are used primarily to enable candidates and political organizations to develop positions and campaign strategies. Potential candidates often rely on these studies to help make their decision whether to run for public office. The benchmark poll, as the term suggests, provides the baseline for any subsequent polling that is conducted during the election. The role of the pollster in this process is to generate a reliable overview of the current situation and offer an interpretative analysis that will contribute to a winning campaign (Goldfarb and Axworthy, 1988).

Political pollsters usually replicate their research during an election campaign by also conducting *tracking studies* which are comparative in nature and are used to monitor the performance of candidates or changes in voters' perceptions; as the campaign evolves they are used to test voting intentions. Tracking proceeds on the basis of fixed intervals leading up to the issuing of the writ for the election. Then, it is custom-ary in provincial and national campaigns for the political parties to commission a *rolling-tracking polling program*. This involves surveying a new sample of the electorate every two or three days or even every night to build a total weekly sample. The goal is to track changes by means of a moving average over the specified time period. Critics of this approach have said that the prohibitive cost of political research often means that tracking is done with only small samples and thus sacrifices accuracy for the ability to assess movement (Taylor, 2000).

In addition, we should be aware of the difference between an opinion poll or survey done during a political campaign and voter identifica-tion. To assess voter identification, respondents are asked about their voting intentions. This may simply involve indiscriminate calling to any residents in an area or calling to verify lists of party members. However, there is no attempt to identify a representative group of residents and very few questions beyond voting intention are ever asked. When expensive campaigns run short of resources and volun-teers, a more productive use of funds is to contract out this activity to call centres or polling firms. Nevertheless, there is often confusion, and voter identification calls may be perceived to be short polls. They are not and have no claim to be considered as scientific studies.

One last type of political poll that deserves our attention is the *exit poll*. These are interviews with a random selection of voters that take place as they are leaving their voting places. In exit polls, respondents are asked for whom they have voted and about how the candidates have handled the leading issues of the election. The goal is to establish the reason for the respondent's voting preferences. Most often the media use the findings from exit polls to project winners on election nights before the actual vote has been counted and to aid their analysis of the results. Their use by news media to predict the outcome of the vote on election days has been criticized in many western countries. In Canada, research done for the Royal Commission on Electoral Reform and Party Financing assessed the impact of the media use of exit polls on voting behaviour in terms of their potential effect on voter turnout, as well as their ability to create bandwagon effects which swing voters to the predicted winning party (Lachapelle, 1991, p. 64). This research also noted that the debate about exit polling has a special significance for Canada. Given Canada's vast size and the number of time zones which must be taken into account during election broadcasts, those who reside in the western provinces might not bother voting at all if they perceive that the outcome has been determined by eastern voters before they have even voted. There was a controversy surrounding advance publication of election results that occurred after the 2000 election, when Elections Canada indicated that a Nova Scotia resident who had used the internet to post actual results across the country before voting had been completed would not be allowed to do so during the 2004 election. However, before the vote it was decided that he would not be restrained from doing so.

The feature of exit polls that generates controversy is how and when they are used. The Royal Commission on Electoral Reform and Party Financing recommended that exit polls be prohibited (Lachapelle, 1991, p. 154). This recommendation was based on the concern they do not employ a representative sampling strategy. Indeed, the *Canada Elections Act* of 1993 banned the publication of exit-poll results three days before an election. However, this was challenged in 1998 in the Ontario Courts by the Thompson newspaper chain on behalf of the *Globe and Mail* and the three-day ban was struck down. The amended *Canada Elections Act* of 2000 emphasized the need to publish methodological information about polls and prohibits the release of all poll results until after polling stations close on the day of an election.[3] In any case, American political researchers, Bardes and Oldendick (2003) observe that attempts like

---

3 Durand (2005) shows that media compliance with the *Act* during the 2004 election was uneven.

this to limit publication of political polls may ultimately not succeed because they will be identified as attempts to limit the freedom of the press.

Two other public opinion research designs which are usually identified with market studies deserve mention here since they have been applied in public opinion studies and by pollsters to assess voting behaviour: *panel studies* and *intercept studies.*

Panel studies are constructed by selecting a sample of participants based on variables known to have an effect on some outcome like the results of an election, the formation of a policy, or the purchase of a product. The objective is to be able to specify causation more precisely by exploring the effects of relevant variables. Once a population of interest has been identified, the panel or sample is created to reflect the variables of interest and their attitudes are explored at specific time intervals. Consumer panels composed of individuals with characteristics related to product preferences may be consulted by product manufacturers for their opinions whenever a new product or a change to an old product is introduced. Alternatively, political panels may assess leaders' performance at intervals during a campaign. The point is to consult the same group of people each time so that the causes of change in opinions should be more observable. One problem with this design is representativeness; the panel does not yield a true probability sample since the type of participants has been pre-selected for inclusion; this of course also raises questions about how generalizable any findings are likely to be. We will discuss this in more detail in the next section. A frequent concern is the likelihood that the composition of the panel will change as people drop out, thus making comparison by time intervals more unstable. Finally, there is what Nachmias and Nachmias (1987) refer to as 'panel conditioning' that is also associated with unrepresentativeness. Participants may react to questions differently than they would if they were in a random sample because they perceive they are now 'experts.'

In addition to panels, intercept surveys are a common alternative when a list of a population is unavailable to choose a sample. This method of data collection is also called a 'mall intercept study' and requires that a person-to-person interview be conducted with a specified number of respondents, often shoppers, who are drawn at random during a time of day when those who meet the criteria for participation in the study are most likely to be accessible for interview. In marketing studies, opinions about product packaging, price, and the like are sought out. However, this technique is also used by the media to assess public reactions to controversial issues or as 'filler' for nightly news programs. Despite the claim that respondents are randomly selected, this design has serious problems with accuracy. No intercept is likely to be able to access a representative cross-section of an entire population of citizens, either shoppers or voters. Moreover, this approach suffers from a high refusal rate as there is little incentive for most people to allow themselves to be interrupted by interviewers to answer their questions. On the other hand, scholarly assessment of the response rates to a mall intercept interview compared to the more standard telephone-based method shows a greater willingness among intercept respondents to participate in the study, thus yielding higher response rates. It also shows that respondents in mall intercepts are more likely to complete all of the interview rather than ending them part way through (see Bush and Hair, 1985, p. 162).

The latest tool to be adopted by the opinion research industry is the *internet poll*. The use of the internet to conduct polling has been described as the greatest innovation in marketing and opinion research since the Gallup polls of the 1930s as it offers a totally new way of collecting data (Taylor et al., 2001). It was first used for public opinion research in the late 1990s to predict U.S. elections by *The Harris Poll*, and correctly predicted 95 per cent of the time with accuracy equal to telephone surveys. In a way, internet polling extends the logic of panel studies and uses the technology of the internet in order to 'intercept' respondents online. Since more individuals and households are now online, it is argued that this form of data collection can represent the demographics of most populations. Certainly internet polls would appear to offer the opportunity to collect data from large groups of respondents in a relatively expeditious way. In fact, Burnham et al. (2004, 198–201) identify several advantages of internet (online) polling which may increase its popularity as a technique for opinion research:

- It may make it easier to contact hard to reach respondents such as those from higher socio-economic backgrounds who are not readily accessible by telephone or in person.
- It offers an opportunity for a respondent to reflect on answers before providing a response, as is rarely the case in telephone surveys.
- It reduces the potential for bias if respondents attempt to provide socially acceptable answers to interviewers.

On the other hand, this technique has been criticized for under-representing those without internet access, such as those with lower incomes and less education who have no email address. Concern has also been raised about lower response rates compared with those from mail and telephone surveys because emails inviting participation may often be treated as junk mail and simply deleted. However, Schaefer and Dillman (1998), who conducted a comparative analysis of response rates to regular mail surveys and internet surveys, found that when the two techniques follow similar procedures for contacting respondents (that is, notices, reminders, and thank-you notes), the response rates produced were nearly identical. Indeed, they found that an email letter requesting participation in a survey was slightly more effective for generating a completed questionnaire than a written letter. Respondents in the internet survey returned more completed questionnaires in a shorter time than respondents to the regular mail-out study.

For a typical survey, a randomly selected panel is sent an email invitation to participate in a survey. This contains information to access a secure web site where the respondent can answer the survey questions. Yet, because it is not strictly based on probability sampling, as respondents who qualify may be 'invited' to participate, critics argue that the results are biased. Moreover, any subsequent analysis would have to employ weighting procedures to overcome the additional bias if some who are selected refuse to participate. Moreover, this approach almost demands short questionnaires in order to keep the attention of respondents and reduce the possibility of confusion, particularly since there is no interviewer to clarify and focus the interview. In order to use the technique, a considerable investment in technology may be required at the outset to access the population and administer the study.

Nevertheless, the ease of application and speedy turn-around time of a web-based survey offers many advantages over telephone and personal interviews. The internet allows researchers to replicate a telephone survey at a considerable reduction in cost. The internet also enables a researcher to access large samples of respondents. Moreover, because respondents can participate in the study at their convenience it is expected that refusal rates will be lower. This approach is in the early stages of its application and may eventually grow to become the normal method for gathering opinion in the future. Readers should, however, be cautioned that some internet polls are completely unrepresentative and thus are not scientific polls at all.

*Focus Groups*

One more type of research needs to be mentioned before we move on. Much has been written about the use of *focus groups* in gathering opinions. This qualitative type of opinion study is in frequent use among market researchers and political pollsters to develop an in-depth understanding of how people feel about an issue or event. Focus groups are used to pre-test creative concepts for an advertising campaign, explore ideas about improving a government program, or to measure reactions to a political event. Babbie comments that focus groups offer a more natural setting for collecting data; 'whereas laboratory experiments are often criticized for being too alien to everyday life, an attempt is made in focus groups to simulate the bull sessions people commonly have when they discuss some topic' (Babbie, 1999, p. 227–8). An open discussion often generates new ways of looking at an issue that may be the basis for developing questions which are used in surveys later.

In a typical focus group, eight to twelve individuals come together to discuss their opinions and attitudes on a predetermined subject. The groups follow a set time limit, usually 90 minutes to two hours. The discussions are always led by a moderator whose job it is to put respondents at ease and keep the discussion on track, and later analyse the results. Groups follow a structured format where the moderator follows a pre-determined 'guide' to ask the questions and probe respondents for unambiguous answers. A skilled moderator will introduce a variety of probing questions to get at basic feelings and attitudes and not be content to accept superficial comments.

Those who are contacted to become participants in a focus group usually share social and demographic characteristics that are believed to influence opinions on the subject under consideration. For example, they may have used the same product, worked for the same company, or voted in provincial elections. Recruitment of participants is careful to ensure people do not know each other and to select participants who are willing to open up and express their opinions. Financial incentives are also offered to motivate participation in the sessions. Focus groups are not 'mini-surveys,' however, because the participants do not statistically represent larger populations and therefore their views are not generalizable. Nevertheless, focus groups make significant contributions to understanding public opinion when they are used to generate ideas for questions for survey research or alternatively when used to elaborate on opinions collected in quantitative studies.

## Populations and Sampling

*Who Is the Target?*

The objective of conducting survey research on public opinion is to measure what a large number of people think about a subject of general interest. The first step in meeting this objective is to identify a target group of individuals who are most likely to be informed on the subject. These are referred to as the *population*. For example, to learn about voting behaviour one should attempt to collect the opinions of eligible voters. To assess opinions about the impact of Sunday shopping on a community one should consult shoppers who are all residents of the community. By contrast, to learn about the value of living on campus one should probably talk to university students rather than members of the general community. Or, to assess the appeal of Diana Krall as a musician, it would be more helpful to identify a population of consumers of jazz rather than of those who prefer country music. The point is that the members of an identified population of individuals share a common characteristic which is relevant to the research problem.

Obviously some populations are huge and the effort required to contact them would be extremely demanding and very costly. Consider the problems with any attempt to interview the population of those who are residents of Ontario. To begin with, it would be impossible to identify them all. Moreover, some populations cannot be studied directly because they are not easily contacted; residents of the widely dispersed communities of Nunavut in northern Canada, for example (see Frideres and Gadacz, 2005). Therefore, surveys are usually conducted on only a part of the population or on a *sample*; inferences are then made about the population from opinions expressed by those in the sample. This subset is assumed to have the same characteristics as the whole population. Any form of survey research must ensure that the sample represents the target population accurately. As we have noted earlier, knowledge of how representative samples are is essential to understanding the predictive power of opinion polls.

A useful way of thinking about representativeness is to remember that complex societies are not homogeneous aggregates as pre-industrial societies are likely to be. A representative sample must therefore account for diversity in a target population. As Labovitz and Hagedorn (1976) remind us, one vial of crude oil may exhibit all the properties of many barrels because the chemical composition of crude oil is the same from barrel to barrel. However, gathering the opinions of one or two Canadians is not likely to yield an accurate picture of the views of all Canadians because the social and cultural composition of Canada is not captured in this kind of sample. Several textbooks on research methods, which are well worth consulting on this subject, have emphasized that sampling that is precisely representative of diverse populations is probably not fully achievable because survey researchers never really know all the characteristics of a complex society. Instead, researchers must be confident that the procedures for deciding who will be studied can provide a level of representativeness which is acceptable (see, for example, Gray and Guppy, 1999, p. 152). When that is not the case, we say that the method has produced a biased sample. Again, this simply refers to the fact that the sampling method employed in the study did not offer an equal opportunity for all of the different types of individuals who make up a population to be selected for inclusion in the sample.

*Sampling Accurately*

At this point one might well ask how unbiased samples can be collected. The answer is to have as much information as possible about the population. It would be useful to have a list that approximates a population. Collecting the opinions of automobile drivers requires at least that one can identify individuals who drive vehicles. This is quite possible if, for example, one is able to access current lists of individuals who are in possession of a valid driver's license. The list may not include everybody, since people move without notifying the authorities of address changes. Some drive without a license, while others keep their license and never drive a vehicle. Nevertheless, such a list could accurately reflect the characteristics of any population of drivers. Any list of a population of interest is called a *sampling frame*; when one is available, a sample may be drawn from the names of individuals identified on it. Companies that specialize in building databases make their lists available for sale to those who do survey research. However, public opinion researchers must choose these databases very carefully as only the most commonly known populations are likely to be available in this manner. Despite the proliferation of telephones in our society, for example, telephone books may not even provide an accurate sampling frame for telephone users because not every user is in the book. Some choose to have unlisted numbers, cell phone numbers are rarely, if ever included, users move and get new numbers, and so on. Moreover, there are simply no lists for some populations. Consider the problem of obtaining a list of residents of Manitoba who support privatized health care. What about the problem of identifying a population of consumers of Canadian wines? The absence of lists is one of the reasons why surveys are conducted using a mall intercept to collect data.

Another method commonly employed in telephone surveys is to make a large number of calls and screen out respondents who do not fit the profile of the population under study. We will discuss this approach more fully below. In any case, acquiring a good sampling frame is the first step in conducting valid public opinion studies. The next step is to collect a *random sample*. We have already referred to this as using a probability procedure to select the sample in order to ensure random selection of potential respondents. This means that each member of the population stands the same chance of being included in the sample. Technically if we cut out all the names from a sampling frame and placed them in a drum, each name would have an equal chance of being pulled out of the drum and selected for inclusion in the sample.[4] The advantage of a random sample is its ability to reduce error when a sample does not completely reflect the characteristics of the population. The characteristics of the sample and the population – the average age, the range of household incomes, or the ethnic composition – should be mirror images of each other. If they are not, steps must be taken to account for the sources of the error.[5]

However, simple random samples can only reflect the people as they are. Minorities in any population may not be selected in the same proportion as majorities. Consider the case of a national survey of Canadian voters. Even in a large sample, it is very unlikely that the opinions of many residents of Prince Edward Island would be part of the study because there are so few people in that province. Indeed, it is much more likely that most of the respondents would be selected from

---

4 When names are drawn from the drum, probability theory would insist they be 'replaced' into the drum to ensure that *all* names have the same chance of being selected. This is called *sampling with replacement*. Yet it also means that the name could be drawn more that once, giving a more than equal chance of being selected. Thus, researchers may choose to sample with or without replacement. For a discussion see Gray and Guppy (1999).

5 As much as researchers try to control sampling errors, they do happen. Therefore techniques like a mathematical 'correcting' of results are often employed to make a sample's characteristics resemble those of a population, especially when they are known in advance. This is discussed by Jackson (1999, p. 391).

Ontario unless the number of Islanders in the sample is magnified. To reduce sampling error one could interview more individuals from Prince Edward Island or add a weight to the number of Islanders' opinions to make them proportional to the national population. Alternatively, one could reduce the weight given the larger number of Ontario opinions, so they do not dominate the findings. This can be effective but does not completely solve the problem of accounting for diversity in large populations. To deal more effectively with this, the standard approach is to create pools of homogeneity in populations and draw samples within them.

The standard approach was discussed earlier under quota sampling, a technique that is based on knowing which characteristics of the electorate would be most likely to explain their voting behaviour. The predictive power of public opinion polling in the early years of the last century was attributed to the ability to collect samples composed of a certain percentage of respondents from each of the relevant quotas. The problem with quotas is that all the factors influencing the way people vote are hard to determine and keep changing. Once upon a time, demography explained a good deal about voting behaviour; an individual's age, ethnicity, or religion was a good indicator of how they would vote. However, as Michael Adams (1997) has indicated in his work on changing Canadian values, 'demography is not destiny' and pollsters can no longer be content that their data will predict future behaviour by relying on the demographic variables that seem to account for the way people have behaved in the past. Nevertheless, studies which identify quotas to build samples continue to be conducted, based on the theory that one may deal with representativeness in diverse populations by building samples from pools of similarity.

Another procedure that follows from this technique is referred to as *stratified random sampling*. To take a stratified random sample the population is divided into homogeneous groups called strata; clearly, some information about the composition of population is needed to decide which strata would be helpful. However, once a stratum is identified it becomes the basis for its own sub-sample within the overall sample. For instance, in a study of university students' opinions about the quality of residential accommodation on campus, we might assume that there would be differences along gender lines, so a sub-sample would be selected to account for each gender group. Alternatively, the age of the students may influence opinions on the issue, so the sampling technique would need to take students' ages into account as a variable which should be used for a sub-sample of age groups. The point is that in a stratified random sample, the presence in the population of characteristics that are likely to create important 'cross-pressures' on opinion, as identified by Paul Lazarsfeld (1944) many years ago, will have a chance to show up when the findings are analysed.

When the relevant strata have been identified, sub-sampling within them may be done either *proportionately* or *disproportionately*. Going back to our example of the opinions of university students about the quality of university accommodations, this means that in strata like gender or age, the sub-sample of respondents will be selected in the proportion they are found in the population, or, as in our earlier example of collecting a national sample of the Canadian population, more respondents will be selected to ensure their opinions show up in the analysis. Suppose we are interested in the effects of discipline on opinions about university accommodations and know that being a Sociology major has an effect on those opinions. We may wish to ensure that the opinions of Sociology majors are taken into account in the analysis particularly if there are relatively few of them. We have the option of mathematically correcting the sample to magnify those opinions or we could 'over sample' the sociologists to allow for a more precise analysis.

Most national public opinion studies employ a *multi-stage random sample* technique. The first stage of the sampling procedure usually involves the division of the national population into geographic regions. A second stage may involve identifying broad groupings within these sampling units, such as census subdivisions which are then randomly selected from within the geographic regions proportionate to their size. Within the census subdivisions, neighbourhoods or city blocks may be selected and a simple random sample of respondents identified. Contemporary opinion polls which involve telephone-based interviews draw numbers randomly from telephone directories or use a more sophisticated procedure of drawing samples from switching centres which provide the lines for telephone service on the basis of the first three digits of the telephone number, known as an NNX. From the combination numbers which are part of the group of numbers of a selected switching centre, telephone numbers are randomly generated by a computer.

As George Gallup had warned all poll watchers, no sampling procedure can ensure absolute representativeness: 'Whenever the range of differences is great – either in nature or man – the sampling process

must be conducted with great care to make certain that all major variations or departures from the norm are embraced' (Gallup, 1972, p. 48).

*Does Size Matter?*

One question that troubles those who are interested in the findings from
public opinion studies is whether enough respondents have been interviewed to represent a population adequately. In other words, was the
size of the sample sufficient to warrant confidence in the study. There
are two related issues: optimal sample size and the amount of sampling
error that can be tolerated in order for the findings to make sense.

Size matters, because in principle the larger the sample the more
accurate it will be. That is, the sampling error will be smaller when a
larger number of the population is investigated. We also noted above
that a few cases may be sufficient to reflect accurately on a population
where most are very much alike with respect to the relevant characteristics such as being members of the same religious order or of a military
unit, but this is not the case for a dissimilar population. However, you
will remember from the last chapter that size alone will not guarantee
accuracy. The imprecise straw polling conducted by the *Literary Digest*
magazine in 1936 was based on an enormous sample of over two
million Americans and yet the polls failed to predict the outcome of that
presidential election correctly. This happened because the samples did
not represent the diversity of the American voters.

Realistically, the size of a sample in public opinion research depends
on how much error can be tolerated, given the objectives of the study,
and how much the data-collection costs are likely to be. A sample of a
few hundred may be quite sufficient to reproduce the opinions of an
entire Canadian province if the sampling error is not responsible for
misleading conclusions. Measuring the opinions of Nova Scotians about
the value of the Kyoto Protocol on global warming may require much
less precision than a prediction about which political party will win the
next provincial election; therefore greater sampling error is acceptable.
When a public opinion survey or poll is designed, there are two methods for estimating the size of the sample required; one can either carry
out a mathematical calculation or consult a sample size table such as the
one below. A mathematical calculation of sample size is beyond the
scope of this book; readers should consult one of the many texts on
quantitative methods in the social sciences (see Jackson, 1999). We will
use the sample table in our examples below.

One first decides how confident one wishes to be in the results. Any random sample of individuals in a public opinion poll is an outcome of just one of an infinite combination of names that can be drawn from a population list. Therefore, it is necessary to be sure that the sample is accurate for the population most of the time. A high level of confidence in the sample is usually presented as being accurate 99 per cent or at least 95 per cent of the time.

Second, one takes into account the diversity of the population with respect to a relevant characteristic. In the table below, a 50/50 mix represents a diverse population, while an 80/20 mix identifies a relatively homogeneous population. In a political-riding study, for example, knowing that a majority of individuals traditionally support the Liberal candidate allows one to identify the riding as homogeneous population. In practice, however, many populations, such as those who read the *Globe and Mail* newspaper, must be assumed to be a highly diverse group so the estimate must account for an equal chance of difference.

Third, the calculation of sample size must also take error into account. Error can result in imprecise information about the population, such as having a poor sample frame, or from poorly designed questions or badly done interviews. There is always error that interferes with how closely the sample approximates reality. Accuracy is thus a matter of determining how closely the sample value reflects the population value given the certainty of some error in the sample. This is expressed mathematically as the *margin of error* or the estimate of the real population value from the sample. It is reported in public opinion studies as a range of points within which the sample values and the population values overlap. Studies that require precise estimates may need to be within ±5 points of the true population value 95 per cent of the time if the sample is to be statistically accurate. Imagine a political poll which shows that candidate A is supported by 43 per cent of the voters and candidate B by 48 per cent, with confidence that 95 per cent of the time the error will be no more than ±5 points from the value obtained. It means that the real vote for candidate A could be as high as 48 per cent or as low as 38 per cent rather than the predicted 43 per cent. Correspondingly, candidate B, who is predicted to have 48 per cent of the vote, could have as much as 53 per cent or as little as 45 per cent. In order to increase confidence in findings like these, one option is to increase the sample size.

Gray and Guppy (1999) identify three practical considerations when calculating the sample size for any survey: response rates, subgroup

Table 2.1 Sample size table

| | Sample size for the 95 per cent confidence level | | | | | |
|---|---|---|---|---|---|---|
| | ±3% Sampling error | | ±5% Sampling error | | ±10% Sampling error | |
| Population size | 50/50 Split | 80/20 Split | 50/50 Split | 80/20 Split | 50/50 Split | 80/20 Split |
| 100 | 92 | 87 | 80 | 71 | 49 | 38 |
| 250 | 203 | 183 | 152 | 124 | 70 | 49 |
| 500 | 341 | 289 | 217 | 165 | 81 | 55 |
| 750 | 441 | 358 | 254 | 185 | 85 | 57 |
| 1,000 | 516 | 406 | 278 | 198 | 88 | 58 |
| 2,500 | 748 | 537 | 333 | 224 | 93 | 60 |
| 5,000 | 880 | 601 | 357 | 234 | 94 | 61 |
| 10,000 | 964 | 639 | 370 | 240 | 95 | 61 |
| 25,000 | 1,023 | 665 | 378 | 244 | 96 | 61 |
| 50,000 | 1,045 | 674 | 381 | 245 | 96 | 61 |
| 100,000 | 1,056 | 678 | 383 | 245 | 96 | 61 |
| 1,000,000 | 1,066 | 682 | 384 | 246 | 96 | 61 |
| 100,000,000 | 1,067 | 683 | 384 | 246 | 96 | 61 |

Source: Priscilla Salant and Don A. Dillman, *How to Conduct Your Own Survey* (New York: John Wiley and Sons, 1994), p. 55; used with permission.

analysis, and costs. Not everyone selected for the sample may partici-pate in the study because they refuse or cannot be reached for inter-view. This is called *non-response* and it needs to be considered because incomplete surveys produce bias. When 500 cases are selected and 20 per cent of interviews attempted fail to be completed, the sample is not likely to be representative of the population. To overcome this problem, additional efforts may be undertaken to complete interviews with those originally selected. Alternatively, it may be necessary to select an over-sample of several hundred respondents using the same sample design in order to reach the 500 case sample size calculated for confidence in the sample. Pollsters who do telephone surveys have been criticized for not revealing how many calls it takes them to collect the required sample sizes, especially since telephone-based surveys are being done so frequently. Refusals are becoming so prevalent in some areas that it is argued if it takes 1000 contacts to achieve 500 interviews, one is more than likely to collect a biased sample.

Gray and Guppy also maintain that the need for *sub-group analysis* should be a determinant of sample size. Very often opinion polls are

Bruce MacKinnon

*Chronicle Herald*, Halifax, Nova Scotia, 14 March 2004. Reprinted with permission from the Halifax Herald Limited.

designed where the estimate of accuracy is based on the total sample and yet sub-group differences such as by province, religious group or socio-economic status are an important basis for reporting findings. The breakdown of the sample into sub-samples thus compromises precision and increases the sampling error in the subgroup selected for additional analysis. To overcome this problem a sample must be collected which is of a sufficient size that the level of confidence in the sub-samples is taken into account when decisions on sampling are made.

The third consideration for sample size, *cost*, is straightforward. The sample size is a reflection of the total budget available for the survey. Data-collection costs on large national sample of 1500 cases may be hundreds of thousands of dollars depending on the method of interviewing selected. We will explore this further in the next section. The addition of other project costs, such as fees for questionnaire design, analysis, and project administration, can make a large sample prohibitively expensive no matter what the advantages are in increased accuracy. It is also well worth noting that many public opinion studies dealing with social issues are commissioned by governments at the local, provincial, and national level. From the viewpoint of a client like a provincial 'government department the costs have to be defended; expensive sampling costs may not be easy to justify. In 2003, Nova Scotia Premier John Hamm was hard-pressed to defend the costs associated with his government's use of opinion polling to gauge the intensity of support for and opposition to Sunday shopping.

## Questionnaires and Interviews

*Choosing the Questions to Ask*

Effective public opinion research comes down to asking the right questions. There are two kinds: *open-ended* and *closed-ended* or *fixed-choice* questions. The former give the respondent the option of answering according to their own interpretation of the question and allows them to provide a detailed answer. An example of this type of question is 'In your opinion, what is the top issue facing the people of your area right now?' Here the respondent is free to choose the issue, go into any amount of detail about it, and freely interpret 'people of your area.' By contrast, in the other type of question, the closed-ended or fixed-choice question, the number of possible answers has been predetermined by the researcher. An example of this would be the question 'Which of the following best describes how you feel about the economy? Would you say the economy is currently in a severe recession, a mild recession, a period of moderate growth or a period of strong growth?' The respondent is required to think about the economy within the frame of reference provided by the researcher and is forced to choose an answer from a list which has a limited number of alternatives that may not be those the respondent would immediately choose to answer the question.

Open-ended questions may be very useful if the public opinion survey is about an issue or event where there is limited data available and lots of time to collect it. They may also provide the detail for designing a more structured questionnaire. A disadvantage is their non-standardized format which makes comparisons between the answers of various respondents very difficult and time consuming. Usually the data obtained has to be *coded* or categorized in some manner so that responses can be compared. It is also difficult to impose measurement precision as answers collected do not easily lend themselves to the construction of scales and indices.

The fixed-choice design is commonly employed in surveys using telephone interviews because of their ease of application and the lower costs associated with data collection on large samples. Comparisons are facilitated by the standardized range of responses and precision is increased by the fact that the context is the same for each answer.

A public opinion poll will usually include both open-ended and fixed-choice questions. Questionnaires sometimes begin with a 'top problem' question such as the one given above because they help an interviewer to establish rapport with the respondent. Top-problem questions are general and non-threatening to a respondent. The questions that follow may use a fixed-choice format sequenced from simple to complex issues or they may include a mix of both types so that respondents will stay motivated to provide answers for them.

After decisions have been made about how the questions will be asked, the next most important consideration is the wording of the questions. There is a considerable literature about the best ways to design questions. (A review is beyond the scope of this book but this literature should be consulted if you are about to create your own questionnaire.)[6] Writers of questionnaires are usually advised that there is a minimal set of conditions for a questionnaire to be effective. First, it is almost axiomatic that the wording should be clear and straightforward for respondents to provide the information being sought without being confused by the question. Pollsters assume that questions will be most meaningful if they are phrased in everyday language and will only introduce complex terminology if it is fully explained to respondents. The use of obscure expressions and technical jargon is usually avoided. The terms used in questionnaire-based interviews may be taken quite literally by respondents; if they are not clear, they may yield unexpected answers as this example from George Gallup illustrates: 'People are extremely literal minded. A farmer in Ontario, interviewed by the Canadian Gallup Poll, was asked at the close of the interview how long he had lived in the same house; specifically, the length of his residence there. The answer which came back: "twenty-six feet and six inches."'

A related concern is that the question not be beyond the respondent's level of knowledge. For example, many respondents may not know much about their provincial government's health care policy and may not be able to provide answers that are carefully thought out. The

---

6 A useful discussion of questionnaire construction and particularly of the mistakes to avoid when wording questions is provided by deVaus (1994, pp. 83–4).

danger is that they may choose to offer any answer that comes to mind rather than appear to be uninformed about the topic. Anthony Wilson-Smith observes that politicians are even encouraged *not* to give straight answers when they are asked questions: 'Rule one of spin doctors is to never answer the question at hand; answer the one you wish you'd been asked' (Wilson-Smith, 2004).

Another issue to consider is whether or not questions will be taken the same way cross-culturally. Canada is an ethnically diverse country which requires that wording be easily understood not only in the two national languages but also by new Canadians who do not have the same level of familiarity with everyday French and English as those who have been residents of the country for a longer period. For this reason also it is usual for public opinion questionnaires to be worded simply.

Despite the claim of some pollsters that providing background information to inform respondents before a question is presented is the best way to get beyond knowledge gaps, there is general agreement that this practice may produce *leading questions.* These are questions that are phrased in such a way that a respondent can tell that the question leads to a particular conclusion. They have been described as having an opinion attached to the question (deVaus, 1991). The following question, for example, suggests an answer: 'Would you agree or disagree that cheaper public auto insurance would be better for people like you than a more expensive private auto insurance system?' Respondents who have deep concerns about the cost of living would find it difficult not to agree that public insurance is preferable.

Political pollsters describe this process as using *projective questions* which are worded to be biased in favour or against an issue (Moore, 1995). It is justified by the argument that in their everyday lives people are bombarded with biased information which contributes to the way they ultimately form their opinions. They say that asking questions which are skewed both negatively and positively on a subject helps to reveal real opinions as opposed to superficial views which are produced by questionnaires containing only objective items. We discussed this earlier when considering the use of *push polls* to gather opinions on an issue or about a candidate for office and we noted that the problem is that leading questions increase error by providing information which more likely reflects the opinion of those conducting the poll rather than the opinions of the population being studied.

A third issue to consider when wording questions is to avoid questions which are perceived by respondents to be offensive or threatening. Public opinion research is sometimes on topics which are highly invasive of personal lives, where the promise of confidentiality or the assurance of anonymity by using only aggregate responses may not be enough to encourage respondents to provide answers. For some people, for example, it is difficult to give frank answers about the basis of their religious convictions or about their sexual behaviour. Several years ago, I was associated with a study of attitudes and beliefs about AIDS for a government task force. One of the objectives of the study was to assess perceptions of the way AIDS affects life-styles and sexual preferences. Respondents were asked several questions about the way the spread of AIDS had influenced their sexual habits relative to perceived risks of the disease and were asked: 'Based on your current sexual habits, to what extent do you feel you are at risk of contracting the AIDS virus? Are you at great risk, some risk, little risk or no risk at all?' The clients were somewhat surprised to find that the data showed that over 93 per cent of respondents indicated they perceived little or no risk of contacting AIDS. In fact, they concluded there had clearly been little change in sexual habits in the population probably because most people continue to be in long-term monogamous relationships. However, another conclusion is that nothing was learned since the question may have been perceived as offensive and many respondents were not prepared to provide any information which would impinge on the privacy of their sexual behaviour.

Consider as well the difficulty of asking people questions about their mental health; many would also view this to be threatening. Even an indirect question such as 'Could you identify those factors about the current mental health treatment system which you think need to be changed in order to provide improved patient care?' may appear threatening to some respondents because it implies they have had some acquaintance with patient care. Clearly, there are no insurmountable obstacles in wording questions but it requires that researchers design them with care and recognize that sometimes sensitive questions simply require that a skilled interviewer be available to ask them.

One other important subject related to the content of questionnaires has to do with the framing of issues in the poll. The concept of framing comes up again in Chapter 3. It refers to the use of an organizing theme for fixed-choice responses to items on a questionnaire which is consistent with the overall objectives of the research. The public does not decide which questions about issues or events are important, and the public will usually not have an opportunity to interpret patterns from responses. Critics argue that public opinion is constructed from fragments, since the opportunity for free expression is strictly limited by the predetermined choices on the questionnaire, which are derived from prevailing frames of reference and often are the views of opinion leaders. 'As a cultural form, opinion polls provide partial, short clues to the world they signify, even as we lose whole dimensions and many details. Polls do not so much stand for "the public" as signify it within a carefully structured frame' (Lewis, 2001, p. 29).

According to this line of reasoning, polls simply reproduce existing opinions about the significance of public issues and what should be done about them. In Chapter 4 we shall look at public opinion about health care in Canada. However, it is important to note that the issue framing which informed many polls on health care was that the system had become unsustainable and needed to be changed because there was a growing loss of confidence in the way services were delivered. Indeed, some polls asked respondents directly whether confidence in the health care system was rising or falling. Not surprisingly, polling showed that a growing majority perceived that the system was failing and supported changes in the way the government was handling health care. The criticism directed at polling by writers like Lewis is that public opinion is being constructed by the methodology, which involves an a priori decision to ask questions that imply there is a problem with health care.

## Methods for Administering Questionnaires

There are three kinds of questionnaires commonly used in public opinion studies: self-administered questionnaires are sent out to respondents and are either returned by mail or an arrangement is made to have them picked up; structured interviews are conducted on a face-to-face basis with respondents or by telephone, but in each case involving an interviewer; and web surveys involve controlled or uncontrolled techniques for questionnaire delivery on the internet without an interviewer. In this section we shall describe each of these methods and consider the merits of each one.

As we noted in the last chapter, in the early years of public opinion research pollsters favoured a self-administered questionnaire sent by mail to respondents, but were often disappointed by how few were returned since it compromised the representativeness of their samples.

Despite this, the use of mail surveys has continued. The reasoning behind the method is straightforward enough: researchers can reach a large sample at a relatively modest cost by sending an unsolicited questionnaire in the mail with an appeal for help from the respondent and including a self-addressed return envelope, usually stamped, in which the questionnaire can be returned. On the other hand, success also depends upon the respondent's motivation to complete the questionnaire. A cover letter stating the worthiness of the study and the immense value placed on the willingness of the respondent to participate may not be sufficient. If the questionnaire is short and on an interesting topic, say about music preferences, there may be sufficient reason for the respondent to oblige. Sadly, however, the value of opinion studies is not always recognized by the public and opinion studies may not have the same appeal as other social surveys, such as those conducted by university researchers. Moreover, most public opinion studies tackle controversial issues and frequently include a large number of questions. Therefore, the motivation to even open the envelope may be quite low, especially since the potential respondent may already be inundated with requests for interviews from surveys being conducted by telephone. One can take steps to engage the interest of respondents. One option is to offer incentives for participation, such as prizes or cash payments, which may work well enough if the costs of doing it are not prohibitive. A more usual approach is follow-up reminders to respondents and a second mailing may be required for those who don't return the questionnaire. A good return rate from a standard mail survey may not exceed 60 per cent but follow-up mailings can increase this to 85 per cent (Dillman, 1978). Dillman suggests that the return rate can be improved by up to three follow-up mailings and a telephone reminder if necessary, making the implementation phase of a survey quite time-consuming.

Beyond this, there is also a problem with controlling the administration of the survey. Because interviews are not standardized, comparison of responses is more difficult. For example, respondents may consult with others while answering or may give little attention to the way they fill out the questionnaire. Both can produce vague opinions. Moreover the response rate, or the numbers of questions which respondents will actually answer, is very difficult to determine.

All in all, there are real problems with this method but there are some advantages too, beyond the lower cost of collecting opinions by mail. Despite the problem with returns, this method is suited to studies of very large, accessible populations. You will note that the census in

Canada is successfully conducted by mail. However, in the case of the national census, respondents are required by law to return their questionnaires. Moreover, the anonymity of the mail questionnaire can be an advantage when collecting opinions on controversial subjects. If representativeness can be assured by achieving a reasonable response rate, including low levels of missing data, the mail survey method can be very effective.

Opinion surveys using structured interviews usually yield higher quality answers and attain better response rates. There are two styles: face-to-face and telephone interviews and both rely on the personality and skill of someone who understands the aims of the questionnaire and has the personality to connect with respondents to ensure that questions are asked as they are intended by the researcher. Indeed, the method of choice in many academic studies – the face-to-face or interviewer-administered survey – can yield dependable results. This is chiefly because the questionnaire is delivered in a standard way on each application and motivating respondents to answer all the questions is less of a problem. Moreover, the interviewer can help clarify any misunderstandings about questions as the interview proceeds and is there to ensure that questions are answered in the order they are asked. The level of detailed information that can be generated when using even small samples also makes this an ideal tool for pollsters who conduct what are known as elite interviews, or in-depth interviews, usually with opinion leaders, to study the complexities of policy decisions.

Of course, all of this will be reflected in the costs of the survey, since interviewers have to be found, trained, and paid. Collecting the data will also be more time consuming, making the study even more costly. This can be prohibitively expensive if respondents are asked openended questions which take longer to answer and to analyse. Bardes and Oldendick (2003, p. 66) estimate that in a sample of 800, with a questionnaire that contains fifty-five fixed-choice and five open-ended questions, the cost of a face-to-face interview is more than five times the cost of a telephone survey and more than eighteen times the cost of a mail survey. Thus, it is rare that public opinion studies conducted by consulting firms will opt for this method despite the quality it may be able to deliver. Academics more commonly use face-to-face interviewing as they can take the time to train student interviewers or can wait longer for data collection to be completed than commercial researchers.

There are several other disadvantages with face-to-face interviews. One is its limited applicability to a geographically dispersed population. Cost alone makes data collection very complicated when respondents are not immediately accessible and have to be tracked down for appointments from community to community over large distances. Moreover, the physical setting for interviews may also make it difficult to control respondents' attentiveness. Moore (1999) mentions that interviewers have sometimes had to ask their questions whenever they can find respondents, and in rural areas interviews have taken place with individuals even while they are engaged in everyday tasks on farms. Gender differences may matter as well. Bischoping (1993) provides an empirical analysis of gender differences in preferences for conversation topics; women prefer topics about the opposite sex and men conversations about work and money. This suggests that matching interviewer and interviewee is likely to be quite important in survey research, especially on sensitive topics in face-to-face interviews. Sending younger males to administer questionnaires about menopause to older females would probably result in more refusals.

Telephone surveys have become the most popular method of administering public opinion studies during the past twenty-five years, primarily because of significant developments in the telephone-computer interface which facilitates data collection. Researchers have taken advantage of the ability of technology to overcome the expenses and inconveniences associated with reaching large populations at a distance. Telephone surveys also rely on trained interviewers to administer a questionnaire-based interview in a supervised environment. A large number of interviewers calling from a centralized location, such as a call centre, all working at the same time, can accelerate data collection to the point that a public opinion survey involving 800 interviews and 55 questions may be completed in a matter of two or three nights of calling. Alternatively, if the nature of a study requires that interviewing be done during the day, such as with customer satisfaction surveys, the call centre will arrange for a shift of telephone interviewers to phone during business hours. Centralization reduces error by standardizing the calling process and controlling for the dishonesty caused by interviewers who do not place calls.

As we noted above, the structured interview done via the telephone can provide the same level of detail as the face-to-face interview but is not encumbered by the need to keep scheduled appointments and find street addresses. On the other hand, it requires that a minimum of rapport be established quickly with respondents to enable the interview to proceed. Clearly, there is less incentive to participate in a telephone survey, especially if the request for interview comes during an evening meal. Moreover, willingness to participate will be determined by perceptions of how long the interview will take. In my years as a public opinion consultant with national public opinion research firms, I have always been amazed that respondents are willing to participate in the quarterly questionnaires on public issues, which sometimes cover well over 100 items. Nevertheless, interviews that last over 25 minutes are not the norm when conducting telephone surveys.

*The Telephone-Computer Interface*

It is important to remember that samples can be generated only as long as telephone numbers are available for relevant populations. Contacting an appropriate sample has now been made easier by the computer technology currently being used by most opinion polling firms. The most common application of computer technology to public opinion research is computer-assisted telephone interviewing (CATI). CATI replaces the pen and paper questionnaire interview with a keyed-in interview that involves personalized questions based on the answers to previous questions using automatic branching for contingency questions. When computerized telephone stations are set up in a call centre, they can be monitored electronically to ensure consistency and determine that questions are being interpreted as expected and fielded in a courteous manner. The CATI allows for a significantly reduced turnaround time for interviewing since the CATI software package selects the telephone numbers from a sampling frame which has been entered into the computer or by randomly dialing numbers from telephone exchanges which have been specifically selected for the sample. A related technology, the predictive dialer determines when the interviewers become available, thus determining the optimal rate at which to launch calls. It does this by

- dialling the telephone numbers and recognizing the call results (busy, no reply, answering machine, fax, modem, and so on);
- supplying only connected calls to the interviewer ; and
- recording in a database the result of each non-connected call for rescheduling.

This method of administering a questionnaire allows for immediate data entry rather than the tedious process of coding associated with the other methods of data collection. In fact, some programs provide researchers with the frequencies for response categories even as the data collection is underway. This may, for example, allow questions which show no divergence in response to be reviewed for misinterpretation or other interviewer error.

Despite the advantages of the CATI system, telephone surveys tend to have lower response rates than face-to-face interviews. Clearly, it is easier to hang up the telephone on a stranger interrupting an evening meal than it is to say no to a carefully crafted letter from a researcher requesting an appointment to conduct an interview on a 'vitally important' public issue. Moreover, a respondent's motivation to participate will be more likely to depend on the length of time the call will take and the kinds of questions that will be asked. For these reasons, telephone surveys favour fixed-format rather than open-ended questions and this has led to the criticism that they can yield only superficial or 'top-of-mind,' unreliable answers. Yet, the success of the telephone survey method cannot be denied; Gray and Guppy (1999) observe that the interview may produce fewer measurement errors, since the body language of an interviewer can sometimes be a factor influencing the way questions are interpreted in face-to-face interviews.

Finally, it is also possible to conduct entire surveys by creating an Internet website where respondents may access a questionnaire by logging on to complete the survey. Web surveys offer the potential to reach very large samples without employing interviewers or mailing out questionnaires. In situations where the population of interest has access to computers, this approach may have considerable merit. As is the case with mail surveys, however, there are challenges that must be recognized. Error can be attributed to lack of computer access, sampling, and non-response because of poor question comprehension or technical problems. Dillman (2000) argues that motivation to respond to a web survey can be improved by the respondent-friendly design and layout of web questionnaires. There are two ways of attracting respondents to participate in this type of survey; one follows the style of the straw poll done by the media; a pop-up window on the web invites a potential respondent to click on a site and participate in a survey. The second type uses a sample where selected individuals are provided with a pin number and are directed to a secure site where the questionnaire is available to them. Again, among the conditions for successful participation is security, since personal information may be requested. This technique has proven to be especially effective in collecting data in surveys of employee satisfaction. Because it allows for greater anonymity, it is also used in customer-satisfaction studies conducted by the major banks.

*Maclean's* (see Figure 2.1) used a variation of this procedure to conduct its 2004 university survey. Oddly enough, the medium chosen to

Figure 2.1 *Maclean's* graduate survey November 2004

## THE *Maclean's* UNIVERSITY GRADUATE SURVEY: HOW IT WAS DONE

The graduates were randomly selected from the classes of 1999, 2000 and 2001. They were chosen by each of the universities using guidelines developed by *Maclean's* and its advisers. Angus Reid, president of Angus Reid Consultants, developed a stratified random sampling plan for each of the 46 participating universities. These guidelines specified the number that would be invited to participate, both at the

undergraduate and graduate level, by year and program, and how the sample was to be chosen. Each university then sent letters to the selected grads, inviting them to participate. To ensure that only those who had been chosen could take part, each grad was provided with a unique personal identification number. This PIN and the accompanying university identification number were required to access the telephone-based interactive voice response (IVR) survey.

In the end, there was a 17-per-cent response rate. The results, when presented for all universities, were accurate within 1.15 per cent, 19 times out of 20, while the individual institutional accuracy varied from plus or minus 4.5 per cent

to plus or minus 8.85 per cent. It should be noted: when interpreting results, there may be non-response biases if certain groups of grads were less likely to participate. In order to minimize these biases, the survey data were statistically weighted by program within each university.

According to Reid, the overall response rate exceeds industry norms for this type of survey: "It's rare to obtain better than a 10-per-cent response rate from surveys sent through the mail. The innovative use of the telephone and the obvious interest of graduates in this important subject likely accounts for this high rate."

Getting this survey up and running involved experts in Canada, the United States and Mexico. In

Toronto, the project specifications were designed by McDougall Scientific Ltd., the data management firm in charge of the survey. McDougall Scientific partnered with Telanet Canada Inc. to launch a project-specific IVR system one of the first of its breed in Canada. The programming was outsourced to a division of No Networks Ltd., based in Bohemia, N.Y. in conjunction with Nortel developers in Mexico City. Before launching the survey, *Maclean's* commissioned an independent ethical review of the project. This was handled by the ethics review committee of ethica Clinical Research Inc. of Montreal. The committee gave the survey its unconditional approval.

SURVEY CONSULTANTS: Angus Reid (Angus Reid Consultants); Shahrokh Khorram (Nordic Research Group)

TECHNICAL TEAM: Janet McDougall, Hong Chen, Drew Finnie (McDougall Scientific Ltd.) Dan Silverman (Telanet Canada Inc.)

Source: *Maclean's*, 15 November 2004.

complete the survey was the telephone. Although some may query the level of non-response being reported, the survey did attract 12,334 respondents.

## Reporting the Numbers

*Why the Numbers Don't Speak for Themselves*

Reporting the findings that emerge from a public opinion study may appear to be straightforward, but the numbers alone are rarely useful unless they are explained. In fact, numbers do not speak for themselves and no one should listen unless they know something about the numbers. Consider the finding that a majority of Canadians were opposed to the invasion of Iraq by the United States and its allies. It means very little without some discussion about the source of the finding and of the reasons for support and opposition to the war among different Canadians. Charles Ragin (1994) refers to this as 'constructing images from evidence' by making connections between social phenomena in order to tell a story from the numbers. Essentially this involves describing any general tendencies that have been found in the data and making projections about likely outcomes if they continue into the future. However, it is acknowledged that in constructing images, presenting evidence depends on two things: how the numbers were collected and who interprets them.

To make it possible to assess the quality of evidence from numbers, the overall purpose of the study – including the key ideas under investigation – is provided when the findings are reported. Moreover, the full questionnaire is attached if it is an actual report or the individual items relevant to the analysis are given if it is a media release. This is because knowing the questions that were asked allows the reader to judge whether the conclusions are reasonable. The target population and the size of the sample are identified, along with the sampling list or any other method by which the units in the sample were selected. We should remember that the sample must resemble the population in its socio-demographic composition. It should not, for example, be biased toward any demographic segment that may have been more willing to be interviewed: females, seniors, or unemployed people, for example. Weighted numbers are not real so it is wise not to generalize too much from small samples. Much of this is captured in reporting the margin of error which estimates the overall confidence in the sampling procedure.

Reporting the period for data collection contributes to understanding the numbers; as we noted, lengthy interviews may not engage respondents, especially in a telephone or mail survey. Indeed, the time taken to reach the required sample size is important as well, since public opinion changes over time and issues have a habit of losing their poignancy as events render them less urgent. The snapshot of public opinion provided by a survey is authentic only if the data is collected quickly, otherwise it becomes less meaningful and can only be considered a tracking study of the ebb and flow of opinion during a specified time frame.

Understanding the methodological basis for polls also allows one to understand why they may show contradictory results even when they are conducted on the same populations. Although many studies use similar questions, the nature of the interviews may not be directly comparable: political questions are sometimes included in multifaceted telephone surveys that explore social issues, consumer confidence, and marketing concerns. Sampling strategies vary from study to study: the strata used in a multi-stage sample design may not be directly comparable and sizes are not uniform either, since they may depend on the costs of the study. In sum, taking polling data at face value is dangerous: sketchy information leads to faulty conclusions particularly when the specifications of a survey or poll are not known.

While it is beyond the scope of this book to offer even an elementary review of the application of statistics to numerical data, the way statistics are used to make arguments deserves a brief comment. Misleading interpretations often occur when numbers are converted to percentages. Knowing, for example, that one in five Albertans (20 per cent) is 'strongly in favour' of having that province secede from Canada is meaningful only if we also know how many Albertans participated in the study. In a sample of 100 cases, 20 per cent represents very few people. Moreover, even in a small sample the point would be made more forcefully by comparing the percentage of respondents who are strongly opposed to the idea to those who strongly support the idea. At least the magnitude of the polarization of opinions would be observed.

Invalid conclusions may also result when numbers are summarized in a single statistic. The idea is to express the most typical value in a set of numbers that easily conveys the most common finding. Although three averages are used in quantitative analysis, the *mean*, the *median* and the *mode*, most think of the mean as the average. A problem with the mean is that it is really only useful for quantitative data such as amounts of income or years of education. It is difficult to measure a mean of attitudes, despite the most precise use of scaling procedures. Moreover, a mean is prone to instability by the inclusion of extreme scores. Consider a grade distribution where five students received 25 per cent, 25 per cent, 25 per cent, 28 per cent and 29 per cent; two students received 40 per cent and two students received 95 per cent and 96 per cent respectively and one outstanding student received 100 per cent. The results would suggest that most students passed the course since the *average* mark could be reported as about 50 per cent. Yet a majority of the students received a failing grade. The explanation is that three high scores distorted the average because the clustering of scores at the lowest grades was not accounted for, thus creating an inappropriate conclusion from the data. The alternative average score, the *median*, is the point at which the distribution of grades is cut in half, in this case at 29 per cent since four of the students received marks below this mark and four were above it. This average presents a totally different picture of student performance, showing more accurately that most have failed. Finally, an even more crude average is obtained from the mode which is the score obtained most often by students. In this case it is 25 per cent, but again this average neglects a good deal of information and doesn't seem to offer a better picture of student performance than the median does. At any rate, the point of these simple illustrations is that statistics can be manipulated to make points and that is why they should not be taken at face value.[7]

## Interpreting Numbers and Giving Advice

As we said earlier, numbers are not really absolute. They are subject to interpretation. An interpretation usually involves two things: first, with the goals of a study in mind, to answer research questions. Take an opinion poll or survey based on the following question: How do Canadians view current immigration policies? The analysis will not only present descriptive information on the opinions of Canadians about immigration but will usually explain these opinions in context. That is, the analysis will be considered in terms of the relationship between two or more different opinion items (variables). The procedure most fre-

---

7 For an informative and amusing consideration of manipulating statistics see Huff (1954).

quently used in exploring them is referred to as a *crosstabulation*, which has sometimes been described as exploring 'the way things go together' (Labovitz and Hagedorn, 1976, p. 101). In essence, interpreting the data is using crosstabulation to derive a story from relationships among opinions: finding, for example, that a larger percentage of respondents who are in favour of increasing immigration levels also are in favour of increasing the foreign-aid budget. Alternatively, a survey may show that a greater percentage of respondents who support additional funding for university education also agree that the federal government should increase funding for multicultural centres in Canadian communities. Exploring these relationships allows the public opinion analyst to demonstrate other attitudes and opinions associated with opinions about immigration. There are statistical procedures which allow the strength of relationships to be estimated, these are known as *correlation*.

Secondly, interpreting numbers involves giving advice relative to findings. In the case of the example used above, it might be about how to improve public awareness of the economic advantages of increased immigration, especially if the study was conducted in advance of a planned policy change. The political use of polling to forecast electoral success has reinforced advice-giving by pollsters. Contrary to a popular misconception, interpretation is not a matter of telling politicians what they wish to hear. When political polling is conducted to contribute to campaign strategies, conclusions about the effectiveness of those strategies are expected to be scientific. Political pollsters are often in the position of making recommendations about how to win, but it is their data which should be doing most of the talking. Campaigns and elections make big demands on pollsters because they are expected to have crystal balls when it comes to interpreting the mood of the electorate. Sometimes the message is not well received. Many politicians who find that the electorate does not support them will conclude 'the members of the public just don't understand' and act despite the polling data. Yet they may find that if they ignore public opinion advice they do so at their own peril. 'The art of the pollster has made the life of politicians much more difficult, not easier. The pollster has added a new dimension or responsibility to the decisions of the politician. The crisis politicians frequently face is that while they know what may be popular, they want to act on the basis of what they think is right and the two are often in conflict. This is a crisis which the art of the pollster has intensified' (Goldfarb, 1988, p. 16).

## Summary

This chapter has been about the 'nuts and bolts' of polling. To understand the nature of public opinion polling, readers must have a basis for evaluating how the numbers have been obtained. Clearly, the application of a good measurement strategy is a critical first step since most polls use quantitative designs which rely on complex rules to assess differences and similarities among opinions. We have also identified the study designs which are effective in reducing errors and can determine the authority of any polling information that is being presented.

The curse of a bad poll is having a biased sample which misrepresents a target population. Good sampling requires attention to procedures which will attain representativeness. On the other hand good samples are not the only consideration; we have also shown that accurate assessments of public opinion require asking the right questions in a manner that will yield truthful answers from respondents. In the conduct of polling, question content may be quite controversial: what is asked determines what is found. Usually, public opinion research is based on administering structured questionnaires by telephone interviewers, but, as we have shown, this method may lead to reporting opinions that are merely constructed from the content of a questionnaire and are not a reflection of what the public actually thinks about issues.

Although considerations about the reporting of the data are the topics of the chapters that follow, it is important to remember that pollsters claim that their numbers will never speak for themselves: the numbers have to be interpreted relative to the objectives of a study. Depending on the content of the data collected, presenting findings is sometimes a matter of creating meaning in a good story. In order to do that successfully, pollsters may rely on a variety of statistical techniques to find connections and commonalties between the opinions collected, or they may put the emphasis on theories and insights developed from their analysis. As we shall soon see, this can be part of the entertainment value of opinion polls and, depending on who does them, may exercise a significant impact on society.

# 3 Public Opinion and the Mass Media

Just as love is often wasted on the young, so polls are often wasted on the media.

– Jeffrey Simpson

## News, Issues, and Opinions

The mass media occupies a central place in Canadian society, selectively creating awareness of social issues or events and interpreting them for the formation of public opinion. When we refer to the mass media, we mean the institutions both public and private, such as newspapers, radio, television, the internet, movies, and advertising agencies, that communicate information to a large number of people in our society. Marshall McLuhan used the phrase 'the medium is the message,' to describe the ability of technology to bring about change in human thinking and social relationships (McLuhan, 1995). He thought the message of technology is its potential to change our lives. McLuhan believed mass communications technology had considerable power to produce conformity in the way we think and act. Our purpose in this chapter, then, is to discuss connections between mass communication and the formation of public opinion, in terms of both how information is being reported, as well as how issues or events are portrayed when the media present the news in such a way as to make it interesting enough to engage us. As Arthur Siegel comments about media reporting, 'they not only gather information, but also package it to make it at once manageable, palatable and interesting' (Siegel, 1996, p. 180). Moreover, a discussion must also consider the advertising industry, which is an adjunct of the communications media, since it also aims to influence opinion when it is used to promote the sale of products to consumers, for example. In fact, advertising is sometimes directed at our opinions of ourselves. Consider, for example, the television commercials which encourage us to buy medications to overcome sexual dysfunction or reduce the effects of aging. Effectively these are attempts to manipulate the image we have of our own bodies. In packaging the presentation of the kind of information we receive, the mass media has considerable power to determine the way we experience the world. Indeed, many years ago C. Wright Mills observed that the mass media has the power to shape and reshape our identities: 'they have provided us with new identities and new aspirations of what we should like to be' (Mills, 1962, p. 217).

## Media Polls and News Management

The sociologist Hans Zetterberg (2004) has described public opinion polling as 'a child of the newspaper world' because poll results were originally a central element of news features designed to interest readers in public affairs. As we noted earlier in this book, in the early years of media polling there was a desire to present political information in a non-partisan way for the benefit of the public and because it helped to sell newspapers. Communications that were designed to be relevant to a mass audience tended to compress factual information in favour of creating a social context in which abstract subjects like social issues would have an immediate appeal. In fact, it is sometimes argued that today news is managed in order for it to have the maximum impact on the way individuals will respond to the information being communicated to them. We often see this in the media coverage during elections when the story is centred on the personality of candidates or the likely outcome of the contest rather than the basic policy positions they represent. However, Dyck (2004) describes news management as a deliberate manipulation of information which is reflected in the emphasis given to different stories using sensationalism in presentation and a preference for covering controversy rather than policy. In the case of contentious decisions taken by government or business, for example, management of a story can sometimes involve the use of 'friendly' experts such as scientists, celebrities, or former executives; these individuals are judged to be more believable as spokespersons for the information being presented than government officials and usually appear in the media coverage to provide their interpretations of the decision, thereby allowing the message to be managed in a way that it is made more acceptable because of the trust we have in them.

News may also be managed in the way a story is framed. As we noted earlier, framing involves choosing a broad organizing theme for linking the fragments of the story together in order to make a point. For example, a recent concern about individuals who have claimed to be political refugees being allowed to enter Canada was framed in the media coverage as a story about the situation of political refugees and current immigration policy. This was done by linking together the values of religious tolerance, a bureaucratic approach to waiting lists for immigration, and a decline in the birthrate leading to labour shortages: all as key elements of the story about refugees. By managing the story in this way, sympathy towards the refugee claimants could be expected from readers. Yet the broader issue of immigration policy, including the issue whether it takes too long for all applicants to be processed through standard immigration procedures, was not a significant element of the story. The issue of fairness in having refugees processed more quickly than those who have been required to follow normal immigration procedures was also not featured in the story.

Another perspective on news management is presented by Fletcher (1991). He writes about the use of image politics in television news coverage during election campaigns, which he argues have become 'contests of television performance.' National election campaigns focus mainly on party leaders as individuals; they treat other candidates as well as policies and issues as less important than the way leaders present themselves to the media. The leader has to a large extent become a substitute for the party he or she represents. Thus the leaders' campaigns are shaped by their own need for media coverage. Correspondingly the news of the election is fed by releases from campaign headquarters which are eagerly consumed each day by the media.

Framing and personalizing as elements of news management are very relevant to our consideration of public opinion, not only because the media have significant impact on the information available to the public, but also because public opinion data is used to help dramatize the significance of the story. The alleged bandwagon effect of media reports about opinion polls reflects the ability of polls to create strong pressures toward conformity, especially when an idea or action appears to be accepted by a majority: as is the case when voting preferences are published. Tracking trends in political preferences by the media over the period of a campaign may stimulate voters to join in and vote with the majority.

The mass media in Canada have become a force for the dissemination of opinions on controversial issues as well as political events. For example, during the past several years *Maclean's* magazine has partnered with leading public opinion organizations in Canada to produce reports on diverse public issues such as the state of national health care, the status of Canadian and American relations, Quebec sovereignty, and Canadians' attitudes towards work and their jobs. Claire Hoy, who wrote about the undue influence of pollsters on politicians and government policy makers in Canada, was highly critical of the widespread use of polling data by the media to define the parameters of public policy issues: 'The 1980s is a decade in which media polling has become an epidemic; in which polling has become not just a political tool, an early warning guidance system but an occasional substitute for policy itself' (Hoy, 1989, p. 39).

Arguments about the media's use and manipulation of public opinion data revolves around the way the data are used in telling a good story. This occurs when major news stories include the results of polling data in 'breaking news' which is reported immediately after the data is released in order to provide dramatic content for the news. Weinreb (2002) notes that to use polls in this manner is to capitalize on the emotion of the situation and produce distorted views from those who are interviewed at the time. An illustration of this occurred when opinions about working in office towers were collected by the media from New Yorkers after the September 2001 attacks on the World Trade Center. Weinreb notes that a year later it was likely that far fewer would have said they were afraid to go into office towers than the number who reported being afraid immediately following the event.

This also happens when opinions about enduring problems are reported in a news format as something that has just occurred. In essence the poll has become the story. Irving Crespi argues that 'poll results are presented as the product of an event – the event being the poll' (Crespi, 1989, p. 110). When this format is followed the developmental nature of public opinion on a complex issue can be overlooked in favour of the event, in this case the numbers being presented.

The Canadian Press story about public reactions to biotech food (reprinted below, see Figure 3.1) illustrates that it is the polling data themselves that are the story. The news clip provides significant dramatic content: 92 per cent of Canadians are concerned about the risks of

Figure 3.1

---

**Canadians suspicious
of biotech food**

OTTAWA (CP) – The vast majority of
Canadians remain deeply suspicious of
biotech food even though they have been
consuming it for years with no evidence
of adverse health effects.

Roughly 90% of people
surveyed for Health Canada last year said
they were concerned about the long-term
risks of GM (genetically modified)
food products.

"Almost all Canadians (92%) indicate
some level of concern with the long-term
risks these products might cause for
human health," says a commentary by
Pollara Inc., the public opinion research
firm that did the survey.

Yet Health Canada has not received a
single report of harm from more than 40
GM products approved in recent years,
including canola, soy beans, corn, rice and
sunflowers.

The Pollara study was based on
interviews with a random sample of
430 Canadians in March, 2004.

---

Source: Canadian Press, 2005.

biotech food, says the pollster's commentary. Yet the fact that no one
has reported being harmed from more than 40 different biotech food
products is left unexplained. Moreover, the data had been collected
almost a year prior to its release to the public; this should have raised
some concerns from the publisher about its current validity.

This story also exemplifies what Bibby (1990) perceives as the media's
tendency to create news when little news is happening. Reporting the

news and creating the news are clearly not the same thing. When polls are used to create news, coverage may emphasize perceptions rather than actual behaviour, as in the contradictory message about biotech food shown in Figure 3.1. W.L. Bennett argues that the fact that only extreme opinions or conflicting opinions tend to be the focus of a news story shows that the news is being managed with the use of opinion polls. 'In the words of Jacobs and Shapiro, the reported results of issue and policy polls often resemble "the journalistic equivalent of a drive by shooting." Only the numbers that support the dramatic focus of the news story tend to be reported' (Bennett, 2003, p. 141).

*Polls, Media, and Moral Panic*

Here we should return briefly to the subject of agenda setting relative to the construction of opinion, particularly when public issues are the content of media stories. As we noted in Chapter 1, Stuart Soroka has explored whether the range of issues that Canadians identify as being the most important to the country are on the public agenda, and are similar to those covered by the media during a comparable time frame. His research has focused on newspaper articles, testing for the degree of consistency among different newspapers in reporting selected prominent issues. He identifies a notable consistency among newspaper coverage of prominent issues, but he has not found that the issues on the media agenda necessarily determine the priority of public issues. Issues like national unity and unemployment affect many Canadians and are not simply driven by media content. On the other hand, sensational issues dealing with crime or health are more likely to become part of the public agenda for the reason that they do receive significant amount of media coverage (Soroka, 2002, p. 117). Thus, the nature of these stories may have a critical role in what the rest of society identifies as urgent social problems that require government intervention. This connection has been specifically recognized in the study of moral panics. Critcher (2003) claims that the media has played a prominent role in constructing moral panics around issues like AIDS and the rave/ecstasy youth culture by exaggerating the risks posed by the issue, stereotyping the individuals who have been identified with the issue, and using the issues as symbols of the public's concern about the threat to public morality. He notes that public opinion may be mobilized by media stories and this generates the sense of urgency associated with a panic. On the other hand, what is on the media agenda does not necessarily grow out of public opinion: 'In moral panics support from the public is a bonus not a necessity. In any case it can be constructed, largely by the media.' In other words the polls themselves do not create moral panic as much as the media's treatment of them (Critcher, 2002, p. 137). We will consider this subject more fully in the next chapter, but the point here is that there is an association between the identification of social problems by the media, the publication of polls about them, and the construction of moral panic that should be recognized in the study of public opinion.

*Shaping Opinion with Spin*

Another aspect of news management involves having the media get out the right messages in order to influence public opinion. As we noted above, one example of this is the way information about products and services is communicated in commercial advertising. However, other messages relating to issues, events, or personalities which are aimed at the public by governments, politicians, and interest groups are equally likely to be managed so that they will be interpreted positively. The term which is commonly used to refer to this is *spin*: delivering a news event in a manner which generates the most favourable reaction to it from the standpoint of the presenter. Those who are responsible for releasing information which will produce this effect are known as spin doctors. Quite often these people are experts in public relations or journalism: they can anticipate potential reactions to a story and attempt to control them.

The most important function of the spin doctor is in dealing with a story about something that has gone wrong, thus sending an unintended message to the public. This is especially true of those who manage political communications, particularly during political crises. The film *Wag the Dog* was a dramatization of spin doctoring at its most ludicrous. The character played by Robert De Niro is a 'fixer' who is called upon to lead the media away from the trail of an American president who has engaged in indiscrete behaviour. In order to direct media attention away from the story about the president, a new event is manufactured by 'the fixer.' In the film, a fictitious war is concocted for the media by White House staff, which enables them to show the public that the president is exercising strong leadership during a time of national crisis. This becomes more important as a news event than the story of indiscretion on his part.

Throughout much of 2004 the Liberal government faced mounting criticism for the way Prime Minister Jean Chrétien's office managed the distribution of public funds for what was called the sponsorship program. The purpose of this program was to promote Canadian unity among residents of Quebec after the near victory by the pro-sovereignty side in the 1995 referendum. The prime minister's office (PMO) was accused of creating a 'slush fund' out of public money which was personally controlled by then prime minister Chrétien. It is alleged that this fund was used to award lucrative contracts to communications consultants with ties to the Liberal party; sometimes, in fact, for doing little or no work. A scandal erupted as up to $100 million of the funds allocated for the program were said to have been spent in a questionable manner, even on frivolous things such as on monogrammed golf balls. Clearly, control of anti–Liberal party and anti-government sentiments were a concern for the PMO and the Liberal government. Thus, despite the possibility of unlawful activity by some, including officials quite close to Chrétien, in an effort to create positive spin, the story was reframed to emphasize the intended purpose of the sponsorship program as an important way to counter a perceived threat to national unity in the post referendum atmosphere in the province of Quebec. Adding more spin to the story offered by the PMO was the declaration that the prime minister's motivation for the program was bona fide patriotism and that he may have been betrayed by staff with interests less noble than his own goal to promote national unity. Indeed the media appears to have accepted this positive spin in its coverage of his appearance before the commission of inquiry into the program:

Former prime minister Jean Chrétien defended the federal sponsorship program at the Gomery inquiry Tuesday, saying it was an important tool to fight Quebec separatism.

But he said he regrets any mistakes that were made, adding that as prime minister he must take ultimate responsibility.

'Those mistakes that were made in good faith can be excused. Any that were made in bad faith are inexcusable. If some people acted in bad faith or for personal gain, they betrayed the prime minister, they betrayed my government and they betrayed the country,' he said in an opening statement.

Chrétien described the events that led to the creation of the program, saying that following the 1995 referendum, in which Quebec separatists nearly won, a strategy was needed to promote national unity and raise federal visibility in the province ...

'I personally committed myself as a Canadian who loves his country ... that it was my duty as prime minister to maintain national unity,' he said. (CBC, 2005)

The significance of this attempt to put a spin on a potentially harmful story should not be underestimated since the responsibility for any wrongdoing could be perceived to rest with the former prime minister. If that were to happen he might be liable to prosecution. If, on the other hand, he were perceived by the public as having been betrayed by those he trusted, his higher motivations might well be accepted and the trail of blame would not lead to his office.

Clearly, for those in powerful positions, spin has become an important instrument to influence public opinion. Yet, considering the skill which is sometimes applied to manipulate ideas or present alternative messages, it is not difficult to believe that the media is sometimes co-opted to deliver the message when it chooses to present only some of the variety of information available to it on controversial stories. The embedding of journalists with the American military during the invasion of Iraq raised questions for many people about the likelihood of spin since the reporters could interpret the military actions primarily from the standpoint of the military units to which they were attached or the information provided by the military commanders. It seemed that the American military had made great efforts to avoid problems caused by coverage with an anti-war spin which characterized much of the media reporting during the Vietnam War in the 1960s.

## Polling as Political Entertainment

Media polls conducted by the television news networks in Canada and the United States offer an interesting example of the entertainment side of public opinion reporting. Earlier in the book we described the emergence of public opinion polling out of a journalistic interest in political prediction: the purpose of polling was to help heighten popular interest in the 'horse race' between candidates for public office. Today, prime time television shows such as *The Passionate Eye* on the CBC in Canada or *20/20* on ABC in the United States often follow a time-honoured tradition of using the results of political polls to inform viewers about the nature of the contest. They also use the poll data to provide contextual information about perceptions of each candidate's personality or their strengths and weaknesses to enhance the entertainment value of the story. Clearly, there are two issues here that we should consider. First, the effect of using polls in media reports to personalize a campaign and make it more immediate for voters. Second, adding the results of polls to dramatize the election as a contest.

It may be argued that watching polls in a news format serves to connect viewers to the event and in a broad sense also to bring together the community. Dayan and Katz (1992) essentially make this point when they write about the power of special televised media events, national coverage of a celebrity wedding, the NHL playoffs, or even a party leaders' debate, to create solidarity in societies. This is because they transcend everyday friendship networks and create a shared experience. Following a race can generate a sense of involvement in the political process which may not otherwise occur in societies where many are isolated from direct participation in politics. Presenting polls as part of the entertainment in the news allows individuals to see where they stand in relation to others within a political community. On the other hand, reporting focused on the personal attributes of the candidates may contribute significantly to voting choice. In American presidential elections for example, it has been shown that the personal attractiveness and likeability of the candidate may add 4 per cent to the net advantage of an incumbent (Erikson and Tedin, 2001). Indeed, they note that President Ronald Reagan's self-deprecating humour and likeability during televised leadership debates with challenger Walter Mondale apparently overcome an initial public uncertainty about his age and the vagaries of his policies and he handily won re-election.

In fact, personalizing an election campaign with polling data is best illustrated by the practice of tracking the party leaders to show who has the most popular position on issues such as delivering health care or managing the economy. To all intents and purposes media coverage in Canada emphasizes the party leaders, while other candidates who must be elected to give the party a chance to form a government are largely ignored. Fletcher has commented on major trends in election coverage and points to 'the notable increase in the amount of direct appraisal of leader performance in the coverage and the greater attention to the personal lives and qualities of party leaders' (Fletcher, 1991, p. 196). This is at the root of the criticism that reporting of political leaders has become preoccupied with the style more than the substance of their campaigns.

According to Arthur Siegel's review of the relationship between politics and the media in Canada, televised public affairs programs present political information in a confrontational style to hold the attention of the audience (Siegel, 1996, p. 180). This explains the increasing weight given to leadership debates, which are an example of the concept of media event advanced by Dayan and Katz (1992). The television coverage given to the debate has almost always been followed by polling to see which combatant is perceived to have won. In fact the debates themselves have been cast as pivotal events in election campaigns, yet they do not always determine the final choice of the electorate. Nesbitt-Larking (2001) observed that in the 1988 televised debate on free trade between Prime Minister Brian Mulroney and former prime minister John Turner (a follow-up to an earlier match, the 1984 debate in which Mulroney 'knocked out' Turner), Turner was perceived to have performed much more competently than the prime minister yet he did not win the election. In 2004, American President George W. Bush was perceived to have been bested by Democratic challenger John Kerry in all three debates, but Bush was re-elected. Nevertheless, these events have considerable entertainment value and influence popular support for the parties. Determining the outcome of the election is another matter. Nesbitt-Larking notes that 'on occasion they have offered some defining moments, but for the most part they have served merely as punctuation. Even the more notable debates have done little to change people's perceptions' (Nesbitt-Larking, 2001, p. 325).

Media coverage of an election sometimes includes an analysis of the latest public opinion poll which the media themselves have commissioned. These polls are used in news not only to inform but also to entertain viewers and listeners: in other words, to dramatize the contest. In this context, the importance of the polling data is primarily as an opportunity for 'analysis': it provides the basis of commentaries by news reporters, pollsters, and pundits who interpret the latest numbers in terms of what they mean to the chances of victory for the various parties or candidates who are running. While the objective may be to make the campaign more meaningful, some have criticized producers of news and current-affairs programs for using the data to focus attention on the human drama in the same way they do in a sporting event. Hoy (1989) has criticized media polling as a misuse of public opinion surveys because the media has turned from reporting the news to manufacturing it.

Many contend that the media's handling of polls may lead to distortions in reporting since the inclusion of poll results in election news produces what Taras refers to as 'sensational audience-grabbing stories' (Taras, 1990, p. 194). He suggests that polls affect the type of story that is done, especially after winners and losers have been declared, as the predicted winner receives most of the media attention. Indeed, reporters may then lose interest in covering other events of the campaign such as press announcements from the parties about their approach to evolving issues. Instead, they concentrate their attention on reporting every change in the final vote standings and on the daily touring of the leader who is expected to win. In fact, when the outcome of the election has been decided by the media, those who are declared to have lost find it more difficult to get much attention. In that sense, then, media polling may have a significant impact on determining the outcome of a campaign, to the extent that a party declared to be losing may have difficulty maintaining the momentum of its campaign.

The publication of a poll done by the media during the final weeks of the 1998 provincial election campaign in Nova Scotia is cited as a classic example of media polling which altered the course of an election. Five days before the end of the campaign in what was perceived to be a very close fight between the Liberals and Progressive Conservatives, polls conducted for the local media by the Angus Reid group showed that momentum had shifted considerably to the Progressive Conservatives and away from the Liberals. In fact, it showed that the PCs under Premier John Buchanan had experienced a virtual resurrection, increasing their lead to eleven points. The effect was dramatic and completely deflated the Liberals who went on to lose the election. This is an example of the way polls done by the media for entertainment can interfere with the election outcome. For this reason, some demand that they be banned during the final stages of elections.

Were these events a result of polling error, biased media coverage, or sensationalism masquerading as news? The answer is probably none of the above. Those who have commented were not privy to the private polls that were being conducted by the Progressive Conservatives at the time. These polls had concentrated on tracking the way voters' perceptions of Premier John Buchanan's leadership would ultimately play a fundamental role in determining their final vote. As a result, the numbers came as no surprise to the campaign and confirmed the direction of the private polls which showed Buchanan's leadership had eclipsed that of the other leaders weeks before election day.

## Mass Communication and Consensus

We have already considered the argument that use of public opinion polls by the mass media may help to connect people to political events:

as such, they are an important element of social cohesion, particularly in culturally diverse societies. This raises the question of whether mass communications that so often involve the distribution of information from studies of our opinions may be contributing to an artificial social consensus. Presenting information about opinion in mass communications has been described as mass persuasion. Neuman (1991) labels it as 'the media cultivation of values.' In both marketing and public affairs, studies collect data which reflect upon our values, yet we do not normally associate this with efforts to persuade us to think and act in one way or another. However, Neuman's phrase gives us reason to consider whether the flow of communications involving our opinions helps to reinforce efforts by different interest groups to define the status quo, whether they involve advertising agencies, politicians, or social activists. Before we draw any conclusions about a conspiracy to create consensus, we need to talk about why opinion polling may be regarded as a medium for promoting it. Indeed, we should not overlook the fact that mass communications are usually received voluntarily in our society: we can choose not to listen and not to read them.

## Opinion and Manufactured Consent

Students of mass society theory argue that the norms of complex urban and industrialized societies – characterized by attenuated family and community involvements and employment in large alienating workplaces, as well as a decline in traditional forms of religious participation – make ordinary individuals more likely to experience social isolation, which in turn makes them less resistant to the power of mass communications (Bell, 1979). According to this line of reasoning, the expansion of media technology and the ubiquity of advertising messages could lead to manufactured consent in mass societies, making traditional politics less relevant to citizens (Neuman, 1991, pp. 22–47).

As far back as the 1920s when Walter Lippmann produced the first significant book on American public opinion, it was argued that political opinion was a reflection of the media's portrayal of political events (see Lippmann, 1922). Lippmann was most critical of the fact that media reporting of the day was often based on partisan interpretations, many of which were designed to win allegiance to the aims of the government. To understand Lippmann's critique it should be remembered that in the years which followed the end of World War I there was a period of rapid social and economic upheaval resulting from the disruptive effects of the war itself and the speed of technological change. It was a time when old norms were being questioned and many people were vulnerable to exploitation because of a climate of insecurity. Lippmann claimed the mass media played an instrumental role in circulating propaganda which took advantage of the level of social anomie in order to gain public consent for the actions of those who held powerful positions in American society. In sum, Lippmann saw the mass media as being complicit in interpreting the decisions of elites to an uninformed and largely indifferent public.

This view of the influence of the media on public opinion has been advanced most completely by Noam Chomsky and Edward S. Herman in their book *Manufacturing Consent*. These authors contend that there is a conspiracy by a wealthy and powerful group who have been able to concentrate ownership of the national media and are thereby 'able to filter out the news fit to print, marginalize dissent and allow the government and dominate private interests to get their messages across to the public' (Chomsky and Herman, 1988, p. 2). Their work follows a model of power which contends that media elites make decisions that are not in the public interest but in their own interests and the interests of members of elite groups in society (see Mills, 1956; Porter, 1967; Clement, 1988).

Chomsky and Herman argue that contemporary media coverage is most likely to be based on interpretations of events which advance the interests of American business and government by circulating state-sponsored propaganda. To support their argument, they allege that the media often suspends critical judgment and even attempts to suppress evidence when providing coverage of events involving injustice or criminality in regimes known to be aligned with the priorities both national and international of the American government. All in all, they see the mass media as uncritical observers of state policy filtering their coverage of any news which could lead to dissent.

More recently this theory has been the subject of research designed to show that the media's description of the results of public opinion polling in news coverage is intended to portray an ideological consensus among the electorate which is not reflected in respondents' answers: 'Majorities consistently support increased government spending in traditionally "liberal" areas such as healthcare, education, environmental protection and even when the word 'welfare' is not used – programs for assisting the poor ... And yet the media's interpretative frameworks tend to suppress the leftist leanings of opinion polls responses, creating a picture of a moderate to conservative citizenry that matches a moderate to conservative political elite' (Lewis, 2001, p. 44).

Lewis agues that what the polls show is often interpreted by reporters to fit the needs of a story that is most likely to be consistent with the thinking of political elites. In other words, when data is presented relative to a public issue it will be 'interpreted' by the media in order to support the framing of the story; which of course he argues will always have a moderate or conservative orientation. Lewis provides many examples of reframing the findings from public opinion studies. For example, on the issue of access to higher education in the United States, Lewis discusses a CBS report which presents polling data showing majority support for universal access to higher education; but it is accompanied by numbers which show that many Americans do not believe the government has a financial obligation to underwrite universal access. He argues that this weakens the original survey findings which could be interpreted as reflecting public support for a liberal value of collective responsibility for higher education, in favour of showing that a more elitist belief in the value of individual responsibility continues to pervade public thinking about the issue (Lewis, 2001, p. 52). In general, Lewis sees the media as being dismissive of findings on public thinking that are not congruent with policies pursued by elites. When these data are used in coverage of issues and events, the media will provide a positive spin to the story with the objective of marginalizing those who express dissent from conventional views.

*Consensus and Elite Opinion*

In an early analysis of structure and control in the Canadian media, Porter (1967) also argued that those who occupied ownership positions vis-à-vis the broadcasting and publishing industry were more likely to share interests with other elite groups in the country. In fact, he showed that the concentration of ownership of the media was indicative of the power of dominant ethnic and class groups in Canadian society. For example, he noted that the English-Canadian media was dominated by those with an English background and included few representatives from French and other ethnic groups. Efforts to achieve and maintain control of the mass media could be seen as a reflection of the process of fusing power between economic, political, and ideological elites in Canadian society. Porter's interpretations do lend support to the argument that consensus is likely to be associated with elite interests. In fact, during the 1970s, concern over the concentration of media ownership caused the federal government to undertake a Senate investigation of the consolidation of ownership. The results were published as the *Davey Report*. This report maintained that ownership of newspapers and periodicals was indeed in the hands of a small business elite. For example, the three largest newspaper chains controlled nearly 50 per cent of the circulation of the daily newspapers in Canada's major cities (Singer, 1995, p. 319). In fact it recommended regulation of future transactions involving mergers, although the recommendation was not adopted. Singer also notes that despite a second review of the issue, completed in the 1980s by the Kent Commission, there was further deterioration of independent ownership of news services in the 1990s.

Does this mean more control of public opinion by elites? Not necessarily. An alternative hypothesis put forward by Neuman (1992) identifies the current web-based, information-technological revolution as offering the potential to reduce the persuasive power of mass media. He describes the web as a 'socio-political force' which may expand political pluralism in democratic societies. This is because the delivery of mass communications is now aimed directly into the monitors of individual computers through email, electronic notice boards, or chat rooms. Consumers of the news may be less passive and naive about what they receive since they have the ability to seek alternative information from a variety of sources, including a worldwide network of news services. Thus, information filters potentially matter less to individual thinking in an environment of globalized mass communications and, more to the point, elite control is at least a more implausible outcome. In sum, web-based communications represents the possibility of considerable user empowerment through greater control of the receipt of messages. 'The user-controlled network enhances the viability of active intermediate social groupings, the classic pluralist response to mass society. Electronic versions of traditional town meeting or informal discussions of politics around the cracker barrel at the general store provide positive and hopeful metaphors' (Neuman, 1992, p. 78).

A critical evaluation of a conspiracy thesis by the media is well beyond the scope of this book, but one would wonder whether a majority of the consumers of information provided by the mass media really accept uncritically what they read and hear; especially when there are so many alternative sources to consult. However, there is another reason to be concerned about the power of the media to create mass

consent: the powerful influence of American media on the way Canadians think.

As most would recognize, Canadians are bombarded on a daily basis
with information coming from media sources originating in the United
States. In fact, it has sometimes been identified as a source of difficulty
in defining our identity as a nation. Canadians may have a taste for
American cultural products but if important elements of culture including drama, literature, and news stories come to us from the perspective
of those who live in another country, the way we see ourselves and the
opinions we hold are likely to be shaped by the way Americans experience life. Winter and Goldman measured the impact of American media
on Canadians by asking students about their knowledge of political and
media figures and found that American news reporters were more
frequently identified correctly than were Canadian news reporters (Winter and Goldman, 1995, p. 207). American political leaders were also
better known by students than were Canadian political leaders. Winter
and Goldman also discuss research that shows that television viewers
seem to know more about the American legal process than they know
about the Canadian judicial system. This is because they derive their
knowledge from American television programming which provides
dramatic presentations of the application of law and the behaviour of
lawyers that viewers in this country accept as typical of the way legal
process works. Moreover, watching major news stories that emphasize
criminal behaviour or racial strife being interpreted by reporters from
CNN in Washington or New York has the potential to create an American perspective on local events, as well as to determine attitudes that
accompany those perspectives. Canadians who decry the increase in
violent crime or oppose gun control may form their opinions from
information received in American news stories. Charles Acland refers
to the effect of the American entertainment media: 'American culture
will colonize Canadian minds' (Acland, 1994, p. 233). On the other
hand, Adams (2003) shows that Canadians have become less comfort-
able with elements of American life and thus their acceptance of popular culture products from the United States may not add up to an
acceptance of American values. Clearly the examples cited do not prove
that Canadian values have merged with those of Americans, yet they
show that imported media has the potential to create some unwanted
effects on public opinion in this country. Moreover, if writers like
Chomsky and Herman and Lewis are correct, Canadian opinions will

be informed not at all by what ordinary Americans think, but by a skilful manipulation of information by the media to reframe views that are more in line with those of elites.

## Advertising and Public Opinion

Theories about the process of influencing mass opinion and creating consensus must also account for the power of advertising to alter or reinforce the way we experience life in society. A television commercial which markets the latest technological features of a new automobile may have the same power as propaganda does to control what we believe and how we will behave. Advertising the latest in automobile technology not only attempts to influence consumer behaviour but also communicates other messages which can determine our beliefs about lifestyles, including how we define status, success, or sophistication. In fact, some argue that the subtlety of commercial messages have even greater power to create opinion than propaganda does. In *The Mechanical Bride,* Marshall McLuhan observed this about the potential danger of advertising messages: 'ours is the first age in which many thousands of the best-trained individual minds have made it a full-time business to get inside the collective public mind. To get inside in order to manipulate, exploit, control is the object now. And to generate heat not light is the intention. To keep everybody in the helpless state engendered by prolonged mental rutting is the effect of many ads and much entertainment alike' (McLuhan, 1995, p. 21).

McLuhan's views have contemporary resonance: he discusses advertising that combines messages about sex and technology and in particular the commodification of the female anatomy in the marketing of technology. In McLuhan's view, technology had become an extension of our bodies. For example, marketing automobiles using human models deceives the audience into thinking about the two entities as similar products. Thus, blending sex with technology creates attitudes about human sexuality as a mechanical process. Similarly, political commercials which aim to influence voting choice may combine political messages with images of families, communities, or the environment. Whether this form of mass communication actually has the power to control the thinking of audiences is debatable. Do we really spend much of our time in an advertising-induced haze as McLuhan argues? Have marketers replaced the community or the family as the main source of values and opinions? On the other hand, since media-based marketing is so omnipresent, he was clearly correct in alerting society to the profound social and psychological impact it may have.

## Audience Research

The most obvious connection between the study of public opinion and advertising is in the methods used by communications organizations to conduct audience research. Broadly speaking, audiences are aggregates characterized by similar tastes or preferences in programming which are often related to their social characteristics. McQuail notes that an audience may be thought of as a public 'when it has an independent existence prior to its identification as an audience' (McQuail, 1997, p. 26). In other words, 'television audience' or 'newspaper readership' refers to a homogeneous social group which derives its connectedness from shared characteristics such as residential location, religious values, or political orientations. An example of this kind of audience would be those who tune in to evangelical Christian programs on radio and television. McQuail also tells us that audiences can be formed from people who share similar lifestyle or consumer tastes. They are members of an audience: they may not belong to a group or have any sense of collective identity although they may have similar demographic characteristics. An example would be the audiences for the various reality television shows like *Survivor*, which has become so popular recently. Research is designed to measure the size and socio-demographic composition of the audiences for these forms of programming. Ross and Nightingale (2003) describe the purpose of audience measurement as two-fold: providing information so media managers can make informed decisions about program timing and content; and allowing advertising firms to assess the effectiveness of product promotion or social communication such as the issue advertising produced for government and business (Singer, 1995).

Audience research was initiated in the United States after the commercialization of radio, mainly to determine who was listening to the programs and what they thought of them. The most widely known form of audience measurement is associated with media decisions and is known as ratings analysis. It counts the size of the audience for various television programs, newspapers, or commercials. The results are usually sold to advertisers and allow them to assess how media selections are made or how loyalty is maintained. The most famous ratings-research company is likely Nielsen Media Research which is best known for its ratings of television audiences. It uses the same scientific methods as other public opinion research including quantitative analysis based on representative samples of a target population, tracking surveys, and consumer panels. In Canada, surveys of audience opinions are conducted by the Bureau of Broadcast Measurement which has conducted media studies since the early 1940s. Newspaper sales and ratings are also monitored by the Newspaper Marketing Board. Its data bank of audience opinion is termed NADBANK; national opinion research firms frequently conduct surveys on an outsource basis for the Board. The two important concepts to understand in ratings research are *share* and *reach* (Ross and Nightingale, 2003). Audience share is a way of estimating the size of the audience exposed to a television program, newspaper, or commercial relative to the size of the target population of consumers during a specific time period. Reach refers to the frequency of exposure of the audience to the program or a commercial during that time period. The ratings are important in determining satisfaction with program options and program content including audience expectations about what they will receive from future programming. In essence, the ratings tell advertisers which program choices are the best to use in order to target marketing messages for products. For example, consider the advertising messages that would be meaningful to audiences of the highly rated and popular television program *Friends*, a situation comedy about 'thirty something,' educated although underemployed single people who live in New York City. The characters are individuals at a life-cycle stage in which they have disengaged from parental families but not established permanent unions and thus have made friendships the core of their socio-emotional needs. In fact, the challenges of personal relationships have been the main entertainment themes of the show. Marketing messages on *Friends* are likely to be most effective when designed around the values and attitudes of an audience who identify with the life-styles of its characters. The products likely to be marketed to that audience relate not only to the demographic attributes of the viewers – age, income, and gender – but also need to be 'ego-expressive' products reflecting the interests of the characters – clothing, haircare products, automobiles, or even Starbucks coffee. Moreover, they may go beyond straightforward commercials and embed marketing messages about these products during the dramatic action in the show.

This example presents the audience as a passive target of advertisers; perhaps they are not that accessible after all. McQuail observes that it is necessary to think about other ways the audience may be influenced by messages in order to assess the relevance of ratings research to advertisers. 'It is clear that the seemingly simple notions of being in the audience and in contact with the media are deceptive and the aspiration to pin down the reach of a medium, channel or message is ultimately likely to be frustrated. With all the developments of research technique, there can never be more than a very approximate estimate of who was (or is being) reached, where, and under what circumstances and in what state of mind' (McQuail, 1997, p. 64).

Nevertheless, ratings analysis such as those provided by Nielsen have had an enormous impact on decisions about how to influence consumer opinions simply because they have the ability to interpret what we are and give it back to us as a form of entertainment.

### Seeing Ourselves through Advertising

Advertising is also linked to understanding public opinion in questions about whether marketing messages simply provide factual information about products or attempt to persuade consumers to view the world and themselves differently (Singer, 1986). Socialization theories teach us that we are rewarded in terms of status, recognition, and wealth for acting in accordance with standards that society considers to be important. We learn what these are by observing and imitating the behaviour of others and we are reinforced when this behaviour has been accomplished successfully (see Bandura and Walters, 1963). Those who have studied the role of communication in mass societies have noted that advertising has also become a particularly influential element of imitative learning, showing individuals how to respond to new situations and telling them how they should want to respond to them, by constructing 'idealized identities and lifestyles' for them to imitate (Singer, 1986, p. 74). Goffman (1979) also discusses the impact of advertising on perceptions of appropriate behaviour using the term *depictions of reality*. He observes that cues or guidelines for appropriate behaviour often come not from actual behaviour we observe but from depictions seen in advertising. In other words, we behave according to the way we perceive people should act when confronted with a situation similar to that seen in an advertisement. Attitudes are learned and cues for them may be derived from both verbal and non-verbal messages contained in a display such as a ritual act of greeting between people. Advertising represents an important form of display which presents an image to show how to think and act. Advertising may indeed create a make-believe world but its presentation of images, people, and products shapes public perceptions and gives meaning to our everyday activities. As Goffman argues, the way we live in the real world reflects how it is presented in advertising messages.

One of the most persistent controversies surrounding those advertising messages concerns the images of sexuality and gender that are presented in them. More specifically, sexuality is said to be socially constructed in a manner that overemphasizes the nature and importance of sex and distorts perceptions of gender behaviour. For example, Jean Kilbourne, an outspoken critic of the power of advertising on interpersonal relationships, has argued that advertisements which mix messages about relationships with consumerism trivialize the nature of relationships, or at least confuse the message about the product with perceptions about people. In doing so, advertising manipulates public opinion about human sexuality. On the one hand, advertising has clearly made a significant contribution to public acceptance of sexuality and sexual pleasure as an expression of interpersonal attraction, but its critics claim it does so in an exploitative way because it associates desires for sex with needs for the consumer products being marketed, thereby creating 'artificial longings' (Kilbourne, 1999, p. 77). For example, in advertising, effective sexual performance is often associated with the choice of an automobile, clothing, or perfume and the message we are encouraged to accept is that it is the use of the product which supplies sex appeal more than the personal qualities of individuals. As Jean Kilbourne has written more recently, 'people in ads like this aren't lovers – they are sexy because of the products they use. The jeans, the perfume, the car are sexy in themselves' (Kilbourne, 2003, p. 175).

In a study of the marketing of men's fragrances, Hubbard (1994) found an increase in the number of magazine advertisements with sexual or sensual content relative to those which feature family, elegance, power, or romance. These sensual or sexual ads emphasize utopian wish fulfilment as a theme, holding out the promise of turning sexual fantasies into realities by choosing the right perfume. Perhaps more importantly, Hubbard observes that in advertising for male fragrances which is of a sensual or sexual nature, the male is often seen to be obsessed with his own need for sexual gratification. The needs of the partner in sexual activity are apparently second in importance to gratification of the needs of the consumer. Kilbourne describes a fragrance ad as creating narcissistic sexual images: 'a celebration of laughter ...

love ... and intense happiness says the ad for Amarige perfume. But all we see is a woman who seems to be in the throes of orgasm caressing her own throat. We don't need any partners any more. This is perfect disconnection' (Kilbourne, 2003, p. 176). Thus, she implies that attitudes towards the need for sexual gratification are being changed by the advertising media to mean that it need not be a social activity at all.

Clearly, this is what is meant by the use of the term *social construction* of sexuality since the commercial presentation of the product also presents norms about sexual performance. Some would argue that attitudes toward sexual partners or expectations of sexual experiences have been created by the fantasy world of marketing and are recognized by many to be quite unrealistic. Others say that marketing with sexual themes has a sinister side because the attitudes towards gender that they convey are essentially exploitative. For example, beer advertising features men in bars where successful entertainment is equated with aggressively 'scoring' a night of casual sex. Similarly women have been encouraged by these advertising messages to accept that their ability to relate to potential partners is almost completely based on their glamour. More recently, however, advertisers have noticed that women also drink beer and so there is a need to mix drinking with sex appeal for women as well. Beer is associated with being sexy and available. All in all, the sensual images of advertising encourage us to view human relationships as we would a commodity.

We should also note that many years ago, Goffman (1979), whose work we have already considered, theorized that displays would be likely to shape our opinions about behaviour appropriate for women and men. In this case he meant pictures in magazine advertising would have the effect of creating stereotypes for male and female behaviour in everyday life. He showed that women in these ritualistic displays were posed in ways different from men; the pictures usually showed women as subordinate to men in a variety of ways, such as being physically smaller, actively involved in socio-emotional work, or being deferential by posing in positions where they were lying down or sitting below men while fully or partly undressed. The conclusion was that advertising involving women presented a range of images reinforcing opinions that women should be flirtatious, submissive sex objects and child bearers. Feminist writers in Canada have sometimes cited Goffman's work to raise awareness of the extent to which this tendency is exaggerated in our culture (see Mackie, 1991).

Perceptions of masculinity which have been reinforced in advertising messages have usually emphasized a macho image. However, television advertising involving males during the past decade has often presented men as wimps or as being child-like people needing a powerful woman to help them deal with life's problems. Consider the ads which show men needing help just keeping their clothing clean and needing to rely on women to find them the right laundry products, or commercials which portray men as overreacting to the symptoms of a simple cold and needing women to tell them how to use medications effectively (Seely, 1994). All in all, current advertising messages like these appear to feed masculine anxiety, which is unusual in a medium which has traditionally favoured powerful and confident male figures.

On the other hand, rather than presenting gender images in reverse, television advertising frequently features women in powerful roles which are not designed to shape new attitudes about gender but are presented to show that they are experts about the products (Twitchell, 2003). The net result continues to be a perpetuation of the social construction of gender through stereotypical displays and, as Goffman observed, these become reality since we think and act in accordance with the representations of reality they make available to us.

## Summary

The relationship between the mass media and public opinion is usually a subject of discussion during the emergence of controversial social issues and political events when critics complain about its power to shape our reactions to them. However, in this chapter we have considered ways that information is managed in order for it to have the maximum impact on consumers, whether they are watching the evening news on television or reviewing the content of commercial advertisements. Managing information in this sense means presenting it in a manner that gets a message across, usually to influence public opinion about the topic. Coverage of news has sometimes been criticized for creating stories where none exist by using sensationalism, personalizing, linking diverse news fragments to make a theme for the story, or providing polling data which confirms the importance of the issue. This can be seen to occur during moral panics: by building the dramatic content in the media coverage, a crisis in public opinion may be created which is usually more than is warranted by the situation. This can also be thought of as message management designed by those who release information on key issues to have the maximum impact on public thinking.

Another argument we have considered here connects the use of polling by the media to effect mass persuasion. Some claim that interest groups and elites manipulate public opinion by using the media and create an artificial consensus on issues when one does not really exist. Yet it is difficult to accept that this can be true given the plethora of information sources that are available in society today. On the other hand, Canadians are subject to many American media products: this has the potential to create perspectives on local issues which are not derived from the experience of Canadians. Stories about crime or politics that come to Canadians from American television networks are clearly influential in creating opinion about justice and political efficacy in this country.

While some are concerned that this will ultimately result in a harmonization of values between the cultures of the two countries, perhaps the greater danger of cultural homogenization comes from the effects of advertising. Given that each day Canadians are bombarded by commercials and embedded marketing messages, it is not surprising that advertising has had a powerful influence on opinions about products and people. Most important is the danger posed by the creation of images about ourselves. Existing analysis of the persuasive power of advertising would lead one to conclude that the subtle messages associating products with people could well contribute to the development of moral panic about representations of sexuality in society. The continued use of sexual images as key elements in advertising, as well as the proliferation of media stories about sexual issues, has from time to time led some Canadians to question whether popular culture has become obsessed with sex. Indeed, a generation of feminist writers has contributed to the development of moral panic about sexuality by drawing attention to negative media stereotyping of body images and by questioning definitions of gender-appropriate behaviour for women and men. All of this has clearly heightened public sensitivity to changing definitions of gender roles in contemporary society. The implications of this relative to the transformation of public opinion about homosexuality will be explored more fully in Chapter 5.

# 4 Public Opinion Polls and Social Policy

The best argument against democracy is a five-minute conversation with the average voter.

– Winston Churchill

Public opinion studies have become important instruments for governance. Politicians may use polls to consult the voters about their approval ratings and to assess the impact of their political decisions on voting intentions. However, they also use survey data to specify the top issues which the electorate expects them to concentrate on while in office. As a general rule, public policymakers, both those who are elected and the bureaucrats, identify public expectations and preferences before they set the agenda for social policy to determine the extent of popular support for policy options. The reactions of the public are also collected when initiatives are being designed to communicate policy and to test public acceptance of these policies.

Contradictory views have developed among academics, journalists, and political pundits on just how polls and issues should be used to shape public policy. Political leaders who have acknowledged the use of opinion polling in their decision making have sometimes been severely criticized. The charge 'government by polls,' which has been levelled at some politicians, implies that those elected to public office do not have a policy agenda and simply do whatever ensures they will retain enough popular support to stay in office. In the 1960s, Key (1961) called the tendency of government leaders to depend on surveys of public opinion before designing national policy 'decay in democracy.'

As we saw in earlier chapters, some see public opinion research based on probability sampling of specified populations as a legitimate medium by which the electorate may have a voice in the policy-making process or even as an exercise in grassroots democracy in a world of increasing political complexity. Others claim, however, that since the public is largely disengaged from social issues, polling does not always correspond to public expectations. Indeed, they argue, it cannot be expected to be otherwise, since the complexity of substantive issues which exist in public policy areas – the national debt, federal-provincial conflicts, or Canada's role in international affairs – demands a depth of understanding which is not possessed by ordinary citizens. They believe that this reflects a growing loss of confidence in government, especially among voters who mistrust political leadership and are not prepared to reward what they perceive to be a wrong agenda with patience and tolerance.

We need to explore the links between public policy decisions and opinion polls to consider whether they are as direct as some observers suggest. Moreover, we must consider whether government priorities are simply defined by the vagaries of public opinion as some observers seem to imply. Critics maintain that the way Canadians perceive the key issues facing the country has essentially been defined by the results of the latest opinion polls.

## Leadership and Opinion Polling

*Government by Polls*

Claire Hoy (1989) considers the 1980s as a period when polling in Canada became an 'epidemic.' Measuring public opinion on an almost-daily basis became routine as it was done not just by politicians and the media but by government departments as well. He recognized that measuring attitudes had a long history in government decision making in this country, but was concerned that the preoccupation with polling by those in authority had become an 'occasional substitute for policy itself' (Hoy, 1989, p. 39). For critics like Hoy, the problem with linking policy decisions to the latest poll data is the belief that elected leaders and governments should have a vision for the future of the country during their mandate. While many assume governments should be responsive to public opinion for identifying issue priorities, they do not expect it to be dependent on public opinion polls when policy decisions are made.

The influence of opinion polls on the operations of government has been the subject of considerable discussion in the literature on politics. Research done on American political behaviour and its relationship to public policy during the 1980s explored the extent to which the public's preferences for policy alternatives and government decisions were likely to be related (Page and Shapiro, 1983; 1989). On the other hand, more recent research shows that the extent of correspondence between actual policy and majority opinion on issues has declined since the 1980s, particularly in matters relating to American foreign policy and the economy (Monroe, 1998). Moreover, one could argue that governments that make decisions based on measuring the importance of particular issues to the electorate and acting in response to them is actually an exercise in democracy because it involves voters in the decision.

In any event, disregarding polls can be perilous for officeholders. In Canada, former prime ministers Pierre Trudeau and Brian Mulroney are both cited as leaders who made major policy decisions while carefully monitoring public anxieties about the top issues of the day with the advice of high-profile pollsters (Laschinger and Stevens, 1992). In the case of the Trudeau government, monitoring a crisis surrounding rising fuel prices in eastern Canada created an opportunity for it to return to office in 1980 after being defeated by the Progressive Conservatives led by Joe Clark. Moreover, it was based on a policy issue. The first budget of the newly elected Conservative government included a tax increase on gasoline. Since Clark had not polled the level of public support for his energy policy, he was unaware of the extent of public concern about rising gasoline costs. The Liberal opposition under Trudeau had discovered through their party polls that the climate of opinion surrounding fuel prices would not support the policies which involved more taxes on fuel proposed by the new government. In fact, they used that as the issue to force an election which followed the defeat of the government's budget in the House of Commons (Laschinger and Stevens, 1992, pp. 66–7).

Similarly, Brian Mulroney was able to win the 1988 election which was essentially a referendum on the Free Trade Agreement with the United States by carefully managing public opinion on the implications of the issue for the economic future of Canada. Since the early days of confederation, Canadians have been preoccupied with the power of American business to undermine the economy of this country. Free trade with the United States has been a highly divisive public issue since a close economic relationship between the two countries has historically been seen to promote continentalism (Nelles, 2004). Despite a century of north-south trade, where each became the other's major trading partner, many Canadians have come to believe that tariffs on American imports protect Canadian jobs, promote higher wages, and maintain the existence of a generous social safety net which might be weakened by free trade.

In the eighties, the business community argued in favour of free trade as a means of ensuring their continued access to the continental market. They maintained that nationalist policies such as those of the previous government of Pierre Trudeau had stimulated protectionism among American politicians and business leaders (Harrison and Friesen, 2004). Moreover, the Mulroney government reinforced this idea through polling data which tracked public concern about the issue, arguing that the Canadian standard of living would be in danger from global competition primarily from products being produced in less developed parts of the world. Free trade would protect access to the American market and was proposed by the government primarily to offset the dangers of globalization which might erode the lifestyles Canadians had come to expect.

The free-trade policy was supported in the 1988 election but by a declining plurality of voters because of its continentalist posture. Some maintain that this was because the campaign mounted by the Mulroney government persuaded them that maintaining secure access to the American economy and culture should not be placed in jeopardy. Doern and Tomlin, for example, observe that the free-trade issue was a 'policy choice rooted in a partisan strategy' in that opposition to free trade was clearly portrayed by the pro–free trade lobby as a vote against the government itself and its policies to create jobs (Doern and Tomlin, 1991). In fact, they suggest many voters supported it without fully understanding all of the implications, including the potential for the loss of some jobs. The opposition parties on the other hand were left on the defensive on this very thorny issue because they were unable able to explain adequately to the electorate why voting for the free-trade proposal was a danger to our economic well-being. 'In the final analysis, neither the Liberals nor the New Democrats were able to come up with politically viable policy alternatives to free trade … both opposition parties were thrown on the defensive by Mulroney's success in capturing the political agenda with his pro-market stance' (Doern and Tomlin, 1991, p. 236).

*Polls and Political Leadership*

According to American political analysts, mixing public opinion polling with the public policy process has become central to the governing
strategy of many contemporary political leaders (Heith, 2004). A leader's
decision to engage in the practice of speaking directly to the electorate
or 'to go public' in order to promote an important issue is often made in
response to longitudinal polls which track good performance ratings
and find the optimal time for direct appeal from the leader to solidify
consensus for action. Samuel Kernell (1986) has also argued that in the
United States, the extent to which a president makes use of public
consultations such as radio broadcasts, television addresses, news con-
ferences, and political travel, is an indicator of the kind of leader he or
she will turn out to be. In essence, presidents who make greater use of
public consultations spend less time attempting to win the support of
congressional representatives. As Kernell concludes, 'going public was
an invention inspired by a policy agenda that would fail if left to the
traditional political process. The ends dictated the means' (Kernell,
1986, p. 226).

Heith (2004) describes this trend toward mixing polling and policy
formulation in American politics as representing a particular style of
presidential leadership in what she terms a 'permanent campaign' environment. It relies on frequent public opinion consults and employs
campaign-style strategy in advance of making policy decisions. The
idea is that in order to succeed in governing, a president must win over
opponents on policy just as he or she does during an election campaign.
In order to accomplish this, the parameters of support or opposition (for
example, age, gender, income level, or value community) must be identified. Communications are then prepared to enhance support for the
decision while countering alternative arguments. They also position the
president as the principal representative for the issue and engage him
in promotional activities such as tours with speaking opportunities that
may be required to enhance exposure to it. However, above all else
there is a careful monitoring of public opinion. 'In this model, public
opinion polls represent more than evaluation, providing a blueprint of
behavior by identifying supporters and defectors, and appealing policy
positions' (Heith, 2004, p. 9).

Yet, as we know, it is argued that many ordinary citizens are not well
enough informed about complex policy issues to offer substantive opin-

ions on them and thus polling does not provide opinions that are representative of what voters think (Althaus, 2003). Some say the design of good public policy may be compromised by polling because polls are usually conducted to provide solutions to political problems such as which issue will have the most voter appeal just as is done in a political campaign. Moreover, the distribution of polling results may be highly selective and carefully interpreted by advisors who rarely circulate raw data to departments of government. In fact they may ensure that bureaucrats are only provided with information on a 'need to know basis.' Indeed, as Heith notes, campaigns are often won or lost due to the skilful mastery of information (2004, p. 32).

In the last half of the twentieth century, public opinion research has become a routine budget item in many government departments in Canada. Pollsters and staff who are experts in understanding communications are retained to manage opinion data on variety of issues for which bureaucrats must recommend policies to political leaders. The Public Opinion Research Directorate monitors all public opinion research for programs, policies, and services contracted by the federal departments of the Government of Canada. According to the annual report of the Directorate, in 2004–5, 364 public opinion studies contracted by the top ten departmental clients had a combined value of $18.5 million (Public Opinion Research Annual Report, 2005). The average value of contracts over the four years reported is $17,853,250.00.

A variety of departments and agencies may conduct public opinion studies (see Table 4.1) but in 2003–4, the largest number of studies was conducted by Health Canada. The Directorate reports that 105 qualitative and quantitative studies on health issues were conducted at a cost of $6.2 million. The issues studied included the reduction of tobacco and drug use, including marijuana; emerging public-health threats such as West Nile virus and mad cow disease; as well as the development of a healthy living strategy. Since a number of studies conducted throughout 2004–5 showed that health care was identified as the top issue facing Canadians, it is no surprise that the largest investment in policy-oriented research would have been on investigating perceptions, concerns and expectations about health issues. The scale of the research undertaken by governments for policy priorities raises the question whether those in positions of authority in government simply redesign policy initiatives around public preferences in an attempt to use polls to find ways to achieve support for the positions they favour.[1] Clearly,

Table 4.1 POR annual reports: Overview of public opinion research in the government of Canada

| | Top departments and agencies for all public opinion research by business volume | | | | |
|---|---|---|---|---|---|
| Department/Agency | Thousands of dollars (Contract Value) | Number of projects | Department/Agency | Thousands of dollars | Number of projects |
| **2004–2005** | | | **2003–2004** | | |
| Health Canada | 6,248 | 106 | Health Canada | 4,866 | 105 |
| Human Resources and Skills Development Canada | 2,033 | 36 | Human Resources Development Canada† | 3,720 | 63 |
| Natural Resources Canada | 1,701 | 39 | Canadian Heritage | 1,758 | 42 |
| Foreign Affairs Canada and International Trade Canada* | 1,415 | 21 | Communication Canada† | 1,459 | 22 |
| Canadian Heritage | 1,392 | 37 | Foreign Affairs and International Trade Canada | 1,337 | 23 |
| Canada Revenue Agency | 1,261 | 26 | Canada Customs and Revenue Agency† | 1,304 | 21 |
| Industry Canada | 1,216 | 34 | Industry Canada | 1,174 | 38 |
| Public Works and Government Services Canada | 1,195 | 24 | Agriculture and Agri-Food Canada | 962 | 20 |
| Finance Canada | 1,051 | 17 | Natural Resources Canada | 912 | 31 |
| Social Development Canada | 1,047 | 24 | Environment Canada | 717 | 27 |
| | | | Treasury Board of Canada Secretariat | 615 | 13 |

*In 2004–2005, the departments of Foreign Affairs Canada and International Trade Canada contracted for POR as a single research unit, hence the contract values are reported together.

†Duties and names of some departments and agencies included throughout this report changed as part of a reorganization of the Government of Canada.

Table 4.1 (concluded)

| | Top departments and agencies for all public opinion research by business volume | | | | |
|---|---|---|---|---|---|
| Department/Agency | Thousands of dollars | Number of projects | Department/Agency | Thousands of dollars | Number of projects |
| **2002–2003** | | | **2001–2002** | | |
| Health Canada | 4,270 | 81 | Health Canada | 4,036 | 88 |
| Communication Canada | 3,176 | 75 | Human Resources Development Canada | 2,614 | 62 |
| Human Resources Development Canada | 2,120 | 60 | Communication Canada | 2,117 | 70 |
| Natural Resources Canada | 1,586 | 28 | Industry Canada | 1,834 | 54 |
| Industry Canada | 1,584 | 42 | Environment Canada | 1,343 | 36 |
| Canadian Heritage | 1,124 | 30 | Canadian Heritage | 1,288 | 36 |
| Foreign Affairs and International Trade Canada | 870 | 16 | Treasury Board Secretariat | 1,228 | 16 |
| Canada Customs and Revenue Agency | 868 | 17 | Foreign Affairs and International Trade Canada | 867 | 18 |
| Treasury Board of Canada Secretariat | 738 | 15 | Natural Resources Canada | 847 | 32 |
| Environment Canada | 710 | 20 | Justice | 810 | 21 |

Source: Public Opinion Research annual reports

policy making that aims to be seen to be sensitive to what the public thinks occurs in Canada too. During the past five years a majority of Canadians have identified health care as their top concern. Moreover, they have usually expressed extreme dissatisfaction with the amount of money transferred to the provinces for health care programs. Provincial governments have, in turn, consistently attributed their problems with health care delivery to reduced spending by the federal government. The federal government has nevertheless been reluctant to engage in additional spending on the health budget because this would jeopardize its accomplishments in managing fiscal affairs. Alternatives such as better management of the existing transfers have received considerably less attention from policy makers than has the need for additional resources.

It is argued that a majority of the electorate accepts the value of a well-funded national health care system and, given the degree of emotion attached to it, that it would be more difficult to convince people that poor management of existing expenditures is an important element of the issue. Thus, an agreement between the provinces and the federal authorities to provide additional spending has become widely accepted as the best policy for sustaining health care.

Leaders who are accused of being overly responsive to public opinion or who are overly careful about their job performance ratings are usually criticized for having too little vision or not having a real plan for governing. When opinion polls are identified with designing policy, critics view this as 'pandering' to public opinion. On the other hand, some American social scientists take the opposite view: that instead of making policy decisions that resonate with what the public thinks, there has been a decline in recent years in responsiveness to public opinion and, more importantly, an increase in attempts to direct public opinion (Jacobs and Shapiro, 2000). These authors argue that leaders are more likely to rely on carefully crafted communications to win support from the electorate for their policy objectives. They do not dismiss the use of polls in policy formulation but suggest that polls are mainly used as tools to monitor the acceptance or rejection of policy

---

1 The data available from the POR Directorate make a compelling argument for the role of government contracts as a reason for the emergence of the opinion polling industry in Canada during the past twenty years. The total value of projects undertaken by government departments and agencies has been consistently above $25 million for the past four years.

options put forward by government and to show the number of those who are amenable to changing their views. In sum, they are used mainly as an adjunct to communications strategies. 'Presidents and legislators carefully track public opinion in order to identify the words, arguments and symbols that are most likely to be effective in attracting favourable press coverage and ultimately 'winning' public support for their desired policies' (Jacobs and Shapiro, 2000, p. 7).

*Tracking Confidence and Trust*

One of the reasons cited by Jacobs and Shapiro for the need for leaders and governments to seek consensus through public opinion polls is recognition that the public has lost confidence in political institutions. It cannot be assumed that once an election is over, those in office will have at least the conditional support of the electorate. Newly elected governments have had to prove during their mandate that they have vision and often must face a cynical electorate when doing so. Indeed, in Canada we have recently witnessed an unprecedented level of mistrust in politicians which has recently threatened the very viability of minority government in the national Parliament. This has been attributed to the actions of the Liberal Party under Prime Minister Chrétien. In what has now been labelled the 'sponsorship scandal,' Prime Minister Paul Martin had to defend the actions of some individuals employed by the former government in a climate of public opinion characterized by scandal. It resulted in the government having to face a confidence vote in Parliament which it survived by just one vote.

The sponsorship scandal was by no means the source of changing political attitudes in Canada. Levels of confidence in the federal government had shown some signs of decline in the early 1980s, as perceptions of the threat of big government were identified. This was measured in terms of the degree to which the federal government was perceived to be likely to make an unwelcome intrusion into lives of Canadians relative to labour and business (Johnston, 1986). Yet this was also a period which included a national crisis owing to the federal government's failure to reach an agreement with the government of Quebec on the constitution. Moreover, the economy had suffered a severe downturn at the time and many Canadians faced job losses. Both of these events might explain weakened confidence in political institutions, as well as a sense that politicians were either unable or unwilling to make the decisions which Canadians believed would improve the situation. This is a conclusion which is supported by Neil Nevitte's (1996) research on value change during that period, which he discussed using the concept *post-materialism*. Nevitte maintained that the 1980s were a turbulent period in all advanced industrial societies, characterized by discontent with governments and a loss of faith in politicians and those in positions of authority. He also argued that trust in government and traditional political behaviour were likely to be replaced by more political activism and public protest, which was reflected in the discontent expressed by the election of members of the Bloc Québécois and the western Reform Party to Parliament.

Notwithstanding the way governments and politicians are viewed by their electorates, public-opinion research is now a necessary tool for making informed decisions about policies. Some ask if this means that polls interfere with democracy and whether governments should not govern and leaders lead without continually having to gauge public support for their actions. Others would argue that polls represent an opportunity for citizens to have a voice in government. Yet in this section we have also observed that policy decisions do not always conform to public preferences, often because most respondents may not understand complex issues and can provide nothing more than vague direction for policy making. Others argue that in any case polls and surveys which are based on quantitative techniques do not allow for much consideration of complex questions. These add up to the conclusion that citizens really have only the most superficial involvement in the policy process. Moreover, it has been suggested that issue polls create a greater likelihood that public opinion will be manipulated by those in authority, especially if messages about policy are crafted and tested to evaluate popular approval and determine the conditions under which it will be secured. This reasoning attacks public participation in decisions on the grounds that the public is being tricked into supporting something which it does not understand. In the final analysis, the public does indeed have the power to control policy decisions, by the most democratic means available: they can throw the rascals out of office.

## Confidence and Crisis in Health Care

*The Emergence of Health Care as a Public Issue*

One of the most critical social-policy questions is how the federal and provincial governments will be able to continue providing for the delivery of public health care at a level which is perceived to be meeting the needs of all Canadians. Over the past five years, public confidence in governments appears to have been linked to perceptions of declining confidence in the quality of health care. The sense of crisis about the issue seems to have been intensified by the release of multiple public opinion polls by the national media which track perceptions about standards of care and frequently provide information on unfavourable comparisons between Canada and the kind of health care systems available in other countries (see Mendelson, 2002). Indeed, *Maclean's* magazine has for some time published an annual health report which measures and interprets the performance of the system in communities on a province-by-province basis.[2] The degree of scrutiny to which the delivery of services has been subject during the past decade raises the question of whether the urgency about fixing health care expressed in public opinion studies has been socially constructed. To understand this point, some background on the condition of the health care system is useful. The delivery of health care is governed by the *Canada Health Act* of 1984 which lays out the conditions under which the federal government transfers money to the provinces to be used to deliver health care. These transfers provide for provincial expenditures on health such as the salaries of physicians and other health care workers in hospitals, as well as the costs of running the hospitals. However, it should be noted that the provinces themselves also contribute to the costs of health care. In addition, the provinces pay for the additional costs associated with prescription drugs, home care, and long-term care (see Romanow, 2002). While the method of delivery varies from province to province, the ability of of the provinces to pay varies, particularly the less populous ones that have a smaller tax base. The purpose of the *Act* is to guarantee universal and accessible health care services.

In the formative years of national medical care in this country, the federal government essentially committed to paying half the cost of health care, allowing the provinces to define the nature of the programs they would offer. However, as Banting and Boadway (2004) note, fiscal transfers have evolved over the years from a formula for cost sharing based on matching grants with the provinces to block grants to the provinces to sustain programs. The change was a consequence of the

---

2 In its inaugural report in 1998, *Macleans* presented an in-depth examination of health care indicators, including spending levels, staffing shortages, the availability of hospital care, working conditions, as well as rating the health status of citizens across the country. (*Maclean's*, 1998, pp. 16–42). In April 2005 *Reader's Digest* retained Leger Marketing to conduct a 'checkup on medicare.'

practice in some provinces of charging patients extra fees for doctors and hospital services, threatening the policy of equal access. The cost-sharing formula was turned into a block grant to provinces when accepted federal definitions for the eligible health programs were not being followed. Moreover, programs and fees not covered in federal-provincial agreements had to be paid for by the provinces themselves. Since the 1980s there have also been disagreements between Ottawa and the provinces about the costs of delivering health care to Canadians; particularly about the increasing fiscal responsibility borne by federal budgets and because of the belief that some provinces were not spending the money for the purposes for which it was intended. For example, it was sometimes argued that the block-grant money was being directed to transportation budgets for road building or that hospitals were being constructed for political reasons in areas where it was not feasible for them to be located.

Partly because of the growing imbalance in the costs allocated between the two levels of government, the funding policy was again changed to a cash and tax-point transfer to the provinces. It was associated with what Banting and Boadway describe as 'a growth of intergovernmental tensions ... this division was to become a slow-acting poison pill in federal-provincial relations, since there was no longer an agreed answer to the question of what proportion of provincial health expenditures was met by the federal government. This poison pill began to take effect as the rate of growth in the transfer declined' (Banting and Boadway, 2004, p. 14).

The government in Ottawa came to view its commitment to maintaining the national health care system as an impediment to its ability to contain the national debt. By contrast, the poorer provinces complained about their ability to maintain national standards in the face of higher expectations from citizens for services which they could not meet. In fact, cost cutting became a reality in 1995 with the introduction of a new transfer arrangement which included a cut to the rate of growth in the transfers. Since that time, provinces have engaged in a very public national debate with the federal government about the most appropriate level of support for the federal government to provide. From the perspective of the ordinary Canadian, there was a crisis since the health care system was perceived to be incapable of providing the level of services required.

The focus of concern about the health care system has been on how much money is being spent on it by governments. The most public

Table 4.2 Public confidence in the health care system (%)

|          | 1998 | 1999 | 2000 | 2001 | 2002 | 2003 | Spring 2004 | Fall 2004 | Spring 2005 | Summer 2005 |
|----------|------|------|------|------|------|------|-------------|-----------|-------------|-------------|
| Rising   | 5    | 5    | 6    | 4    | 4    | 6    | 6           | 6         | 8           | 5           |
| Same     | 35   | 38   | 41   | 41   | 36   | 41   | 43          | 45        | 44          | 43          |
| Falling  | 59   | 55   | 51   | 54   | 58   | 51   | 49          | 47        | 46          | 50          |

Question: Overall, would you say that your confidence in the Canadian health care system is rising or falling, or is it about the same as it ever was?
Source: Pollara (2005).

issues which have emerged are about the availability of hospital beds, hospital closings, and the shortage of medical personnel, particularly specialists in rural parts of the country. For example, in 2001 Ipsos-Reid reported that 78 per cent of Canadians perceived a funding crisis in the health care system; in research conducted by Ekos Research during that same time period, nearly one in four (23 per cent) respondents said they were not confident that they would be able to access the necessary health care services if a member of their family were to become seriously ill (Mendelson, 2002). While anxieties about the state of the health care system appear to have declined among members of the public during a six year period beginning in 1998, it is interesting that in 2004 as many as 47 per cent of respondents in a Pollara (2005) report expressed 'falling confidence' (see Table 4.2). It is also interesting to note that overall the proportion who expressed rising confidence in the system remained virtually unchanged over that period (6 per cent). Mendelson also notes that Canadians have sensed deterioration in the system: 'Concerns about the quality of care, understood as timely access to the best quality care have increased in recent years. "Quality" has gradually become more important to Canadians in the past seven years because they have sensed deterioration in the system ... "Quality" and "equal access for all" are now judged to be of equal importance' (Mendelson, 2002, p. 10).

Indeed, public anxieties about deterioration in the system fed into the political life of the country to the extent that it became the centerpiece of the national election campaign of 2004: all parties promised that a new accord on funding for health care would be concluded if they were elected.

At the same time the lack of confidence may be misguided as the shortcomings of Canada's health care system may have been overstated. In 1998, when perceptions of crisis in health care were most intense and an international comparison showed that a majority (56 per cent) of Canadians believed that fundamental changes were needed in the system (Mendelson, 2002), *Maclean's* reported on a United Nations comparison of health care in the leading industrial nations, including France, Germany, Great Britain, and the United States. Canada was ranked first on a variety of measures of the state of health of citizens and the levels of public spending directed at health care. In fact, *Maclean's* observed that Canada would continue to perform 'above average' on these measures despite reduced levels of health care spending at the time. Considering the ongoing discussion of public health care in Canada, it is legitimate to ponder if the guidelines for policy have become defined by a sense of moral panic which has evidently become part of the issue.

*Health Care and Moral Panic*

A recent headline reads 'Polls show mistrust of government's Medicare spending, widespread dissatisfaction: Health care workers, Canadians want accountability.' The story, written by journalist Mark Kennedy of the *Ottawa Citizen* in December 2000, reported on public opinion research completed by Pollara during a time of heightened anxiety about sustaining the health care system in Canada. It concluded that governments had lost the confidence of the public in their ability to make the right decisions. Perceptions of diminished quality despite the money being spent were reported by both the public and health care workers themselves. The problem was attributed to an ill-advised attempt by governments to impose reforms because of the belief that the system had become virtually unsustainable. Other polls had shown that Canadians placed a high value on having a public health care system which they could trust and they were searching for reasons which would explain the problems with it. Given that a majority identified the parameters of public concerns regarding the issue, as well as the intensity of media coverage which has been associated with it over the past decade, it is interesting to speculate whether the forces at work had created a moral panic about health care in this country. We have used this concept previously in this book to explain how public opinion may coalesce around an issue that becomes the source of popular discontent with the direction in which society is perceived to be headed.

The idea of a moral panic to describe this form of collective behaviour was first used to study British youth culture in the 1960s by Stanley Cohen (1972). It is applied to explain a situation when general changes in society have created social confusion. This is much like Durkheim's concept of *anomie*: there is widespread public anxiety until a new consensus is established.[3] In Cohen's definition of the concept, 'a condition, episode, person or group of persons emerges to become defined as a threat to societal values' (Cohen, 1972, p. 9). In Britain, jazz, drugs, and rock music were perceived to be leading youth to sexual promiscuity and to societal decay. Furthermore, these elements of youth culture had become perceived as a threat to existing values. It is important to understand that moral panics tend to emerge when the source of the problem is widely recognized and is easily understood by the public. If changes in behaviour become defined as a threat to core values, some corrective action or moral regulation by those in authority is seen to be required. According to Goode and Ben-Yehuda (1994), the reaction may be exaggerated given the nature of the event itself. However, the term 'moral panic' captures the intensity of emotion which is associated with a perceived threat to normative order even if it is not real. It also accounts for the nature of the reactions by the public, the media, and legal authorities to the perceived threat. For example, during the spring of 2005 in Halifax, Nova Scotia, a number of 'swarming' incidents produced what Cohen would identify as moral panic. These incidents involved several youth surrounding, roughing up, and robbing their victims. The events were widely reported in the local media as examples of armed youth violence. Although there were only 15 incidents, reactions from observers ranged from a demand that there be a 9:00 p.m. curfew for youth (which some argued was unconstitutional), to more police patrols in a trendy shopping district where some of the swarmings occurred. There was even a proposal that surveillance cameras should be more widely employed all over the downtown area.

---

3 Émile Durkheim, one of the founding figures in sociology, was concerned about the sources of consensus in society and the moral authority that sustains them. Modern societies experience many and frequent changes which may lead to social unrest. In *Suicide*, Durkheim contrasted social solidarity with *anomie*, a situation where there is widespread confusion about appropriate moral standards. He explained increased rates of suicide during these periods as individual acts brought about by changing social conditions which upset rules for behaviour (see Aron, 1967; Parsons, 1968). Functional theories of social control like this maintain that social stability is a product of an allegiance to a consensus on rules. When that consensus is unclear, forces of disequilibrium may take the form of moral panic.

Although not all unconventional behaviour leads to a moral panic, it is likely to occur when a worrisome change to social institutions is perceived to be happening. Ulrich Beck (1992) identifies modern societies as having a 'culture of risk'; people are aware of the many risks associated with modern living and are concerned about how to manage them. For example, the general technological and social advancements which facilitate international travel bring along with them the risk of spreading disease – currently the concern with the spread of 'avian flu.' Thus there have been worldwide efforts to deal with this risk by making people more aware of the dangers when they travel and encouraging international cooperation to develop a vaccine. Similarly, access to international media such as CNN and the web have played a significant role in disseminating Western culture and ideas to the rest of the world. Yet there is a risk which many non-Western cultures have recognized. The liberal ideas of Western culture have been identified in some developing countries where technological changes have been pervasive as a threat to religious beliefs; thus rising fundamentalism may be occurring as a form of risk management.

Studies of moral panic have emphasized that 'events are more likely to be perceived as fundamental threats and to give rise to moral panics if the society, or some important part of it, is in crisis or experiencing disturbing changes giving rise to stress' (Thompson, 1998, p. 8). Reactions to perceptions of risk could generate a crisis which becomes a moral panic: this seems to have been the case with the initial response by the public to AIDS. Chas Critcher notes that the response had all the features of moral panic; there was a 'gay plague,' with 'folk devils' that challenged conventional morality and sacred institutions like the family. Yet, he shows that while stressful, the AIDS crisis did not become moral panic, at least partly because elite opinion and the media emphasized education about the disease and did not allow it to be portrayed as a health threat to society from a deviant sub-group (Critcher, 2003, p. 39).

On the other hand, this did happen in this country when the quality of health care delivery was being challenged by fiscal reform. As we noted earlier, perceptions of a crisis in the Canadian health care system were accompanied by the argument that universal and accessible health care was in danger. In fact, this threat to the status quo was regularly covered in media reports which emphasized that a large number of opinion polls showed increasing majorities of Canadians were becoming concerned about declining quality and their inability to access services when and if they needed them. The media also reported that many people in various parts of the country had lost significant levels of confidence in their government's ability to find an effective solution to this problem. In the opinion polls about the health care system reviewed by Mendelson (2002), 1,000 survey questions in over 100 opinion polls were identified with this issue. Moreover, confidence in the performance of the system was being regularly tracked and covered in the broadcast and print media. For example, polling from 1998 by Pollara to track confidence in the system has shown that a majority continue to express falling confidence: 59 per cent indicated falling confidence in 1998 and a 47 per cent majority viewed the issue that way in the fall of 2004 (Pollara, 2005). Moreover, the story about the poll results was often covered in a television news frame that used a personal account by some individual who had experienced hardship because health services were not available.

Another way of thinking about this is that the opinion polls and the coverage given to them by the media helped to establish what Thompson (1998) has referred to as a 'collective definition of the problem.' Whether the crisis was real or imagined, a majority of Canadians was clearly emotionally involved in the perceived crisis, mostly because of the value conflict it seemed to bring about. This set the agenda for a national debate about fixing the problem. In all moral panics, public anxieties are usually expressed as hostility towards those who are seen to be responsible for the threat to existing values. In the case of the health care crisis, there has been consensus that all Canadians have been victims of poor public policy imposed on them by both levels of government. In particular, governments have been blamed for not investing the fiscal resources necessary to deal with a shortage of doctors and nurses. Although the shortage of professionals is accepted as a national problem, in reality it is probably a bigger problem for residents of hinterland areas of the country than it is for those in major urban centers. As Goode and Ben-Yehuda explain, in moral panics the perceived extent of the threat is often disproportional to the actual problem it poses to the public. They suggest that depictions of its impact on people tend to be 'wildly exaggerated' (Goode and Ben-Yehuda, 1994, p. 36). At any rate, exaggerated or not, provincial governments have felt compelled to shoulder the funding burden in their health care budgets, albeit with faint praise from the public; while doing so, they have blamed the federal government for the funding deficits which they have experienced.

Thus, the reasons for moral panic here have had much to do with the symbolic or emotional significance of health care as a birthright of a generation of Canadians. Some have described it as an integral part of Canadian identity. Indeed, former federal Liberal Health Minister Monique Bégin, in a very emotional commentary written for the *Globe and Mail* newspaper, saw the need for fiscal reform, but only because it would restore what in her view was 'our beloved medicare' (Bégin, 2000). To understand the purpose of this dramatic component in a commentary by the former cabinet minister, we must recognize that many believe that medicare, more than many others institutions, represents the values which distinguish us from Americans. It is the threat to these values that is the source of moral panic.

You will recall that earlier in this book (Chapter 1) we considered the core values of Canadians and Americans from the perspective of cultural differences which impact on public opinion. In Seymour Martin Lipset's *Continental Divide* (1990), one of his many writings on this subject, Canadian values are described as collectivity-oriented and statist. This means that Canadians are more inclined than Americans to value the role of the state in providing benefits for their lives or to seek group rather than individual solutions to social problems. They also stress the importance of obligations to groups, such as the family and the community, before the rights and freedom of individuals. The extent of the difference described by Lipset has been challenged by some contemporary research as it clearly suggests Canadians have become overly dependent on the state and are much less self-reliant than they should be. Moreover, at least one public opinion analyst has argued that the two cultures are growing even further apart on these values than Lipset's early work showed (see Adams, 2003). Nevertheless, the national public health insurance system in Canada is clearly a reflection of these values. In contrast, the rejection of a public system by Americans is explained by a stronger belief in individual responsibility and a mistrust of government. The basis for cultural differences is best left to another book, but the expression of public outrage from those who sought fiscal reform in health may be understood if these elements of our culture are considered.

In sum, moral panics emerge when a social change which many oppose is probable and may sometimes be the result of value conflicts. The health care issue was essentially a value conflict because Canadians perceived the idea that a universal and accessible system was going to be changed as a threat. Sometimes societies cope with major value conflicts by labelling somebody or something which is threatening as a 'great evil' that is set on demoralizing society. It can then be legitimately defeated at all costs while public opinion is aroused to support whatever action is required to do so.

In the study of moral panics, the term *folk devil* is widely used to explain public reactions when there is consensus about what is undermining the status quo. The perceived threat then becomes the object of increased hostility (Cohen, 1980; Goode and Ben-Yehuda, 1994; Thompson, 1998). Thus the evolution of the health care crisis also involved the identification of folk devils; these were the advocates of private health care, since universality, accessibility, and quality were in jeopardy and funding shortfalls would lead to a gradual acceptance of more privatized health care.

As with most moral panics, when matters become sufficiently urgent because they are perceived to be likely to harm society, authorities must take action. In Canada, with rising levels of public concern and a national election looming, not to mention the complaints of provincial health ministers about the effects of growing acceptance of privatized health care, federal government commissioned two investigations in 2001. Both the Senate and the Romanow Commissions carried out extensive consultations with Canadians from coast to coast, sending a message to Canadians that something was being done to respond to the panic. Central to the findings of these investigations was the high value which the public placed on a universal, accessible, publicly delivered health care system with limited scope for the private, profit-based delivery of health services. The Romanow Commission (2002) recommended a new mechanism to transfer funds to the provinces from the federal government sufficient to provide stability for a five year period. Although the discourse on sustaining quality continues, the panic seemed to subside with the promise of the prime minister during the 2004 election to follow some of Romanow's recommendations and strike a new arrangement with the provincial premiers for a renewal of the promise of universal health care.

## Political Ideology and Public Policy

An important question in the study of public opinion is whether Canadians view social policy like health care reform from an ideological perspective. What is more, can the analyst of opinion data not simply assume that varying levels of support for and opposition to the top issues of the day reflect the political orientations of respondents? Indeed, if this is true, then in the debate about health care we have considered above, those whose political thinking is liberal or socialist in contemporary politics would have been more likely to support a fully universal and accessible national health care system, while those who think conservative would have been more likely to support greater use of privatized health care.[4] We spent a good deal of time in Chapters 1 and 2 exploring variations in the structure of opinions to conclude that the formation of political attitudes about policy is not as simple as this would suggest. Nevertheless, there has been some controversy over the years about the extent to which political ideology is pivotal to understanding how the public thinks about policy.

The study of ideology in understanding public reactions to social issues and government decision making has a long history in American political sociology.[5] Converse (1964), who conducted studies of voting behaviour, argued that American voters did not express views on policy issues from strongly held convictions; indeed they changed their minds about the same issues from one study to another. Converse described these 'flip flop' responses as reflecting 'non-attitudes.' On the other hand, others have explored measurement error as a possible explanation for the volatility of responses over time (Erickson, 1979). As we noted earlier, the idea that in mass societies voters are totally passive about government and have no political ideology that determines their voting choices has been widely expounded during the past 40 years. Without a doubt, those who have written about the 'end of ideology' in Western civilization take this view. This has sometimes been attributed to the decline in the power of religious values and a reduction in social class differences. Indeed theories of mass society also contend we no longer have the passion for strong beliefs such as those which created radical political movements in the early years of the twentieth

---

4 The terms liberal and conservative refers to attitudes and opinions which express ideological differences between the major political parties in Canada. Liberal political values are broadly identified with government intervention, individual choice, and the promotion of nationalism. Conservative political values are often associated with fiscal responsibility, a more-limited government presence, and decentralized federalism. Socialist values have also emphasized government intervention, greater attention to social security, and social equality. For a full discussion of the ideologies of the Canadian political parties, see Jackson and Jackson (2004).

5 For a discussion of the literature on the links between political ideology and orientations towards government policy among the American public see Bardes and Oldendick, 2003, pp. 101–20.

century: Nazism, Marxism, and even the civil rights movement (Bell, 1960; Haber, 1966). Indeed it is argued that the fact that people do not view social process from behind a veil of political commitment any more suggests there is no consistent ideological disagreement between supporters of the major parties on matters of policy.

The question is whether the core values of Canadians determine their political choices. For example, would our party choices reflect our beliefs about the value of tolerance and the rights of others? Some research indicates that support for both the left and right sides of politics is compatible with different expectations on social policy matters, particularly when voters are activist members of the major political parties. Donald Blake (1988) explored this topic by comparing the attitudes of delegates at party conventions to social and economic issues, including regulation of foreign investment, defence spending, foreign-aid spending, support for the social safety net, legalization of marijuana, environmental protection, and immigration. He expected that party activists and delegates would be likely to be more ideological in their thinking than ordinary voters in society. However, while Blake's findings show some differences between activists and voters on most policy areas studied, their views were not strongly divergent on a majority of them. Actually, there was even less disagreement on issues among those who were ordinary delegates than among activist delegates, suggesting that ideology mattered less to how this group viewed policy issues.

However, different views about social issues may not indicate ideological differences. As Richard Johnston observed about the issue differences identified by Blake, positions on policies should also be consistent: when individuals think ideologically, their response to one policy question should predict their response to other questions (Johnston, 1988, p. 58). Johnston's analysis revealed genuine ideological divergence among Liberal and Conservative convention delegates particularly in two policy areas. On economic policy, Conservative attitudes were more consistent in rejecting an anti–big business orientation; on social policy, attitudes were less supportive of bilingualism, although they showed a good deal of internal division on policies aimed at promoting bilingualism. Liberals showed attitudes which were most dissimilar from Conservatives on anti–big business measures and were consistent in their attitudes toward policies that favoured bilingualism. Johnston concluded that divergent opinions among party activists was attributable to political ideology but could also be explained by ethnic, class, and regional interests.

More recent research published by Archer and Whitehorn (2001), involving a comparison of political activists from the three major parties, shows considerable differences between activists of the three parties on policy positions. Most extreme were the ideological differences between Conservative and Liberal/NDP party members on issues relating to bilingualism and language policy. Conservatives were least inclined to support special status for Quebec. The other area of profound difference was between the Conservatives and the NDP on issues relating to economic policy. In particular NDP activists were less supportive of economic policies which increased continentalism and closer trading relations with the Americans. Moreover, NDP activists were clearly distinguished from Conservatives by their opinions about the extent of privatization that should exist in the Canadian economy. Thus, in the context of the policy implications discussed at the beginning of this chapter, the existing research does not immediately allow us to conclude that voters who identify strongly with a political party are more likely to perceive a link with party ideology when they express opinions about public policy. It is not entirely clear that ordinary supporters of a party will be as influenced by ideological thinking as activists may be. As we discussed in earlier chapters, opinions only acquire an ideological tinge when events acquire important meaning. Considering again the public reactions to perceptions of a health care crisis, it is most unlikely that the complicated questions surrounding the delivery of health care have been fully understood by those who express opinions about quality and accessibility. Nevertheless, it is an issue which seemed to have assumed some ideological significance, especially since the federal election of 2004 when supporters of the major parties were claiming to be differentiated by their opinions on the acceptability of private health care. In any case, a year after the election, when passions might be expected to have cooled, it appears that ideology still influences what Canadians think about the issue. In April 2005, Leger Marketing of Montreal conducted interviews with 1500 Canadians about access to private sector health care. According to the Leger study, 52 per cent view greater access to private care as an option the respondents would find acceptable while 42 per cent reject the idea (Montreal Economic Institute, 2005). However, as shown in Table 4.3, support for private-sector health care is significantly greater among respondents who identify themselves as intending to vote Conservative (67 per cent) and for the Bloc Québécois (64 per cent) than among those who intend to vote Liberal (49 per cent) or NDP (35 per cent). One is

Table 4.3 Distribution according to voting intentions

| | Entire population (N = 1,504) | Liberal | Conservative | NDP | Bloc Québécois |
|---|---|---|---|---|---|
| Yes | 52% | 49% | 67%↑ | 35%↓ | 64%↑ |
| No | 42% | 44% | 30%↓ | 59%↑ | 34%↓ |
| Don't know/Refusal | 6% | 6% | 3%↓ | 6% | 2%↓ |

Question: Would you find it acceptable or not if the government were to allow those who wish to pay for health care in the private sector to have speedier access to this type of care while still maintaining the current free and universal health care system?
Notes: 1. Significant statistical differences are indicated using the symbol ↑ if they are higher and by ↓ if they are lower.
    2. Vertical reading
Source: Leger Marketing, April 2005

tempted to conclude that this is also a reflection of the minority situation in the House of Commons at the time the study was conducted.

Clearly, the role of political ideologies in the formation of public opinion about policy on major social issues cannot be overlooked. When controversial issues like health care acquire an emotional meaning, even those who are not active in politics evaluate the options with reference to ideological criteria. The fact that many are not consistently ideological about policy may reflect the complexities surrounding the issues.

## Summary

It is generally recognized that in business, government, and politics today, few policy decisions are made without consulting the target group which will be most impacted by it. In areas of public policy in particular, the voter is routinely requested to give advice on highly complex issues which has raised questions about whether (a) ordinary Canadians have the knowledge to provide reasonable answers to this kind of opinion polling and (b) it has become a substitute for leadership. Some have argued that governments have become so dependent on the use of polling data that they are overly responsive to it, while others have shown that there is very little correspondence between majority opinion and the policy decisions that governments ultimately make. In any case, politicians often test their positions on controversial issues by designing messages which are carefully communicated to selected audiences long before a policy decision is actually taken. They will then have them tracked for acceptability in opinion polls. The goal is to find a basis for popular support and understand the basis for opposition. This practice, so often used during elections, has been likened to running a permanent campaign while in office. Yet it is very unlikely to stop, as controversial elements of a policy agenda which can pose significant threats to the survival of governments necessitate and sometimes demand demonstration of public 'buy-in' in order to proceed. In fact, we have noted just how much this situation has promoted the development of the polling industry in Canada: budget allocation for polls has exceeded $25 million each year for the past four years.

In recent years, public policy decisions in Canada have been dominated by issues about health care. Opinion polls have shown that growing anxiety about the sustainability of a public medical service has been expressed by a large majority of Canadians. Moreover, the emotion associated with health care issues in the context of the mobilization of public opinion suggests a sense of moral panic. There is no doubt that a number of disturbing changes have shaken public confidence in the ability of the system to deliver the level of services expected and the ability of governments to fix it. On the other hand, there may be a level of emotionality inspired by a basic value conflict involving alternative beliefs about the need for a health care system which is exclusively a public one. In 2006 Canadians chose a new federal Conservative government, which of all the major federal parties is the one most likely to consider expanded private health care as an option. However, it is safe to say that any change from current health care policy is almost guaranteed to involve a careful exploration of the current opinions of all stakeholders, as well as a public discussion of the intended changes, long before a policy change takes place.

Additionally we have speculated that beliefs about public policy are likely to be related to political orientations. It is quite clear that ideologies are connected to interest-group behaviour, but political activists do not necessarily represent the thinking of the general public. Most often they are identified with the more extreme views on the impact of policy alternatives. However, their effect on controversial issues is not easily dismissed either. We have seen over and over in Canada that activists have been a strong voice for generating opinions about the clash between private health care and the ability to deliver quality in a public system in this country. This has had a lot to do with the way the public thinks about policy on this issue.

# 5 Change and Stability in Opinions

It is hard enough to remember my opinions, without also remembering my reasons for them!

– Friedrich Nietzsche

Conceptions of important issues and priorities are regularly subject to change. Public opinion is characterized by its dynamic nature and tends to respond when new priorities are identified or when unexpected events in society create an altered view of how things should be. Consider the extent to which fears about international terrorism have changed attitudes about public security and made vigilance a concern for Canadians since the events of 11 September 2001 which resulted in the destruction of the World Trade Center in New York City. These events led to a loss of public confidence in the invulnerability of North American cities to international terrorism.

Major shifts in values and beliefs owing to wide-ranging collective developments in societies, such as those associated with political revolution or economic upheaval, have also impacted on the stability of public opinion. For example, groups that aim to mobilize opinion around an issue may also stimulate change in public opinion, sometimes creating new perspectives and aspirations. In a society that is open to social change, there are many different sources of new ideas to which the public may respond.

In order to extend our understanding of stability and change in public opinion, we will consider in this chapter some of the events during the past several years that have influenced the way Canadians think. Considerable research has been done not only in Canada but also in other Western nations on how opinions about the functions of major institutions and the nature of social priorities have changed. This research suggests that these changes can be attributed to the fundamental cultural, economic, and technological transformations that have occurred during the last twenty-five years that have reduced the influence of key institutions such as the family and the church on the way we think and behave (see Fukuyama, 1999). Finally, demographic changes such as population maturation and internal migration from rural areas to urban areas are associated with changing values (see Foot, 1998). Residents of metropolitan areas may have different priorities when it comes to the availability of public services such as policing, waste management, and retail than those who live in rural hinterlands.

We will begin the chapter by examining some of the significant changes in social relationships in Canadian society and go on to consider how perceptions of important issues and priorities have developed in response to these changes. We will then consider examples of contemporary issues about which opinions have changed and review how dissent has resulted in the mobilization of public opinion for social change through collective action. We conclude with a look at postmodern views about whether it is meaningful to argue that there really are collective opinions or whether there simply are unconnected individual views.

## Some Sources of Opinion Change

Throughout this text we have referred to factors that have contributed to the transformation of Canadian society. These include population change, value change, economic change, and technological change. Clearly these factors are interrelated and account for changes in lifestyles and behaviour. It is often argued that new ideas emerging to challenge convention are the origins of many of the views that Canadians express about issues in public opinion polls; because of that they deserve to be briefly reviewed here. First we will consider population change.

### Population Change

Demography may provide a basis for opinion change because societies experience transformation in the composition of their populations because of aging, internal migration, or cultural diversity from immigration. When this happens there are different expectations of institutions and the services that they provide, as well as different attitudes and consumer behaviour. Research by demographer David K. Foot (1998) shows that the age of the population is correlated with the ebb and flow of demands for products and activities. Moreover, age is also linked to attitudes about spending and investing. According to Foot, changes in the patterns of participation in leisure activities can be attributed to the size of an age cohort. The period between 1946 and 1966 when a large number of children were born in Canada is known as the baby boom generation. This age cohort is believed to have had a significant impact on lifestyles in this country because baby boomers make up a large proportion of the population. For example, active sports such as tennis and skiing were perceived to be important because of the preferences of a majority of baby boomers; their preferences established a lifestyle preference for many others as well. But when a majority of the baby boom population became older, less-difficult physical activities like walking and gardening became perceived to be a more sensible way to spend one's time and money. 'Most people, as they get older become less active and less inclined to engage in strenuous physical activities. As a result, their leisure and recreation habits change. The impacts of these changes on every recreational pursuit from badminton to birding are dramatic ... There is no excuse for a community to spend money on hockey rinks at the millennium that are likely to be empty in 2005, while neglecting to provide the parks and walking trails that an ageing population needs' (Foot, 1998, p. 148).

Foot refers to the decline in popularity of tennis and skiing – extremely popular sports during the 1980s – as a reflection of demographic change. The demand for skiing and tennis equipment and facilities escalated because this 'big generation' of Canadians perceived them to be desirable forms of social behaviour which had the advantage of physical exercise suitable to their age and family situation. Tennis and skiing become the 'in things' to be seen doing with young children in tow. The relative cost of expensive tennis and ski equipment for the whole family was justified especially when Health Canada encouraged outdoor sports like these as a healthy regimen for those in middle age. So a generation in their late thirties and forties bought equipment and spent winter vacations pursuing these sports as an element of popular culture. However, as this age cohort is now approaching their sixties, the tennis courts and ski slopes are much less crowded, partly because the next generation is smaller. However, this is not entirely because older people cannot participate in these sports (Foot notes that a former governor general of Canada, Roland Michener, played tennis in his nineties), but because of the general belief that older people should probably not take the risk to their health or stretch the limits of their endurance by engaging in them. For an older generation, participation in less risky walking sports is perceived to be more age-appropriate. Golf and the social activities that are part of golf now have the attention of the big generation of Canadians. Demography apparently also explains the current passion for exercising the arm muscles at video lottery terminals and other leisure time pursuits found only at casinos; both of which currently enjoy popular support among the boomer generation.

Many assume that consumer behaviour in the stock market and particularly the values of assets in a portfolio are entirely determined by business performance. In fact, during the 1990s, many Canadians invested their savings in the market for the first time based on that belief. They also perceived that continued growth in the value of shares would sustain their investments and increase their savings. At least that is what the stock brokers who advised investors said would happen. Canadians have traditionally not chosen to take chances with their money, preferring instead to invest safely in guaranteed assets like Canada Savings Bonds and Guaranteed Investment Certificates (GICs) which are backed by major banks. You may remember that this has been identified as one of the values which make us different from more risk-taking Americans (Lipset, 1970). Nevertheless, during the 1990s there was a high demand for shares by people who had never before thought of putting their money in the stock market. In fact, the expectations that investments would grow created a considerable boom that lasted almost until the end of the twentieth century.

In Foot's analysis of demographic change, the argument is that middle-aged members of the baby-boom generation had moved from spending to investing for their old age. Stock market prices were a reflection of this phenomenon. However, in this case the issue is whether demography alone can explain the level of interest in investment. It is equally likely that attitudes toward riskier forms of investment had changed since there was a stronger demand for shares than the knowledge possessed by baby boomers of business performance would otherwise have created. Like participation in active sports, investment in the stock market represented a lifestyle change that a majority of Canadians also accepted whether or not they were part of the baby-boom generation. In other words, majority opinion about the value of holding stocks explains the volume of shares purchased in popular companies like those of the technology firms that were active in the development of the fibre-optic equipment necessary to the knowledge-based economy. Firms such as Nortel Networks and JDS Uniphase accounted for a large volume of trading on the Toronto Stock Exchange during that time. Traders who promoted and sold the shares of course assisted in this but it appears that changing attitudes along with changing demography influenced this phenomenon.

Although the stock market is not the only investment vehicle, Foot argues that as this big generation of Canadians gets older they will invest more and spend less and thus determine much of the direction of consumer behaviour. One could speculate that they would do this only if they continue to believe that investment in the stock market is worth the risk. During the past five years, the volume of shares traded has not exceeded those of the boom years of the 1990s. Clearly this is consistent with an argument that attitudes toward riskier forms of investment have changed again especially since the baby boom generation is now nearing retirement. The popular investment strategy of the twenty-first century has been for safer investments in tangible assets, such as real estate or personal property, rather than taking on the vagaries of the stock market again.

Population change may also involve the movement of people from one part of the country to another and from other countries. Interprovincial migration has always been a characteristic of Canadian society. For example, Hiller (2000) notes that historically the more industrial provinces, including Ontario and British Columbia, have benefited from the internal migration of the population; in recent years Alberta has been a popular destination for interprovincial migrants.[1] On the other hand, the Atlantic provinces have consistently lost people through out-migration as more mobile individuals have chosen to relocate in search of better employment opportunities, often with the assistance of friends and relatives who have already migrated to selected destinations (see Beaujot, 1991).

International migration has also been a source of population change for Canada. The government has set immigration targets at about 250,000 people per year and it is estimated that by 2030 immigration will be the

---

1 The 2001 Census shows that about 269,000 people had changed provinces or territories and about 887,000 had moved from one census division to another within their province or territory in the previous year. During this period interprovincial migration was at its lowest level since 1992–3. (Statistics Canada, 2002)

main source of population growth. As the baby-boomer generation start to retire and die, natural growth will not meet societal needs and new Canadians will be required to replace them. As with internal migration, the destination for many immigrants has been the most industrialized provinces and the largest metropolitan centres such as Toronto, Montreal, and Vancouver. Most importantly, however, is the fact that a majority of immigrants who arrived in Canada in the last thirty years have been members of visible-minority groups. According to some calculations, about seven in every ten recent immigrants are members of a visible minority, usually Asian (Chard and Renaud, 2000). At any rate, many sociologists have noted that this level of cultural blending has important implications for how the issues confronting our society are being viewed. Harry Hiller attributes the potential for differences in attitudes to ongoing changes in population characteristics resulting from the realignment of people from rural to urban areas and from new Canadians taking up residence in the country (Hiller, 2000, p. 10). Moreover, some have argued that attracting a greater number of racially and ethnically dissimilar immigrants, in conjunction with Canada's policy of promoting multiculturalism, has the potential to discourage newcomers from full participation in the national society and will reshape the attitudes of minorities about their identification with Canada (Bissoondath, 1994). Indeed, since the bombings in London during the summer of 2005, which have been blamed on 'home-grown terrorists,' some members of the international media have taken up elements of this argument to explain the tragedy, claiming that the marginalization of Muslim immigrants in the ethnic ghettos of Britain's larger cities has led to attitudes of resentment and a rejection of the values of the majority of society.

Kymlicka (1998) shows, however, that most immigrants in Canada do not reject major social institutions. They are more likely to become Canadian than immigrants from the United States or the United Kingdom are. In fact, he points out that the rate of naturalization of immigrants to Canada is almost double that of the United States. Moreover, immigrants do not always isolate themselves from participating in political parties: 'after all, political participation is a symbolic affirmation of citizenship and reflects an interest in the political life of the larger society. Yet there is no evidence of decline in such participation ... More generally, all the indicators suggest that immigrants quickly absorb and accept Canada's basic liberal-democratic values and constitutional principles' (Kymlicka, 1998, pp. 18–19).

On the other hand, as we saw earlier in this book, interest in politics may not in itself be the best indicator of distinctive political opinions. A recent study of candidates seeking to be elected as members of parliament compared the political attitudes of those who are visible minorities and those of anglophones and francophones (Black, 2002). The research explored attitudes on a number of social, moral, and economic issues including questions about environmental protection, perceptions of the welfare state, crime rates, equal rights, abortion, pornography, as well as government intervention in the economy. While the results were not significantly dissimilar in a statistical sense, Black shows that visible minority members do express many attitudes in these areas different from those of candidates from the other cultural groups. For example, visible-minority candidates are more supportive of environmental protection than the other groups but are less likely to favour environmental protection over job creation. Moreover, on social issues, visible-minority candidates are most likely to perceive there is not enough respect for traditional values but were inclined to be more liberal in their views on cracking down on crime or on abortion as a personal choice, as well as in their perceptions about the negative effects of a welfare state. They were also more liberal in their views about individual self-reliance for success than those with European or majority Canadian origins. Black concludes that on the whole, candidates from visible-minority backgrounds are more leftist or liberal in their political attitudes and these attitudes continue to differentiate them from candidates from other cultural groups even when party ideology is taken into account. These data suggest the argument that cultural changes have the power to transform the way individuals think about social issues in our society is persuasive, at least as far as political orientations are concerned. However they do not account for the changes which can be attributed to values.

*Value Change*

Earlier in the book we addressed the subject of core values as presented by expert analysts of public opinion like Neil Nevitte (1996), Michael Adams (1997), and others, who claim that there have been significant changes in the way Canadians perceive important issues. You will recall that Nevitte argues that Canadians have become less deferential than in earlier periods of our history. They are less trusting of governments and politicians and more willing to engage in political protest. He also suggests that because segments of Canadian society have never experienced disadvantage or deprivation, they have been able to embrace new thinking about aspects of our material culture such as economic growth. He contends they are less concerned with acquisition and more concerned with quality-of-life issues. This theory, postmaterialism, has been put forward as an explanation of value change. It draws on the work of Inglehart (1997) who studied the emergence of postmaterial values in several mature industrial societies. It suggests the emergence of a new consensus in these societies that is focused on equality in health care, education, work, and family life. It also posits a transformation of political life, with more participation in protests and more public activism.

In December 2002, *Maclean's* magazine published the results of a national opinion poll on the mood of the country which showed widespread unhappiness among the people of this country, with the headline 'Why So Cranky?' The data showed 41 per cent were more pessimistic about the future, 32 per cent said their financial situation had gotten worse, 43 per cent said they were more negative about the ethics and morality of business leaders, and 59 per cent said the prime minister should step down. The story questioned the negative public mood in light of the fact that at the time domestic economic indicators were stable and unemployment had become less of a concern for a majority of respondents. Relative to other parts of the world, fear of political unrest and terrorism was not an immediate problem and worries about social issues were down. Even national unity was no longer perceived to be a source of controversy. Yet, as shown in Figure 5.1, despite a more-relaxed social environment, there seemed to be a cloud hanging over the pattern of response to the issues.

The occlusions in what should have been a sunny climate of opinion were attributed to a disconnect between public expectations and action by government on their most immediate concerns. In particular the cranky public mood evinced by the data was interpreted to mean that there was growing cynicism about the willingness of those in authority to countenance real change in areas of grave concern. These areas of concern included reform of health care, dealing with child poverty, and, interestingly enough a year after 11 September 2001, more spending on the Canadian military.

Does this reflect the kind of value changes expected if the theory of postmaterialism is correct and does it call into question the basis for a new national consensus? Lower levels of trust in the state and political leadership are identified with attitudes that are part of a postmodern

Figure 5.1  Top issues for Canadians – December 2002

Wandering Worries: Percentages citing specific issues as top concern over the past decade

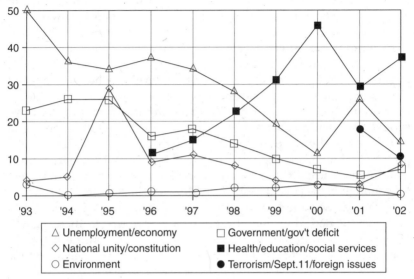

Source: *Maclean's*, 30 December 2002.

view. Several social scientists have explored the declining overall satisfaction with the way Canadian democracy works (Kornberg and Clarke, 1994; Nadeau, 2002). While Canada has usually placed high on international quality-of-life indicators, there is nevertheless evidence of frustration, if not outright dissatisfaction, with aspects of political life in this country. 'Attachment to Canada is weak among Quebec francophones, while confidence in the federal government ... the courts ... and politicians remains divided ... and the number of Canadians identifying with a political party is in decline' (Nadeau, 2002, p. 51).

According to this research, dissatisfaction with the workings of Canadian democracy is linked to things such as a limited choice of parties, the uneven distribution of seats in Parliament, and the representation of women in political life. Another prime source of dissatisfaction is a perception that political leaders are dishonest and lack integrity. In sum, many perceive that democracy in Canada does not work equally well for everybody and their dissatisfaction with the political institutions manifests itself in the opinion that important problems facing the nation are being avoided.

Trends in opinions such as these have been used as evidence of worldwide cultural shifts. In social theory, a transformation from an agrarian society with tradition as the basis for authority towards an industrial society where rationality is a basis of authority is referred to as modernization. At later stages of societal development, modernization is followed by further social and cultural transformation giving rise to postmodernization which at the cultural level involves a 'change of direction in the dominant norms and motivations underlying human behaviour' (Inglehart, 1997, p. 27). Exploring this concept briefly, we should note that modernization also involves the development of an economy based on production, the growth of cities, a decline in the power of religion, and the expansion of bureaucracy in the structure of institutions. The cultural supports in the emergence of modern society are found in values like reason, individualism, liberalism, and achievement. Yet, as we noted above, postmodern theory is a view of society that goes in new directions by giving less priority to these values. However, it also describes a society with less trust in the power of science and new technologies to yield solutions for problems, and the emergence of new ways for individuals to experience religion, politics, sexuality, and human relationships.[2] According to this theory, advanced industrial societies have reached a stage where prosperity and a sense of security have made it possible for many to take basic survival for granted: values associated with the modern era, such as accumulation, are given less priority. The sense of security afforded by governments or even by religious and scientific beliefs is less important than other non-material things. 'In postmodern society this emphasis on economic achievement as the top priority is now giving way to an increasing emphasis on the quality of life. In a major part of the world, the disciplined, self-denying and achievement-oriented norms of industrial society are giving way to an increasingly broad latitude for individual choice of lifestyles and individual self-expression' (Inglehart, 1997, p. 28).

Most importantly postmodern theory also represents a rethinking of the way social relations have been organized. The term most often applied to this is *deconstruction* which refers to re-evaluating and overturning understandings about established structures and how they

---

2 For a comprehensive critique of the theory of modernization and arguments for a postmodern view of society, see Best and Keller (1991).

operate in society (see Boyne and Rattansi, 1990). For example, our acceptance of the idea of consensus or even some basic uniformity of views as a foundation for society is opposed in postmodern thinking in favour of notions about the fragmentation of culture or the relativism of values, as well as a strong sense of the need for personal fulfillment. Moreover, postmodern theory recognizes that boundaries separating institutions and the norms or customs governing social experiences will be regularly violated in society. For example, in artistic expression, a dance performance or a musical composition may incorporate elements of classical, jazz, and hard rock in order to create an interesting new art form. On the other hand, some manifestations of postmodernism in contemporary culture have been deemed to be less acceptable. Critics of postmodernism have expressed concern about the unregulated crossing of boundaries between institutions, such as the introduction into mainstream entertainment of the kind of overt sexuality that at one time was found primarily in pornography (see McNair, 2002). Thus, the presentation of explicit sex scenes, which was once considered out of bounds for mainstream audiences, has become more accepted as an integral part of many highly successful contemporary films and television shows.

In April 2004, *Maclean's* published a special feature on incivility in contemporary society (Gillis, 2004). The story provided many examples of incidents involving bad manners that have become common in day-to-day interaction and it speculated about why incivility has become so much a part of our world.

One of the more interesting details in the story was a reference to a public opinion poll that was conducted in 1999 and showed that 65 per cent of respondents expected manners to deteriorate over the following decade. Experts presented interpretations of this trend, attributing it to increasing sense of anonymity in our lives: family and community beliefs have less power to control our behaviour. The pollster Angus Reid was quoted as attributing it to a growing free-market individualism that had become more widespread in Canadian society during recent years. A related hypothesis was that contemporary child rearing placed too much emphasis on developing children's self-esteem resulting in adults who are overly self-absorbed. These interpretations all refer to value changes relating to social relations in contemporary society. More significantly, the interpreters of this poll conclude that incivility and discourtesy can also be explained as reflecting the diminishing importance of class boundaries in a postmodern society. Since manners have the effect of perpetuating class and lifestyle differences they would be seen as symbols of social relations that were accepted in an earlier era but are incompatible with the way we view each other today.

The work of Michael Adams (1997) also shows that current trends in public opinion are a reflection not merely of changing demography but also of sub-cultural value differences. What we think about politicians, government intervention in our lives, or homosexual unions is derived from the subcultures with whom we identify. In his analysis, Adams maintains that emerging demographic attributes and value and lifestyle differences explain more effectively the sources of opinion segmentation. Rather than sketching a 'character type' as a way of exploring dominant modes of conformity in society, such as presented in *The Lonely Crowd* by David Riesman (1965), Adams shows that shifts in public opinion on social issues or consumer behaviour and even our views about the workings of institutions in contemporary Canadian society can be explained by locating individuals in values communities where outlooks are similar.[3] If this view is correct, the attitudes of tomorrow may be predicted by studying the values communities in which today's youth participate. Nevertheless, it is equally likely that there will continue to be no strong consensus on which solutions are most appropriate to deal with the top priorities of the day.

*Economic Change and Technology*

In theories about social change, values are strongly linked to economic changes. An element of economic change that receives considerable attention is the impact information technology has had on occupations and the way individuals experience their jobs. Some analysts have argued that improved communication technologies have transformed society to the point where competitive advantage is dependent less upon spatial location than upon access to high-speed data lines and the availability of a good telephone-computer interface. While most of the

---

3 The Canadian population was divided into three demographic segments: the oldest generation, aged fifty years and older, is identified as pre-boomers; the baby boomers are those aged thirty to forty-nine; and generation X refers to those who are under twenty-nine. Within the age groups, respondents are classified by whether they evince traditional or modern opinions, particularly about permissive behaviour and whether they show individualistic or social orientations in relations with others. Twelve value clusters are presented within the generational groups.

new jobs that have been created during the past three decades have involved the use of computers and electronic data processing, the expansion of information technology in all areas of the work world has raised questions about how the workplace has changed, especially in white-collar, clerical, and service-sector jobs (see Krahn and Lowe, 2002). Characteristic of the changes involving information technology that have been noted are increased routinization and de-skilling of jobs, making white-collar work more similar to unskilled labour (Braverman, 1974), and loss of control by workers over the tasks which they perform (Rinehart, 2001). Broader reorganization in the knowledge economy such as the globalization of production has also involved flexible labour practices whereby a number of highly specialized firms may be networked through subcontracting arrangements so that work is reallocated among partner firms in the network (Harrison, 1994). The significance of this is that the secondary labour market where pay levels are lower, fringe benefits are less available, and unions less influential has expanded. Flexibility – not keeping products in inventory, for example – has come to mean that there is no need to keep workers either if they are easily accessible during peak periods.

It is important for us to consider how these changes have moulded attitudes about the place of work in people's lives. For example, the transformation of the workplace has meant that jobs have become less fulfilling for many people. Indeed this is sometimes cited as a source of a declining work ethic as people become more discontented with the conditions of their work. Public attitudes about the place of work in people's lives have been explored as part of the cross cultural survey of values described by Nevitte (1996, pp. 157–206). This study of mature industrial nations, including Canada, shows that the number who agree with the view that a decrease in the importance of work in our lives is a bad thing has declined since the early eighties, predominantly among Europeans. Canadians are less likely to agree with the statement than Americans (48 per cent versus 62 per cent). In Canada there was an 8.8 per cent decline in agreement over a ten-year period. This measure is offered as evidence that people are less concerned about the importance of work than they used to be. Moreover, on the basis of a semantic differential scale using self-report information (see Chapter 2) there was a small decline in job satisfaction in Europe and an increase in the United States over the period, while Canada has remained the same. On the other hand, the number who report that they take a great deal of pride in their work increased in every country surveyed in the study

(Nevitte, 1996, p. 163). Nevitte concludes that while the data suggest that attitudes to work as a life interest are changing, these are attitudes that reflect postmaterial values. People who identify with materialist values see work in instrumental terms, that is, simply as a way of making money or as 'hours for dollars,' while those with postmaterialist values see work in terms of security, recognition, or self-actualization. 'From this perspective, people work not because they have to, nor because they see work primarily as providing a source of material comfort, but because the workplace fulfills other goals such as the opportunity to express their abilities. This is the dimension usually identified as the key emerging value orientation within the contemporary work world' (Nevitte, 1996, p. 168).

However, data made available recently by Statistics Canada about workers' overall satisfaction with their jobs and pay levels show that on a nation-wide basis, those surveyed are likely to offer *positive opinions* about their work lives (Table 5.1). The table shows that more than one in three (34 per cent) say they are very satisfied with their jobs although the intensity of satisfaction tends to increase with age and education and is greatest among those in managerial positions. This suggests that jobs in the information economy are perceived to be more interesting and engaging than jobs in resource-extraction industries. On the other hand, workers are considerably less satisfied with the amount they are paid for their work. Once again older more educated workers who are in managerial positions are more likely to say they are very satisfied with their pay.

Understanding the attitudes and experiences of workers is important because it ultimately reflects their sense of well being. Not surprisingly, there is a large literature on the subject of job satisfaction. Of interest is a British study, *Perceptions of Work, Variations within a Factory* (Blackburn and Beynon, 1972). The authors argue that workers' biographies are integral to understanding their attitudes towards their jobs. For example, family responsibilities are a primary factor shaping attitudinal differences. They show that childless workers hold different attitudes to work than those with children, and men have different attitudes than women. They conclude that both the technological and organizational structure of a plant and factors outside the workplace must be taken into account in order to understand these opinions.

Goldthorpe et al. (1968) have explored the way that a worker's basic orientation to work prior to entering a job explains attitudes of instrumentalism and fatalism in workplaces where there is very little possibil-

Table 5.1 Job and pay satisfaction in Canada 2001

| Employee characteristics | % of employees who are satisfied with their job | | | % of employees who are satisfied with their pay | | |
|---|---|---|---|---|---|---|
| | Not satisfied | Satisfied | Very satisfied | Not satisfied | Satisfied | Very satisfied |
| Overall | 10.0 | 55.8 | 34.0 | 23.5 | 57.9 | 18.3 |
| Gender | | | | | | |
| Men | 10.5 | 56.6 | 32.7 | 21.1 | 61.7 | 17.1 |
| Women | 9.4 | 55.0 | 35.3 | 25.9 | 54.3 | 19.6 |
| Age | | | | | | |
| Less than 25 | 14.1 | 58.1 | 27.7 | 27.0 | 56.6 | 16.3 |
| 25–44 | 9.8 | 57.0 | 33.0 | 23.7 | 58.8 | 17.5 |
| 45 or more | 8.7 | 53.1 | 37.8 | 22.1 | 57.1 | 20.4 |
| Education attainment | | | | | | |
| Less than high school | 10.3 | 59.3 | 30.1 | 23.5 | 60.9 | 15.3 |
| High school | 10.0 | 56.0 | 33.9 | 20.8 | 58.5 | 20.5 |
| Some university or post-secondary | 10.4 | 55.8 | 33.6 | 24.8 | 57.3 | 17.6 |
| University | 8.4 | 53.3 | 38.0 | 22.7 | 57.2 | 20.1 |
| Occupation groups | | | | | | |
| Managers | 6.7 | 49.2 | 44.1 | 15.4 | 62.8 | 21.6 |
| Professionals | 9.2 | 52.5 | 38.0 | 25.9 | 57.2 | 16.7 |
| Technical/Trades | 10.6 | 56.7 | 32.5 | 23.4 | 58.2 | 18.3 |
| Marketing/Sales | 10.8 | 60.0 | 29.2 | 24.1 | 59.9 | 15.8 |
| Clerical/Administrative | 8.4 | 56.1 | 35.0 | 25.7 | 52.6 | 21.3 |
| Production workers | 14.9 | 62.9 | 22.1 | 26.5 | 58.3 | 15.2 |

Source: Statistics Canada – catalogue no 71-585

ity for initiative and little variety on the job. They found that high wages and job security are traded off against these negative factors and are responsible for relatively high levels of satisfaction when these conditions are present. In Canada, research by James Rinehart has shown that job satisfaction is likely to be a reflection of individuals' evaluations of their jobs relative to the viable alternatives available to them (Rinehart, 2001).

In a recent study of Canadian call centres, which are often seen to be an important source of employment for many workers in the information economy, Butler and Jarman (2004) explore whether work settings (also known as the type of workplace) influence the way workers view their jobs and particularly their levels of satisfaction with them. The study used a typology of call centres based on important differences vis-à-vis benefit levels, type of technology, as well as working conditions and the kind of job security that different centres are able to provide. Not surprisingly, pay levels emerge as centrally important in determining what makes a person satisfied with a job in a call centre. However, employer loyalty to these workers is a second crucial factor in understanding variations in worker attitudes to their jobs and ultimately reflects how job satisfaction is expressed.

These studies show there are significant changes underway in the way work and ultimately the way life is perceived. However, before concluding this section we must also consider the increasing role of the Internet in expanding public perceptions. The world wide web is an element of the globalization of culture which creates connectivity between peoples, in terms not only of lifestyles such as fashion codes and music or movie preferences, but also of thought patterns. Seeing local issues in terms of global consequences is a good example of this. Tomlinson (1999) discusses the idea as promoting a sense of cosmopolitanism where issues far away from one's everyday experience become more immediate to us. He argues that globalized communication has the power to 'close moral distance' (Tomlinson, 1999, p. 171). By this he means that we do not require face to face interaction to experience empathy for people who live some distance away. We connect with the experience of distant others, personalizing them as we would in any form of interaction, based on images provided by mass communications. Technological innovations such as the Internet thus have the power to homogenize attitudes and interests at a distance. However in this process local cultures may be weakened. In fact, as we noted earlier (Chapter 3), societies like Canada may face significant threats to their sovereignty when they are bombarded by cultural products emanating from outside their borders.

Once while driving through Germany on a summer vacation, I listened to a radio station. The only German spoken during the program was in the introduction: the songs and commentary that made up the rest of the program were in English. Apparently the German radio audience did not care what language was spoken, as long as they heard their favorite pop tunes. In a connected world, therefore, the culture of one's country of origin or ethnic background may have less and less to do with the way we experience life. More and more Europeans think and act like the French, English, and Germans, who are the dominant actors in the European Union (Tepperman and Blaine, 1999, p. 189).

Apart from the possible creation of a virtual community, the Internet also serves as an information medium when other sources have been censored or are unavailable. The Monica Lewinsky–Bill Clinton sex scandal was the first time a major political news story was obtained from the Internet (Bennett, 2003). Indeed, it might not have become the news event that it did, if information about the president's behaviour had been restricted to the usual journalistic channels. Public curiosity was aroused by the unrestricted flow of sensational stories that did not appear in the evening news; this was apparently a significant factor in the formation of opinions that President Clinton had lied about the nature of his relationship with Lewinsky. In any event the Internet has added a new dimension to the coverage of news events like this: stories now have the chance to become global sensations as more and more users spend their time online seeking information from around the world. If there is a basis for the much used term 'world opinion,' it clearly has a foundation in the claim that the Internet has the potential to bring this about.

## Changing Opinions about National Issues

Over the past decade the tide of public opinion has turned on a number of national issues. Fear of free trade with the United States and the threat of Quebec separating from the rest of Canada no longer generate the same emotional reactions in public opinion studies that they did in the early 1990s. This does not mean that attitudes about closer commercial relations with the Americans have completely changed or that we no longer fear for national unity. However, concerns about our survival as a nation without tariffs on cross-border trade seem to be less immediate now that globalization has become a household word. On the other hand, other perceived threats to social stability have shifted the focus of public concern upward on a number of issues. In this section we will examine trends on two public policy issues which have challenged Canadians over the past year or two: the changing nature of our opinions concerning same-sex marriage, which some Canadians perceive to be a threat to the institutions of marriage and the family; and changing opinions towards our right to privacy and the need for increased national security, an issue which has seen an upsurge since the events of

11 September 2001 and especially since the bombings in Madrid and London during the summer of 2005.

## Same-Sex Marriage as a Public Issue

The legalization of same-sex marriage by Parliament has been a controversial issue in Canada in recent years. It appears to entail a significant change in the definition of the family in contemporary society. The growing belief that same-sex couples should be entitled to marry if they wish and be recognized as having the same rights as heterosexual married couples is a reflection of the broad value shifts which have taken place in our society. However, the family cannot be understood apart from other institutions in society. Changes in core values relating to traditionalism, the rights of individuals, and orientations to authority, which we reviewed earlier, have influenced current attitudes toward homosexuality and the meaning of marriage. Indeed, many people view the same-sex legislation as the result of the capacity of the family to adapt to a changing social environment.

Traditional models of family life that provided a frame of reference for negative public opinion about same-sex unions emphasized that marriage is the legitimation of parenthood. For some members of society, marriage is a sacred institution sanctioned by religion: it is the union of a male and a female for the purpose of procreation, as well as for the care and socialization of their children (see Nye and Berardo, 1973). People who oppose same-sex marriage thus see themselves as having a religious duty to protect family values from an increasingly secularized and uncaring society. The family is seen as the source of morality that is protected by religious teaching. According to this argument, societal stability depends on gender differentiation and reproduction. Since same-sex couples cannot produce children, the purpose of marriage is lost to society and thus same-sex marriage is not an acceptable alternative. Some also have the view that when children are a part of a same-sex union, the partners may not provide adequate role models for their children.

Other departures from this family ideal – dual wage earning, rising divorce rates, single parenting, sexual permissiveness, and in vitro fertilization – reveal, however, a fundamental disconnect between traditional views about the functions of marriage and current behaviour. Moreover, as a society we have come to value diversity and choice in many areas of social life, and the efforts of homosexuals to be legally

Figure 5.2  Attitudes toward homosexuality, 1996–2001

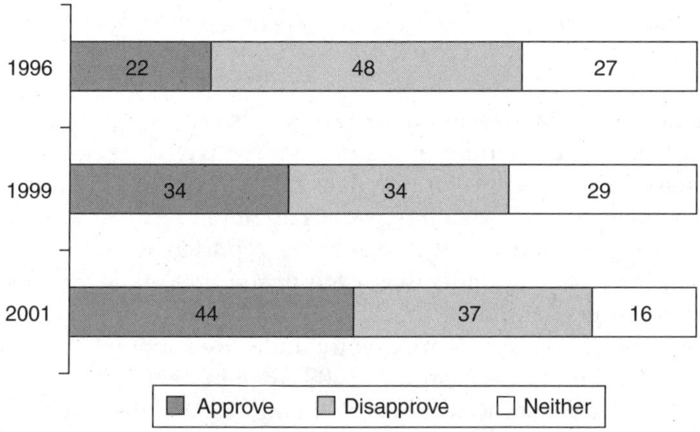

| | Approve | Disapprove | Neither |
|---|---|---|---|
| 1996 | 22 | 48 | 27 |
| 1999 | 34 | 34 | 29 |
| 2001 | 44 | 37 | 16 |

■ Approve   ▨ Disapprove   □ Neither

Base: Total sample (N = 2035)
Source: Environics Research Group, April 2001

recognized may be understood as an effort to make their lives more congruent with current values. For those whose identity as gay persons has been a source of discrimination and who wish to parent children, legalized marriage offers a measure of protection relative to their responsibilities for the support, custody, and adoption of children. Indeed, the argument that the absence of heterosexual role models in same-sex families will produce maladjusted individuals is not supported. The available research literature which compares heterosexual and same-sex couples who raise children suggests that the sexual orientation of the parents has no great effect on child development (Stacey and Biblarz, 2001). Clearly, these data are by no means conclusive since the study of same-sex child rearing has only just begun, but the contradictions are not readily apparent in public opinion.

During the past ten years, public opinion on this policy issue has undergone considerable change. The Environics Research Group of Toronto has tracked the opinions of Canadians about homosexuality and the levels of support for same-sex unions. The data they provide involves a comparison of attitudes over a five-year period from 1996 to 2001. The 2001 data was based on a sample of 2035 respondents and, as shown in Figure 5.2, there was a significant change in attitudes about homosexuality during the five-year period. The proportion of respondents who expressed approval of homosexuality in 2001 (44 per cent) had doubled from 1996. Moreover, they note that in 2001, just over one in five Canadians *strongly approved* and 23 per cent *somewhat approved* of homosexuality.

There were also important socio-demographic differences reported by Environics based on age, gender, and education, as well as region and political orientation. Nevertheless, the data clearly indicated that attitudes of Canadians to homosexuality were changing.

It should also be noted the attitudes being reported were not the views of a majority of respondents at each of the three time periods under consideration. As shown in Table 3, a majority either disapproved of homosexuality or was apparently undecided about it. In fact, 7 per cent more expressed disapproval in 2001 than in 1999. While more were neutral about the issue in both 1996 and 1999, a majority had made up their minds to express their approval by 2001. In fact, intolerance appeared to be eroding and in September 2003, the CBC released results of a survey of 1,015 Canadians sponsored by NFO-CF World Group, a market-information firm located in the United States and Canada, which showed that about 52 per cent were of the opinion that there is nothing morally wrong with homosexuality. Indeed, 57 per cent also believed that same-sex unions do not represent a threat to marriage. However, the data again revealed demographic dissimilarities in opinions. For example it showed females, young Canadians, and those from urban areas as well as those from a higher socio-economic status are more likely to be tolerant of homosexuality than are other Canadians. In sum, as in the Environics findings, there was sufficient evidence of opinion change to conclude that the public debate about same-sex marriage would be largely free from judgments associating homosexuality with depravity.

The Environics study of 2001 also reported that a majority (55 per cent) of Canadians were in favour of allowing same-sex unions within the legal definition of marriage. The finding was consistent with an earlier poll conducted by Angus Reid in 1996. That study also showed nearly half of respondents (49 per cent) were in favour of legal recognition being given to same-sex unions.

On the other hand, one year later, in 2002, a survey by the Strategic Counsel reported that respondents were polarized for and against changing the definition of marriage in the Canadian constitution, although generational differences again explained much of the opposition to the

Figure 5.3 Proportions of Canadians in agreement with same-sex equality, 2000–2005

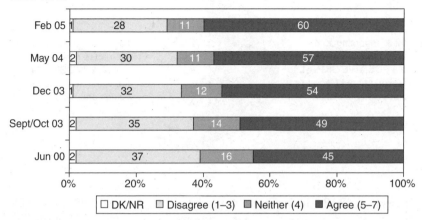

Question: Same-sex couples should have the same rights as heterosexual couples.
Base: Total sample (N = 1046)
Source: EKOS Research, February 2005.

proposal. In sum, since 2000, same-sex marriage has emerged as a significant issue in national political debates and this has been reflected in the public-opinion polls which have been released to the media during this period (see Figure 5.3). The opinions reported in the figure above show growing support for recognizing same-sex equality, as a majority (60 per cent) of Canadians ultimately made up their minds over the period surveyed that same-sex couples should have the same rights as other married couples.

Since 2002, the debate has been focused in the courts. Courts in several provinces, including the Ontario Court of Appeal in Canada's most populous province, have ruled that the definition of marriage includes equal rights and legal protection for same-sex couples. Moreover, the House Standing Committee on Human Rights and Freedoms in Ottawa began a series of public hearings in 2003 on this issue which resulted in the conclusion that the current legal definition of marriage should be amended to reflect the rulings of these courts.

Since that time the political debate has centred on the positions taken by the national political parties on the issue. For example, in 1999 the Reform Party introduced a resolution in Parliament in favour of the traditional definition of marriage, which passed with the support of a

Figure 5.4  Same sex marriage and Canadian values

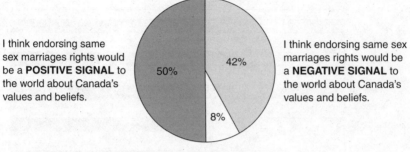

I think endorsing same sex marriages rights would be a **POSITIVE SIGNAL** to the world about Canada's values and beliefs.

50%

42%

8%

I think endorsing same sex marriages rights would be a **NEGATIVE SIGNAL** to the world about Canada's values and beliefs.

Source: EKOS Research, February 2005

majority of MPs, including a majority of those in the Liberal caucus: former prime minister Paul Martin among them. However, after the Liberal government of the day received the recommendation of the House Standing Committee on Human Rights and Freedoms, opposition to changing the traditional definition of marriage largely rested with the Conservative Party of Canada. Liberal MPs along with members from the Bloc Quebecois and the NDP have mainly been supportive of changing the definition of marriage to include same-sex unions. Opposition by the Conservatives is linked to reservations among church leaders about blessing homosexual unions as marriages. However a NFOCF Group survey in 2003 indicated that 48 per cent of respondents rejected the idea that churches should even participate in the political debate.

It is interesting to note that on the eve of enacting in Parliament the *Civil Marriage Act* legalizing same-sex marriage, the February 2005 EKOS survey showed that a majority of respondents indicated that giving legal recognition to same-sex unions would send a positive signal to the rest of the world about current Canadian values and beliefs (see Figure 5.4). However, despite these sentiments and the fact that same-sex marriage is now legal, a Strategic Counsel survey conducted for CTV and the *Globe and Mail* newspaper which was publicly released in July of 2005 shows that Canadians were almost equally split on the issue whether couples in same-sex marriages should be allowed to adopt children. Overall, 46 per cent were in favour of legalizing adoption by same-sex marriage couples and 51 per cent were opposed to the idea (see Table 5.2). Moreover, the table shows a remarkable consistency in opinions across the country.

Table 5.2 Should same-sex couples have the legal right to adopt children
How supportive are Canadians of allowing gay couples to legally adopt children?

| | Total sample (N = 1000) % | Region | | |
|---|---|---|---|---|
| | | Rest of Canada (N = 753) % | Ontario (N = 379) % | Quebec (N = 247) % |
| **Total supportive** | **46** | **47** | **48** | **42** |
| Very supportive | 23 | 22 | 23 | 24 |
| Somewhat supportive | 23 | 25 | 25 | 18 |
| Not too supportive | 16 | 15 | 13 | 18 |
| Not at all supportive | 35 | 35 | 37 | 36 |
| **Total not supportive** | **51** | **50** | **50** | **54** |
| DK/NA/Ref | 3 | 3 | 2 | 4 |

Source: EKOS Research February 2005

Overall, the data presented on this complex public issue in this section clearly shows that opinions, and perhaps attitudes as well, have changed significantly since 2000 towards both homosexuality and the rights of same-sex couples. The most important finding is the degree of agreement expressed by at least 50 per cent of Canadians that endorsing a revised definition of marriage would demonstrate our belief in inclusiveness to other nations in the world. On the other hand, there is no consensus yet on how the family is to constitute itself in the future. While the public has not evinced strong opposition to allowing same-sex couples to adopt children, many continue to view it as inappropriate. The roots of this opinion may be both political and religious, reflecting a general uncertainty about the future of traditional family arrangements in the face of social change. However, if it is recognized that same-sex couples are guaranteed equal treatment under the Canadian constitution, the trends we have reviewed show that, barring a constitutional challenge to redefining the family, public ambivalence is likely to fade away and adoption will become a normal process for same-sex families.

*National Security as a Public Issue*

Since the end of the Cold War in 1989, national defence typically has not been a priority for Canadian governments nor a significant concern of many Canadians. Although the Mulroney government reorganized the armed forces and increased spending on new ships and planes during the 1980s, the most allocated for this purpose since the end of the Second World War, our national governments have ultimately relied on the American military to help defend Canada. However, the 11 September 2001 attacks on the World Trade Center in New York City and the Pentagon in Washington D.C. by Islamic terrorists have apparently made Canadians more attentive to matters of personal and national security. A survey conducted by the Strategic Counsel in August 2005 reported that 62 per cent of Canadians believe a terrorist attack will occur in the next few years. Moreover, a majority are willing to trade civil rights for security from such an attack (Strategic Counsel, 2005). Indeed, concern has filtered into political and economic thinking as politicians and business leaders have begun to assess the impact of Canada being a target of terrorism.

During the cold war, Canadian public opinion was easily mobilized in support of efforts to resist the spread of Communism throughout the world. In this task the government of Canada allied itself with American foreign policy and adopted an approach to national security which involved us in continental defence with the American military should Soviet nuclear weapons be used to attack North America. In some situations, these agreements put Canadian forces under American command. Nevertheless, there is little evidence to show that these policies were viewed as something which created problems with our sense of national identity, although intellectuals such as George Grant (1965) warned that agreements on trade and foreign policy would inevitably draw us closer to American domination. Whitaker and Marcuse (1996) argue that the anti-Communist consensus that permeated public opinion during the Cold War years was essentially ideological. There was a perceived communist threat to democracy presented by Soviet Russia that needed to be resisted. Meeting this threat demanded absolute loyalty from all citizens or the North American way of life could be eroded. In other words, as Whitaker and Marcuse maintain, opinions on national security were based on 'the politics of fear ... Canadians were urged to "stand on guard." They were not encouraged to ask what exactly they were standing on guard *for*. It was enough to know what they should be on guard *against* ... the effect of the efforts of opinion leaders, public and private was to encourage a public opinion based above all upon *fear*' (Whitaker and Marcuse, 1996, p. 279).

Apparently most Canadians had no idea about the real meaning of the threat of Communism and rarely considered it or identified it in opinion polls as one of their top concerns. Instead, during this fearful time, they preferred to express opinions about bread and butter issues like housing and taxation. Nevertheless, they accepted the government's argument that the spread of Communism was a serious problem that required vigilance and they supported the authorities responsible for our protection like the RCMP and the military.

Canadians have usually demonstrated respect for authority. You will recall that earlier in this book we discussed this as one of the value differences by which we are sometimes differentiated from Americans (see Lipset, 1990). Canadians are described by Lipset as being disinclined to resent intrusions by governments in their lives and as showing less interest in individual freedom than Americans do. The mood of insecurity during the Cold War simply built on an underlying respect for law and order among Canadians at that time.

During the decades which followed, there is little evidence that attitudes about national security had changed, in terms either of the unwillingness of Canadians to have their tax dollars directed at military spending or their acceptance of the government's direction when any threat to national security was identified. Perhaps the best-known example of this is the October Crisis of 1970, when terrorists from an extremist element among Quebec separatists known as the FLQ kidnapped and held for ransom the British trade consul and a well-known provincial cabinet minister. In the days that followed, the kidnapped minister, Pierre Laporte, was murdered by the terrorists. The prime minister declared Quebec to be in the midst of a situation of 'apprehended insurrection' and enacted the *War Measures Act* which brought the army and tanks to the streets. It also brought about the suspension of civil liberties allowing the police to detain those suspected of any form of criminal activity for 21 days without being charged with committing a crime (see Landes, 1995, pp. 86–7). However, the public did not meet the suspension of liberties with widespread disapproval. There were objections by intellectuals and some opinion leaders, but most people greeted it as a temporary condition and some even approved of the rounding up of suspicious persons. A Gallup Report released in December 1970 indicated that 87 per cent approved of the government's action in bringing forward the *War Measures Act* to handle the crisis (Canadian Institute of Public Opinion, 1970). The Report noted that the decision had majority support among both English and French speaking Canadians and, interestingly, among the better educated: that is, from nine out of every ten respondents who had high school and university education.

Public deference and compliance with the authority as a culture trait has apparently undergone considerable change since then. According to Newman (1995) this was a watershed period, if not one of revolution, since trust and confidence in institutions were cast aside in favour of incivility, suspicion, and even open defiance. As we noted earlier, Gregg and Posner (1990) interpreted the change as showing that the status quo was no longer acceptable to a public that expected new solutions to old problems. Alternatively, the changes in opinion may indicate that national security was not really an immediate concern for a middle power like Canada. 'Acknowledging the improbability of our ever becoming a military or economic leader, we defined ourselves increasingly in terms of what the United States was not: where it was warlike, we were peaceable; where it was strong-willed, we were tolerant; where it was mean-spirited, we were charitable. Against the conventional wisdom about our inferiority complex, the 1980s saw Canada develop a sense of superiority. If not a military or economic leader, Canada would be a moral leader. If we were to lead, it would be by example' (Gregg and Posner, 1990, p. 13).

While Canadian support for organizations such as the NATO continued to be strong, 60 per cent of Canadians said they would rather live under Soviet Communism than risk a nuclear war: a new type of thinking about security was evolving. Indeed, only a minority of Canadians agreed that the emphasis of the government should be on military spending rather than social spending. Just over one in four (29 per cent) of respondents in the data collected by Decima Research (1989) and reported by Gregg and Posner in their book endorsed more military spending (Gregg and Posner, 1990); instead the majority expressed the view that the money would be better spent on non-military technologies. Three out of four Canadians indicated that our international relations should be directed at reducing the arms race and dealing with world poverty. In sum, Canadian thinking during this time showed that we were no less fearful about the possibility of international conflict but more willing to embrace policies that would promote world peace.

In Michael Adam's presentation of the evolution of Canadian and American values, derived from polls conducted during the 1980s through 1996, the changes in this country show us moving away from insecurity, which he sees as continuing to dominate American culture. For Canadians, international tensions were best faced with new solutions. We have rejected an ordered lifestyle and traditional rules in favour of idealism and more control of our own destiny (see Adams, 2003, pp. 196–200).

Moreover, we have become more concerned with inner fulfillment, autonomy, flexible lifestyles, and in a new Canadian model of peace, good government, and less order. To support this point, it is worth mentioning that in two polls, both based on interviews with a national sample of 1,500 Canadians, one released in the spring of 1987 and the other released in winter of 1989, only 1 per cent of respondents mentioned national defence as an important problem facing Canada (Decima Research 1987; 1989). The top issues were still material: the national debt, the cost of living, and unemployment.

Adams observes that as the new millennium began, a growing awareness of international terrorism and the terrorist attacks on the United States during 2001 had a noticeable impact on the sense of tranquility inherited from the late eighties. There was renewed belief in the need for greater security and vigilance. Yet Canadians have not been eager to participate in a war that they are not convinced is connected to any threats to our domestic security. In 2003 EKOS Research Associates tracked support and opposition to Canadian participation in an attack on Iraq. Their data shows that throughout that year a majority consistently opposed Canadian involvement with the U.S.-led campaign. They also show that 71 per cent of those interviewed supported the government's decision not to be part of the international coalition fighting the war (EKOS Research, 2003).

More recently in August 2005, the *Globe and Mail* announced the results of a poll on national security: 'Canadians want strict security. Most favour video cameras everywhere and deportation of terrorist sympathizers.'[4] The survey concluded that Canadians had become quite security conscious (Strategic Counsel, 2005). Indeed 72 per cent of respondents supported placing video cameras in public places and 81 per cent were in favour of deporting or jailing those promoting terrorist activities. The study showed that about 62 per cent fear that terrorists will attack Canada within the next few years (see Figure 5.5). Moreover a majority (48 per cent) perceived that Canada is not well prepared to deal with an attack by terrorists. It also shows that we are prepared to give a good deal of power to authorities if the national interest is threatened. The Strategic Counsel study indicates that while not a majority, many Canadians are likely to support legal restrictions on freedom of speech, accept surveillance and possibly even detaining

4 The survey used a sample of 1000 Canadians 18 years and older. The interviews were conducted in the first week of August 2005.

Figure 5.5  Perceptions of a threat from Muslim terrorists in Canada

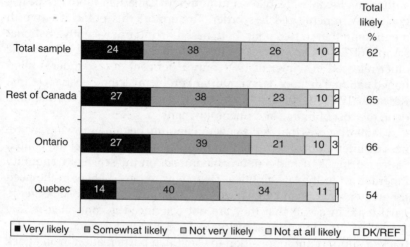

Q.7. How likely do you think it is that an act of terrorism will take place in Canada within the next few years?
Base: Total sample (N = 1000)
Source: The Strategic Counsel, *Immigration, Terrorism and National Security*, 7 August 2005

suspected terrorists without trial when they are identified as a danger to public security (see Figure 5.6). However, apparently we have not abandoned our belief in a sense of global responsibility, since a majority (53 per cent) oppose placing restrictions on immigration from Muslim countries and are undecided about the need for our government to engage in espionage on members of suspect ethnic groups in Canada. Nevertheless, an Ipsos-Reid opinion study conducted before and after the July 2005 bombings in London showed that nine out of ten (89 per cent) Canadians expressed concern that the government should take the threat of Muslim terrorists operating in Canada more seriously (Ipsos-Reid, 2005).

Do these opinions reflect real change and show we have not in fact abandoned the security consciousness that had been thought of as a core value in Canadian society? Some argue that they do: they show that there is continued belief in the role of the state to provide social, economic, and political protection. Nevertheless, during the past twenty-

Figure 5.6  What measures against the war on terrorism do Canadians support?

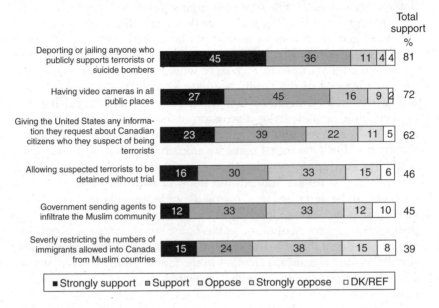

Total
support
%

| | | Total support % |
|---|---|---|
| Deporting or jailing anyone who publicly supports terrorists or suicide bombers | 45 / 36 / 11 / 4 / 4 | 81 |
| Having video cameras in all public places | 27 / 45 / 16 / 9 / 2 | 72 |
| Giving the United States any information they request about Canadian citizens who they suspect of being terrorists | 23 / 39 / 22 / 11 / 5 | 62 |
| Allowing suspected terrorists to be detained without trial | 16 / 30 / 33 / 15 / 6 | 46 |
| Government sending agents to infiltrate the Muslim community | 12 / 33 / 33 / 12 / 10 | 45 |
| Severly restricting the numbers of immigrants allowed into Canada from Muslim countries | 15 / 24 / 38 / 15 / 8 | 39 |

■ Strongly support  ▣ Support  ▢ Oppose  ▢ Strongly oppose  ▢ DK/REF

Q 12-17 As part of the war on terrorism, would you strongly support, support, oppose or strongly oppose the following measures?
Base: Total Sample (N = 1000)
Source: The Strategic Counsel, *Immigration, Terrorism and National Security*, 7 August 2005

five years, *opinions* about the urgency of national security as a government priority have clearly fluctuated. Clearly we were not as concerned about it twenty years ago. As we noted in Chapter 2, research itself may be a source of biased results. Asking respondents about a controversial issue during a period of heightened sensitivity – immediately after a terrorist attack, for example – is not likely to yield an objective assessment. However, the data on this issue suggests that over the longer term, while opinions about national security as an immediate priority may show considerable variation, the strength of belief in a secure and protection-oriented society remains constant.

*Same-Sex Marriage, National Security, and Moral Panic*

In our consideration of same-sex marriage and national security we suggested that changing attitudes about flexible lifestyles and world peace were representative of wide-ranging value changes which have had consequences for Canadian society. Clearly, they are both issues that have generated a great deal of public interest, yet they have not become moral panics. In the first example, although some interest groups have claimed that same-sex marriages would create a threat to conventional definitions of the family, we have shown that this view is not widely shared by Canadians. Gay rights activists might argue that the politicization of the public discussion about equality, the *Charter of Rights and Freedoms*, and the implications for same-sex couples was designed to instigate moral panic by arousing passions against homosexuality. This apparently has not succeeded to any degree with a majority of Canadians. Indeed, the trend of national opinion on this issue cannot be described as showing a 'fundamentally irrational' concern, which of course Goode and Ben-Yehuda (1994) maintain is a distinguishing feature of moral panic. Same-sex marriage was not perceived as a direct threat to the stability of current family arrangements, simply because significant changes in the family have been under way since the sixties. Nor was it widely perceived to have been a denial of human rights since even heterosexual common-law unions have become more accepted by society in recent years and have been recognized under the law.

The reaction to same-sex marriage was also not a moral panic because it cannot be seen as having been disproportional to the threat posed to our values. There was not an exaggerated level of public concern about the sanctity of the family or the rights of individuals. There is no question that religious leaders and politicians have claimed that the definition of marriage should be reserved for heterosexual unions, but the notion that same-sex marriage is evil has not resonated with public opinion most likely because, like heterosexual marriages, these unions are perceived to involve people who feel affection for each other and are prepared to be responsible for each other. Indeed, many have contended that to deny same-sex couples the opportunity to marry if they wish is inconsistent with our view of ourselves as a tolerant and accepting nation. Moreover, by and large the media treatment of the issue has also been even-handed. There has not been an obvious attempt to create a consensus in news coverage of the issue. The media coverage of the published polls has attempted neither to generate hostility towards the behaviour of homosexual couples nor to demonize those who are opposed to the idea to the extent seen in the discussion of health care delivery. All of which leads one to the conclusion that the conditions which are normally present in a moral panic were not there in public reactions to same-sex marriage, which explains why it has clearly not been depicted as a moral crisis for Canadians.

Issues relating to national security were sensationalized during the summer of 2006 because of the arrests of several young Canadians in Ontario who were alleged to be connected to Islamic extremist groups promoting international terrorism. The subsequent media interest focused on the sources of discontent among some Muslim youth and called attention to the potential for violence against others in the country. Despite a general recognition that violence could become a reality, there has as yet been no major grassroots reaction against Muslims of the kind that could lead to moral panic. It can be argued that our security against terrorism is still not identified in public opinion terms as a national emergency, certainly not in the way the delivery of heath care services has been. Quite simply, there has been no panic about national security because terrorism is not perceived to be a threat to the moral order. We have shown that many Canadians understand the potential threat of terrorism, but because there has been no champion for the cause of security, and no prominent interest group promoting fear, there is no clear consensus on the urgency of the problem. Why was public opinion readily mobilized against the threat of attack during the Cold War but not now? First, because nuclear annihilation was widely perceived to be possible in the 1950s and 1960s. Many recognized the threat of nuclear bombing from the skies as they had witnessed it at the end of the Second World War. Second, there were agreed upon enemies or, as we have termed them, 'folk devils' in the form of representatives of a communist ideology widely believed to be set upon world domination to destroy the kind of society we were. Third, the immediacy of media coverage of international tensions during the period was more limited and there was far more uncertainty about issues. Indeed, for many parts of the country media coverage was virtually non-existent. Often it was supplemented by rumour and clearly was not delivered by embedded reporters. Moreover, as we suggested above, our current values have made us more reluctant to agree to adversarial roles in international conflicts.

This is not to dismiss the fact that many realize that Canada could be a target for terrorism. Suspected Islamic extremists have been stereotyped and this may well lead to them being perceived as folk devils in developing moral panic. Media coverage of international terrorism has been plentiful but it is usually reporting what has happened in other countries and this is remote from concerns about security for many Canadians, particularly those who reside in hinterland areas. In terms used by those who analyse moral panics in a risk-conscious culture, the risk-anxiety level (Critcher, 2003) associated with national security is ambiguous relative to the risk perceived to be associated with a health care delivery system that is not working. Moreover, until now the media has not endeavoured to characterize the risk from terrorism in an exaggerated manner nor has it attempted to construct a basis for a moral panic by using opinion polls to quantify the risk. As we have seen, Canadians continue to perceive protection to be of primary importance to them and they expect governments to provide it. Yet they have a much broader understanding than national security in a military sense. This perhaps explains why our response to the threat of international terrorism has been more measured than that of our neighbours.

## Postmodernism and Public Opinion

Postmodern theory has implications for understanding changes in public opinion beyond a consideration of moral panic. It raises questions about our understandings of what public opinion is. Specifically, it challenges our frequent reliance on quantitative techniques to assess opinions and interpret the numerical data once it has been collected. As Lewis (2001) has asked, 'what is the meaning of polls?' His answer is that polls are a numerical representation rather than an actual measure of public opinion: polls construct reality in order to persuade us to accept media and elite depictions of consensus.

### Deconstructing Opinion Polls

As we noted above, social theory is usually identified with the work of Max Weber on legal-rational authority, or the scientific management procedures of Fredrick Taylor. It equates the modernization of cultures with the emergence of numeration procedures. Susan Herbst (1993) argues that one of the consequences of these procedures has been an increasing reliance on research techniques that emphasize information based on calculation and specificity of measures rather than those which emphasize a more qualitative expression of opinions. In the field of polling, this has happened in order to bring greater objectivity, precision, and standardization to public opinion research. However, the need for these procedures means that numeration has all but replaced other ways of gathering opinions. It has valorized quantitative research to the point where real meaning is potentially lost as aggregated numbers are used to represent opinions. 'Numerical descriptions of phenomena and statistical analysis enable the accomplishment of certain types of goals but neglect the achievement of others ... For example, when newspaper journalists use the sample survey to describe public opinion on an issue, they are less likely to conduct in depth interviews with knowledgeable citizens and political activists. One could argue that political activists, who are informed and passionate about issues provide more valuable data than do the anonymous individuals included in the typical opinion poll sample' (Herbst, 1993, p. 19).

While this may be so, consulting knowledgeable individuals may not necessarily lead to objectivity since the views they hold may not be representative of the diversity of opinions in a complex society. Nevertheless, the criticisms offered by Herbst illustrate the problem postmodern thinkers have with numerical analysis. An example to illustrate this problem is the tendency of pollsters to apply mathematical weights to categories of opinion. This is commonly done when a sample actually under-represents some groups in a population (see Chapter 2). The difficulty with this procedure is that mathematical weights are not actual opinions but they tend to be given the authority of opinions in quantitative research. Herbst is illustrating a problem which occurs because our society accepts legal-rational authority over other forms; thus calculations based on numbers are the standard for knowledge. Statistics provide considerable power to present numeric data as truth. In sum, polls are consistent with the drive to rationalization in a modern value system; they are assumed to be an objective, value-free way of generating scientific information.

On the other hand, the postmodern view associated with writers like Michel Foucault and others is that knowledge calculated from numbers which are anonymously collected from individuals and then moulded into a representation of reality through categorization and correlation simply shapes that reality rather than finds it. Moreover, Foucault would maintain that such techniques give considerable power to those who have the polling data to control what we think. In this context polls may be thought of as a form of surveillance of the public. The availability of polls ensures that opinions are constantly being monitored and the data are presented for public consumption or used to mobilize public consensus in desired directions.

Deconstructing quantitative opinion polls leads one to give greater consideration to the complexity of opinion since a culture that challenges and sometimes rejects rational authority would challenge the validity of opinions based on quantitative research techniques as well. From a postmodern perspective, numerical calculations represent the mood of the public in only the most superficial way. Non-survey methods would provide a medium for a more free expression of opinions than a structured questionnaire might permit. As discussed in Chapter 2, focus groups which allow the researcher to observe the formation of opinions in the context of group interaction, or even participant observation where researchers engage in intensive involvement in the formation of opinions over a lengthy period of time, would allow for more penetrating analysis than numerically based polls.

The old caution, 'figures lie and liars figure' may also capture a desire to deconstruct opinion polls. Given the often contradictory findings which are produced in quantitative surveys, usually blamed on poor study designs, unrepresentative samples, and incorrect conclusions from correlation analysis (see Jackson, 1995, p. 39), it could be argued that polls are not that useful in measuring opinions. Shiraev and Sobel (2006) report that confidence in poll numbers has undergone considerable change since the early years of opinion surveys when a majority viewed their predictive powers to be highly accurate. They show that even in the 1990s, two out of three Americans believed that polls work in the public interest. However, by the year 2000, a majority of those (55 per cent) questioned about the value and accuracy of polls said that they get it right only some of the time. 'Americans these days tend to be more skeptical about polling accuracy. When Fox news asked registered voters whether opinion polls represent what people think about important issues, two-thirds of respondents were skeptical. Almost one-third nevertheless believed the surveys are accurate' (Shiraev and Sobel, 2006, p. 47).

In summary, a deconstruction of opinion polling reveals some of the shortcomings of the accepted basis for reporting how the public thinks. It also raises questions about the empowerment of the individuals and groups who have used polls to present their definition of social reality. From this perspective one of the social consequences of polling is the ability to create the impression of a consensus on issues which may not be there at all. The most potent example is the presentation of polls on social issues as a basis for making public policy decisions. Postmodern theory would suggest that the idea of an opinion that is shared by all those who are considered to be the public cannot be accepted because of changing definitions of the term public. The operational definition, which is used in most polls, is to include anybody in a relevant population who is over eighteen. However, even this definition of the public means only those who are of interest relative to the issue being researched in the poll, i.e., the 'population' which has been selected for study, rather than the entire population who may have opinions on the issue under investigation.

Another problem raised by those who deconstruct opinion polls is imposing structure on data. There is a fundamental contradiction between interpretation and letting the poll speak for the public. As we noted above, numerical representations of individual opinions and beliefs that are categorized and calculated is seen as imposing a structure on them that may not exist. Many would argue that data cannot speak for itself. However, interpreting the meaning of opinion data by looking for relationships between variables, such as the internal consistency among a battery of opinions on an issue or correlating political attitudes to opinions on other social issues, presumes they are somehow related in an orderly way. This premise is rejected by those who do not see underlying rationality among the opinions people express and would argue that opinions are volatile and interests are transient. In other words they would not accept that the method used can yield a structure in public opinion which may not always be present.

## Summary

Understanding public opinion in Canada is difficult because it is frequently subject to change. In this chapter we have considered some of the sources of change and stability in Canadian society which have both influenced and been influenced by public opinion. We have considered how demographic change has influenced our cultural makeup as a nation, what we value, how we spend our time, as well as the sources of our satisfaction or discontent with day to day life. However, Canadians are differentiated by the value communities which can be identified by varying lifestyles and opinions as much as they can by demographic characteristics.

The dynamics of change and stability in public opinion are illustrated by tracking the way national policy issues have been viewed during recent years. We have shown that opinions about same-sex marriage have changed significantly, going from widespread disapproval of these unions to a belief by the majority that same-sex couples should have the same rights as other married couples. Yet these opinions also reflect continued support for marriage and the family. We have also shown that Canadians who have usually not been concerned about threats to national security have recently shown a greater willingness to accept a policy of greater security arrangements It is premature, however, to conclude that these opinion changes reflect moral panic rather than a typically Canadian moderate reaction to current events.

Postmodern theory is seen by many to offer the best way of explaining the complexity of the cultural changes and continuities that are often reflected in public opinion. But postmodern theory has also raised fundamental questions about the quantitative techniques by which opinions are collated and then offered as an expression of shared beliefs. It raises questions about the power of analysts to interpret adequately the diversity of individual opinions on the basis of snapshots of numerical information. And, since the data do not speak for themselves, the analyst is left to create an underlying order where none may exist. Thus it leads some to ponder what opinion polls actually tell us.

# Conclusion: Polling and Public Opinion

Public opinion polls are an important medium for understanding life in contemporary Canada. This book was written to appeal to those who wish to know more about polls and develop some familiarity with the tools used by those who are engaged in doing them. One objective has been to show readers that the relationship between public opinion and polling extends well beyond politics and the study of voting. Public opinion research, which had its roots in political-attitude studies, has assumed a central place in other subjects of social investigation. In fact, we have explored the art and science of polling in a variety of contexts, ranging from polls dealing with controversial issues which are conducted by governments or interest groups and the media to consumer opinion studies that are conducted by business about products and markets. Throughout these chapters we have focused upon the social basis of public opinion in order to show that views which have been expressed in polls can never be disconnected from community experiences that individuals share. In fact, recognizing this principle is essential to an understanding of change or continuity in public opinion and makes it possible to predict opinion trends in large populations.

Another objective of this book has been to provide readers with information about the meaning of numbers that have largely become the symbols of opinions whether they are presented by the media, by politicians, or in celebrity endorsements. Remember, marketing organizations concerned with consumer attitudes and behaviour as well as political parties that want our reactions to leaders and platforms use quantitative techniques to show what the public thinks. To make sense of the information we are given, we must know something about how the information was acquired and whether accepted rules of science have been followed. Indeed, in this book we have argued that a concentration on techniques of quantification and the ability to convert opinion polls into numbers which can be manipulated mathematically has given a great deal of power to users of this form of measurement. Users of polls can usually manage to make sense of central tendencies in collected views much less ambiguously when they are based on numbers rather than on phrases. More importantly, the value of a good public opinion pollster often depends on an ability to extract the very essence of popular views and give them a voice in a good story much as if they were being expressed by individual respondents. This can be done more readily when numeric comparisons are possible. On the other hand, we have also talked about the dangers of being overconfident that numeration reflects more than a construction of opinion and examined the views of critics who claim that it yields an inaccurate representation of public opinion, simply because numeration interprets answers to superficial questions as a meaningful reality.

Another objective of the book has been to describe the relationship between mass communications and public opinion polls. We have argued that the use of polls in media reporting or as the centerpiece of coverage about controversial issues may involve sensationalism masquerading as news. We have tried to show that the mass media bears some responsibility for attempting to lead public opinion when it uses polls in this manner. Correspondingly, the polls have simply become entertainment when they are used this way; particularly when they are employed in reporting election campaigns to enhance the interest of voters who might otherwise not pay much attention to the campaign. However, the relationship between the media and public opinion is important not simply because the media report controversial news, but also because the media creates opinions and sometimes stimulates discontent when none is present. Above all the media's use of polls in order to manufacture news may contribute to moral panics. As we have shown in earlier chapters, this is particularly likely during a period of unrest, when a steady stream of information about threats to the status quo can inflame passions on both sides of a public debate.

In particular we have drawn attention to the influence of American media on the way Canadians may think about world events. Since international tensions have increased during the past few years, Canadians have become more sensitive to the impact of these events on our own security. And because of the position of Americans on these events, we often turn to American media sources for information and opinions.

In recognizing the importance of these media sources, there is no suggestion that Canadians accept American views uncritically. Yet, when we are exposed to a bombardment of news which is interpreted by American reporters, who not only provide us with American pronunciations for the names of countries but usually evaluate the countries themselves relative to American interests, it is difficult not to be influenced. There is little doubt that what we as Canadians think about world events is associated with the content of news coverage that we receive.

Advertising as another form of mass communication may also be seen as an attempt to steer public opinion in a certain direction by those engaged in promoting a point of view. However, in this case it is about our opinions of products. Advertising sends both direct and subliminal messages about our culture. In many ways it has a more subtle but no less powerful ability to influence or create a frame of reference for lifestyles, aspirations, and needs. The point we made in Chapter 3 is that advertising has enormous potential to construct social reality, in some cases ordering us to act and think according to norms defined as important by those who want us to buy their products. It is as important in influencing the public agenda in Canada as any other type of communication, given the prominent place occupied by advertisements in the various entertainments available today.

This review of public opinion and polling encourages readers to consider why polls are significant to the social policy agenda in Canadian society. Critics have said that acting in response to polls is indicative of a leadership vacuum. Those who interpret polls are said to have too much influence over decisions relating to public policy. We have shown that leaders may be very responsive to information derived from public opinion polls, yet the literature reviewed has not provided clear evidence of policy decisions based exclusively on polling. On the other hand, we have drawn attention to the role the polls have played in identifying strong views among Canadians on what the government should do about controversial national issues, like health care and national security, which clearly have influenced actions taken by political leaders. The implication is that polls are likely to have a permanent place in devising strategies to communicate public policy, but that Canadians won't accept polls as the only basis for government decision making about public policy.

Finally, the book addressed the subject of change and continuity in public opinion. In doing this we confronted the limitations of polling.

The meaning attached to public opinion polls is how well they capture our shared views. We argued that while opinions are situational they are related to enduring societal values. On the other hand, we have also seen that our values may be transformed in response to new technologies, economic circumstances, or even cultural conflicts. Diverse conditions make possible vast differences in values; thus it is of interest to consider whether the notion of world opinion has any real merit. For example, does cultural diversity preclude the possibility of any international consensus on the environment, or will opinions on environmental issues always be ethnocentric? Some argue that a global economy, in which trade depends on good relationships between nations, means that world opinions matter. For example, the opinions of nations about the internal relations within another country now matter a great deal to the way it is viewed as a trading partner. Indeed, it is less likely today that a nation which oppresses its citizens will be a business partner acceptable to other more democratic societies. Moreover, there is evidence for the ability to mobilize the power of world opinion in the efforts of the United Nations to achieve solutions on least on some global issues, such as the AIDS epidemic in African nations. Despite arguments about the erosion of nationalism because of a globalized economy, a positive outcome of more cosmopolitan lifestyles and shared popular cultures is the emergence of similar outlooks and opinions among peoples of different nations.

In concluding this book, I would observe that there is no evidence public opinion polling will become a less acceptable method for the study of collective behaviour in the years ahead. Nevertheless, accepting that polls are best at providing snapshots of today but only estimates of tomorrow should be a guiding principle for those who seek the insights they always offer.

# References

Acland, C. (1994). Cultural survival: Sleeping with the elephant. In D. Glenday & A. Duffy (Eds.), *Canadian society: Understanding and surviving in the 1990s*. Toronto: McClelland & Stewart.

Adams, M. (1997). *Sex in the snow: Canadian social values at the end of the Millennium*. Toronto: Viking Press.

Adams, M. (2003). *Fire and ice: The United States, Canada and the myth of converging values*. Toronto: Penguin Press.

Althaus, S. (2003). *Collective preferences in democratic politics: Opinion surveys and the will of the people*. Cambridge: Cambridge University Press.

Altschuler, B. (1982). *Keeping a finger on the public pulse: Private polling and presidential elections*. Westport, CT: Greenwood Press.

Anderson, K. (1997). Gender and public opinion. In B. Norander & C. Wilcox (Eds.), *Understanding public opinion*. Washington, DC: CQ Press.

Archer, K., & Whitehorn, A. (2001). Opinion structure among party activists: A comparison of New Democrats, Liberals and Conservatives. In H.G. Thorburn & A. Whitehorn (Eds.), *Party politics in Canada* (8th ed.). Scarborough, ON: Prentice-Hall.

Archer, K., et al. (2002). *Parameters of power: Canada's political institution* (3rd ed.). Scarborough, ON: Nelson.

Aron, R. (1967). *Main currents in sociological thought*. New York: Basic Books.

Babbie, E. (1999). *The basics of social research*. Toronto: Wadsworth.

Baer, D., Grabb, E., & Johnson, W. (1990). The values of Canadians and Americans: A critical analysis and reassessment. *Social Forces, 68*(3), 693–713.

Bandura, A., & Walters, H. (1963). *Social learning and personality development*. New York: Holt, Rinehart and Winston.

Banting, K., & Boadway, R. (2004). Defining the sharing community: The federal role in healthcare. In H. Lazer & F. St-Hilaire (Eds.), *Money, politics and healthcare*. Montreal: Institute for Research on Public Policy.

Bardes, B., & Oldendick, R. (2003). *Public opinion: Measuring the American mind*. Belmont, CA: Wadsworth.

Beaujot, R. (1991). *Population change in Canada: The challenges of policy adaptation*. Toronto: McClelland and Stewart.

Beck, U. (1992). *Risk society: Towards a new modernity*. London: Sage.

Bégin, M. (2000, 2 June). Funding not the only crisis in health care. *Globe and Mail*. Retrieved 1 June 2006 from http://www.utoronto.ca/hpme/dhr/commentaries/begin_June2.htm

Bell, D. (1979). 'Communications technology – for better or for worse?' *Harvard Business Review*, May–June, 20–42.

Bennett, W. (2003). *News: The politics of illusion*. New York: Addison Wesley Longman, Inc.

Berelson, B., & Janowitz, M. (Eds.). (1996). *Reader in public opinion and communication*. New York: Free Press.

Berelson, B., & Steiner, G.A. (1967). *Human behavior*. New York: Harcourt, Brace & World.

Best, S., & Keller, D. (1991). *Postmodern theory: Critical interrogations*. New York: Guilford Press.

Bibby, R.W. (1990). *Mosaic madness*. Toronto: Stoddart.

Bischoping, K. (1993). Gender differences in conversation topics: 1922-1990. *Sex Roles, 28*(1-2), 1-18.

Bishop, G.F., Oldendick, R.W., Tuchfarber, A.J., & Bennett, S.E. (1978). The changing structure of mass belief systems: Fact or artifact? *Journal of Politics, 40*(August), 781–787.

Bishop, G.F., Oldendick, R.W., Tuchfarber, A.J., & Bennett, S.E. (1980). 'Pseudo-opinions' on public affairs. *Public Opinion Quarterly, 44*(Summer), 198–209.

Bissoondath, N. (1994). *Selling illusions: The cult of multiculturalism in Canada*. Toronto: Penguin.

Black, J.H. (2002). Representation in the Parliament of Canada: The case of ethnoracial minorities. In J. Everitt & B. O'Neil (Eds.). *Political behaviour: Theory and practice in a Canadian context*. Toronto: Oxford University Press.

Blackburn, R.M., & Beynon, H. (1972). *Perceptions of work: Variations within a factory*. Cambridge: Cambridge University Press.

Blake, D. (1988). Division and cohesion: The major parties. In G. Perlin (Ed.), *Party democracy in Canada*. Scarborough, ON: Prentice Hall.

Blankenship, A.B, Chakrapani, C., & Poole, W.H. (1985). *A history of marketing research in Canada*. Toronto: P.M.R.S.

Blumer, H. (1948). Public opinion and public opinion polling. *American Sociological Review, 13*(October), 542–554.

Blumer, H. (1960). Public opinion and public opinion polling. In D. Katz, D.

Cartwright, S. Eldersveld & A.M. Lee (Eds.), *Public opinion and propaganda*. New York: Holt.

Boyne, R., & Rattansi, A. (1990). *Postmodernism and society*. New York: St. Martin's.

Braverman, H. (1974). *Labor and monopoly capital*. New York: Monthly Review Press.

Breton, R. (1990). The effects of institutions in ethnic communities. In J. Curtis & L. Tepperman (Eds.), *Images of Canada*. Scarborough, ON: Prentice-Hall.

Burnham, P., Gilland, K., Grant, W., & Layton-Henry, Z. (2004). *Research methods in politics*. New York: Palgrave Macmillan.

Burstein, P. (2003). The impact of public opinion on public policy: A review and an agenda. *Political Research Quarterly, S6*(1), 29–40.

Bush, A.J., & Hair, J.F. (1985). An assessment of the mall intercept as a data collection method. *Journal of Marketing Research, 22*, 158-167.

Butler, P.M., & Jarman J. (2004). *The importance of pay and employer loyalty: Job satisfaction among workers in the call centre industry in Atlantic Canada*. Paper presented at the Work, Employment and Society Conference, University of Manchester, England, 1–3 September.

Canadian Institute of Public Opinion. (1970). *The Gallup Report*. Toronto: Gallup, 12 December.

Canadian Broadcasting Corporation. (2005). Chrétien defends sponsorship program. 10 February. Retrieved 10 February 2005 from http://www.cbc.ca/story/canada/national/2005/02/08/newsponsorship05028.html.

Chakrapani, C. (Ed.). (2000). *Marketing research: State of the art perspective*. American Marketing Association.

Chard, J., & Renaud, V. (2000). Visible minorities in Toronto, Vancouver and Montreal. In *Canadian Social Trends* (Vol. 3). Toronto: Thompson Educational Publishing.

Chomsky, N., & Herman, E. (1988). *Manufacturing consent: The political economy of the mass media*. New York: Pantheon Books.

Clement, W. (1988). *The challenge of class analysis*. Ottawa: Carleton University Press.

Cohen, S. (1972). *Folk devils and moral panics: The creation of the mods and rockers*. New York: Blackwell.

Cohen, S. (1980). *Folk devils and moral panics: The creation of mods and rockers*. (2nd ed.). New York: St. Martin's Press.

Converse, P.E. (1964). The nature of belief systems in mass publics. In D.E. Apter (Ed.), *Ideology and discontent*. New York: Free Press.

Converse, P.E. (1970). Attitudes and non-attitudes: Continuation of a dialogue. In E.R. Tufte (Ed.), *The quantitative analysis of social problems* (pp. 168–189). Reading, MA: Addison-Wesley.

Converse, P.E. (1987). Changing conceptions of public opinion in the political process. *Public Opinion Quarterly, 51*(Winter), S12–S24.

Cook, F.L., et al. (1983). Media and agenda setting: Effects on the public, interest group leaders, policy makers, and policy. *Public Opinion Quarterly, 47*(1), 16–35.

Crespi, I. (1989). *Public opinion, polls and democracy.* Boulder, CO: Westview.

Critcher, C. (2003). *Moral panics and the media.* Philadelphia: Open University Press.

Dawson, L. (1998). *Comprehending cults: The sociology of new religious movements.* Toronto: Oxford University Press.

Dawson, R., Prewitt, K., & Dawson, K. (1977). *Political socialization.* Boston: Little Brown.

Dayan, D., & Katz, E. (1992). *Media events: The live broadcasting of history.* Cambridge, MA: Harvard University Press.

Decima Research. (1987). *Decima Quarterly Report.* Toronto: Author, June.

Decima Research. (1989). *Decima Quarterly Report.* Toronto: Author, December.

deVaus, D.A. (1991). *Surveys in social research* (3rd ed.). London: UCL Press.

Dillman, D.A. (1978). *Mail and telephone surveys: The total design method.* New York: Wiley.

Dillman, D.A. (2000). *Mail and internet surveys: The total design method* (2nd ed.). New York: Wiley.

Doern, G.B., & Phidd, R. (1983). *Canadian public policy: Ideas, structure, process.* Toronto: Methuen.

Doern, G.B., & Phidd, R. (1992). *Canadian public policy: Ideas, structure, process* (2nd ed.). Scarborough, ON: Nelson Canada.

Doern, G.B., & Tomlin, B.W. (1991). *Faith and fear: The free trade story.* Toronto: Stoddart.

Durand, C. (2005). Opinion polls and the Canada Election Act. *Electoral Insight, 7*(1), 28–31.

Dyck, R. (2004). *Canadian politics: Critical approaches* (4th ed.). Scarborough, ON: Thomson Canada.

EKOS Research. (2003). *Toronto Star/La Presse* Poll. http://ekos.com/admin/articles/2/feb2003.pdf.

EKOS Research. (2004). *Press release Federal Election Campaign 2004: Approaching stalemate?* Ottawa: Author.

Elkin, F. (1975). Communications media and identity formation in Canada. In B.D. Singer (Ed.), *Communications in Canadian society* (2nd ed.). Toronto: Copp Clark.

Emery, C. (1994). *Public opinion polling in Canada*. Canada: Library of Parliament Research Branch.

Erikson, R., Tedin, K., & Luttbeg, N. (1980). *American public opinion: Its origins, content and impact* (2nd ed.). New York: Wiley.

Erikson, R., & Tedin, K. (2001). *American public opinion: Its origins, content and impact* (6th ed.). New York: Addison Wesley Longman.

Erskine, H. (1971). The polls: Women's role. *Public Opinion Quarterly, 35,* 275–290.

Everitt, J., & O'Neill, B. (Eds.). (2002). *Citizen politics: Research and theory in Canadian political behaviour*. Oxford: Oxford University Press.

Firestone, O. (1970). *The public persuader: Government advertising*. Toronto: Methuen.

Fletcher, F. (Ed.). (1991). *Media, elections and democracy*. Toronto: Dundurn.

Foot, D.K. (1998). *Boom, bust & echo 2000: Profiting from the demographic shift in the new millennium*. Toronto: Macfarlane, Walter & Ross.

Fox, P., & White, G. (Eds.). (1991). *Politics: Canada* (7th ed.). Toronto: McGraw-Hill Ryerson.

Frideres, J.S., & Gadacz, R.R. (2005). *Aboriginal peoples in Canada* (7th ed.). Toronto: Pearson Prentice Hall.

Friscolanti, M., Gatehouse, J., & Gillis, C. (2006, 19 June). Homegrown terror: It's not over. *Maclean's*, 18–26.

Frizzell, A. (1991). The perils of polling – as exemplified in the '88 election. In P. Fox & G. White (Eds.), *Politics: Canada*. Toronto: McGraw-Hill Ryerson.

Fukuyama, F. (1999). *The great disruption: Human nature and the reconstitution of social order*. New York: Simon & Shuster.

Gagnon, A.G., & Tanguay, A.B. (Eds.). (1989). *Canadian parties in transition: Discourse, organization, and representation*. Scarborough, ON: Nelson Canada.

Gallup, G. (Ed.). (1972). *The Gallup poll: Public opinion, 1935-71*. New York: Random House.

Gallup, G. (1985). *The Gallup poll: Public opinion 1984*. Princeton: Gallup.

Gatehouse, J. (2002, 30 December). Why so cranky? *Maclean's*, 24–28.

Gibbins, R. (1994). *Conflict and unity: An introduction to Canadian political life*. Scarborough, ON: Nelson Canada.

Gidengil, E. (2005). Missing the message: Young adults and the election issues. *Electoral Insight, 7*(1), 6–11.

Gillis, C. (2004, 5 April). The rude age. *Maclean's*, 28–32.

Goffman, E. (1967). *Interaction ritual*. New York: Pantheon.

Goffman, E. (1979). *Gender advertisements*. New York: Harper & Row.

Goldfarb, M., & Axworthy, T. (1988). *Marching to a different drummer: As essay on the Liberals and Conservatives in convention*. Toronto: Stoddart.

Goldthorpe, J.H., et al. (1968). *The affluent worker: Political attitudes*. London: Cambridge University Press.

Goode, E., & Ben-Yehuda, N. (1994). *Moral panics: The social construction of deviance*. Malden, MA: Blackwell.

Grabb, E., & Curtis, J. (2005). *Regions apart: The four societies of Canada and the United States*. Don Mills, ON: Oxford University Press.

Graber, D. (2002). *Mass media and American politics* (6th ed.). Washington, DC: CQ Press.

Grant, G. (1965). *Lament for a nation: The defeat of Canadian nationalism*. Toronto: McClelland & Stewart.

Gray, G., & Guppy, N. (1999). *Successful surveys: Research methods and practice* (2nd ed.). Toronto: Harcourt Brace.

Greenberg, A., & Rivers, D. (2001). Pioneer days: The promise of online polling. *Public Perspective, 12*(March/April), 40–41.

Gregg, A., & Posner, M. (1990). *The big picture: What Canadians think about almost everything*. Toronto: Mcfarlane, Walter & Ross.

Grenier, M. (Ed.). (1992). *Critical studies of Canadian mass media*. Toronto: Butterworths.

Gwyn, R. (1962). Ad-men and scientists run this election. In P.W. Fox (Ed.), *Politics: Canada*. Toronto: McGraw-Hill of Canada.

Hannigan, J.A. (1995). Canadian media ownership and control in an age of global megamedia empires. In B.D. Singer (Ed.), *Communications in Canadian Society*. Toronto: Nelson.

Harrison, B. (1994). *Lean and mean: The changing landscape of corporate power in the age of flexibility*. New York: Basic Books.

Harrison, T., & Friesen, J.W. (2004). *Canadian society in the twenty-first century: A historical sociological approach*. Toronto: Pearson Prentice Hall.

Hawaleshka, D. (2002, 17 June). Measuring health care. *Maclean's*, 23–30.

Heith, D. (2004). *Polling to govern: Public opinion and presidential leadership*. Stanford: Stanford University Press.

Hennessy, B. (1970). *Public opinion* (2nd ed.). Belmont, CA: Wadsworth.

Herbst, S. (1993). *Numbered voices: How opinion polling has shaped American politics*. Chicago: University of Chicago Press.

Hill, K.Q. (1998). The policy agendas of the president and the mass public: A research validation and extension. *American Journal of Political Science, 42*(4), 1328–1334.

Hiller, H.H. (2000). *Canadian society: A macro analysis* (4th ed.). Toronto: Pearson Prentice Hall.

Hinckley, R. (1992). *People, polls, and policymakers: American public opinion and national security.* New York: Lexington Books.

Hovland, C.I., Janis, I.L., & Kelley, H.H. (1953). *Communications and persuasion.* New Haven, CT: Yale University Press.

Howlett, M. (1997). Issue-attention and punctuated equilibria models reconsidered: An empirical examination of the dynamics of agenda-setting in Canada. *Canadian Journal of Political Science, 30*(1), 3–30.

Hoy, C. (1989). *Margin of error: Pollsters and the manipulation of Canadian politics.* Toronto: Key Porter.

Hubbard, R.C. (1994). Sex and the selling of male fragrances. In L. Manca & A. Manca (Eds.), *Gender & Utopia in advertising: A critical reader.* Lisle, IL: Procopian Press.

Huff, D. (1954). *How to lie with statistics.* New York: W.W. Norton & Company.

Inglehart, R. (1997). *Modernization and postmodernization: Cultural, economic, and political change in 43 societies.* Princeton, NJ: Princeton University Press.

Ingelhart, R., & Norris, P. (2003). *Rising tide: Gender equality and cultural change around the world.* New York: Cambridge University Press.

Ipsos Reid. (2005). Canadians offer opinions in wake of attack in London. 16 July. http://ipos-na.com/news/press-release.cfm?id=2736.

Jackson, R.J., & Jackson, D. (2006). *Politics in Canada: Culture, institutions, behaviour and public policy* (6th ed.). Toronto: Pearson Prentice Hall.

Jackson, W. (1999). *Methods: Doing social research* (2nd ed.). Scarborough, ON: Prentice Hall Allyn and Bacon Canada.

Jacobs, L., & Shapiro, R. (2000). *Politicians don't pander: Political manipulation and the loss of democratic responsiveness.* Chicago: The University of Chicago Press.

Janis, I. (1972). *Victims of groupthink.* Boston: Houghton-Mifflin.

Jennings, M.K. (1992). Ideological thinking among mass publics and political elites. *Public Opinion Quarterly, 56*, 419–441.

Johnston, R. (1986). *Public opinion and public policy in Canada: Questions of confidence.* Toronto: University of Toronto Press.

Johnston, R. (1988). The ideological structure of opinion on policy. In G. Perlin (Ed.), *Party democracy in Canada.* Scarborough, ON: Prentice-Hall.

Jones, N. (1995). *Soundbites and spin doctors: How politicians manipulate the media – and vice versa.* London: Cassell.

Kagay, M. (1999). Public opinion and polling during presidential scandal and impeachment. *Public Opinion Quarterly, 63*, 449–463.

Katz, D. (1972). The functional approach to the study of attitudes. In J.B. Cohen (Ed.), *Behavioral Science Foundations of Consumer Behavior.* New York: Free Press.

Kennedy, M. (2000, 14 December). Polls show mistrust of governments' medicare spending. *Ottawa Citizen*. Retrieved 1 June 2006, from http://www.pollara.com/Library/News/mistrust.html.

Kernell, S. (1986). *Going public: New strategies of presidential leadership*. Washington, DC: CQ Press.

Key, V.O., Jr. (1961). *Public opinion and American democracy*. New York: Knopf.

Kilbourne, J. (1999). *Deadly persuasion: Why women and girls must fight the addictive power of advertising*. New York: Free Press.

Kilbourne, J. (2003). Advertising and disconnection. In T. Reichert & J. Lambiase (Eds.), *Sex in advertising: Perspectives on the erotic appeal*. Mahwah, NJ: Erlbaum.

King, Henry. (1968). The beginning of marketing research in Canada. In W.H. Mahatoo (Ed.), *Marketing research in Canada*. Toronto: Thomas Nelson.

Kohut, A. (1986). Rating the polls: The views of media elites and the general public. *Public Opinion Quarterly, 50*(Spring), 1–9.

Kornberg, A., & Clarke, H. (1994). Beliefs about democracy and satisfaction with democratic government. *Political Research Quarterly, 46*, 537–564.

Krahn, H.J., & Lowe, G.S. (2002). *Work, industry and Canadian society*. Scarborough, ON: Nelson Canada.

Kumar, K. (1995). *From post-industrial to post-modern society: New theories of the contemporary world*. Oxford: Blackwell.

Kymlicka, W. (1998). *Finding our way*. Toronto: Oxford University Press.

Labovitz, S., & Hagedorn, R. (1976). *Introduction to social research* (2nd ed.). Toronto: McGraw-Hill.

Lachapelle, G. (1991). Polls and the media in Canadian elections. *The Collected Research Studies*, Royal Commission on Electoral Reform and Party Financing. Toronto: Dundurn.

Landes, R.G. (1995). *The Canadian polity: A comparative introduction*. Scarborough, ON: Prentice Hall.

Laschinger, J., & Stevens, G. (1992). *Leaders and lesser mortals*. Toronto: Key Porter.

Lazar, H., & St-Hilaire, F. (Eds.). (2004). *Money, politics and health care: Reconstructing the federal-provincial partnership*. Montreal and Kingston: The Institute for Research on Public Policy.

Lazarsfeld, P., Berelson, B., & Gaudet, H. (1944). *The people's choice*. New York: Columbia University Press.

Lazarsfeld, P., Berelson, B., & Gaudet, H. (1948). *The people's choice* (2nd ed.). New York: Columbia University Press.

LeBon, G. (1896). *The crowd: A study of the popular mind*. London: Ernest Benn.

Lewin, K. (1947). Frontiers in group dynamics. *Human Relations, 1*, 5–41, 143–153.

Lewin, K. (1948). *Resolving social conflicts*. G. Weiss Lewis (Ed.). New York: Harper.

Lewis, J. (2001). *Constructing public opinion: How political elites do what they like and why we seem to go along with it*. New York: Columbia University Press.

Li, P.S. (Ed.). (1999). *Race and ethnic relations in Canada*. Don Mills, ON: Oxford University Press.

Lipmann, W. (1922). *Public opinion*. New York: Harcourt Brace.

Lipset, S.M. (1970). *Revolution and counterrevolution* (2nd ed.). Garden City, NY: Anchor.

Lipset, S. (1990). *Continental divide: The values and institutions of the United States and Canada*. New York: Routledge.

Mackie, M. (1991). *Gender relations in Canada: Further explorations*. Markham, ON: Butterworths.

Manca, L., & Manca, A. (Eds.). (1994). *Gender & utopia in advertising: A critical reader*. Lisle, IL: Procopian.

Marchak, M.P. (1988). *Ideological perspectives on Canada*. Toronto: McGraw-Hill Ryerson.

Margolis, M., & Mauser, G. (1989). *Manipulating public opinion: Essays on public opinion as a dependent variable*. Pacific Grove, CA: Brooks/Cole.

Marshall, R. (1998, June 15). The health report. *Maclean's*, *111*(24), 16–42.

McClosky, H., & Zaller, J. (1984). *The American ethos: Public attitudes towards capitalism and democracy*. Cambridge, MA: Harvard University Press.

McCombs, M.E., Danielian, L., & Wanta, W. (1995). Issues in the news and the public agenda: The agenda-setting tradition. In T.L. Glasser & C.T. Slamon (Eds.), *Public opinion and the communication of consent*. New York: Guilford.

McLuhan, E., & Zingrone, F. (Eds.). (1995). *The Essential McLuhan*. Concord, ON: Anansi.

McLuhan, M. (1995). Understanding media. In E. McLuhan & F. Zingrone (Eds.), *The Essential McLuhan*. Concord, ON: Anansi.

McNair, B. (2002). *Striptease culture: Sex, media and the democratization of desire*. New York: Routledge.

McQuail, D. (1997). *Audience analysis*. Thousand Oaks, CA: Sage Publications.

Mendelsohn, M. (2002) *Canadians' thoughts on their health care system: Preserving the Canadian model through innovation*. Kingston, ON: Queen's University.

Mills, C.W. (1956). *The power elite*. New York: Oxford University Press.

Mills, C.W. (1962). *The Marxists*. New York: Dell.

Monroe, A.D. (1975). *Public opinion in America*. New York: Dodd, Mead.

Monroe, A.D. (1979). Consistency between public preferences and national policy decisions. *American Politics Quarterly*, *7*(January), 3–20.

Monroe, A.D. (1998). Public opinion and policy. *Public Opinion Quarterly*, *62*(Spring), 6–28.

Montreal Economic Institute. (2005, April). *The opinion of Canadians on access to health care*. Montreal: Leger Marketing.

Moore, D.W. (1995). *The superpollsters: How they measure and manipulate public opinion in America*. New York: Four Walls Eight Windows.

Moore, D.W. (1999). Daily tracking polls: Too much 'noise' or revealed insights? *Public Perspective, 10*(4), 27–32.

Nachmias, D., & Nachmias, C. (1987). *Research methods in the social sciences* (3rd ed.). New York: St. Martin's.

Nadeau, R. (2002). Satisfaction with democracy: The Canadian paradox. In N. Nevitte (Ed.), *Value change and governance in Canada*. Toronto: University of Toronto Press.

Nelles, H.V. (2004). *A little history of Canada*. Don Mills, ON: Oxford University Press.

Nesbitt-Larking, P. (2001). *Politics, society, and the media: Canadian perspectives*. Peterborough, ON: Broadview.

Neuman, W. (1986). *The paradox of American politics: Knowledge and opinion in the American electorate*. Cambridge, MA: Harvard University Press.

Neuman, W. (1991). *The future of the mass audience*. Cambridge: Cambridge University Press.

Nevitte, N. (1996). *The decline of deference: Canadian value change in cross-national perspective*. Peterborough, ON: Broadview.

Nevitte, N. (Ed.). (2002). *Value change and governance in Canada*. Toronto: University of Toronto Press.

Newman, P.C. (1995). *The Canadian Revolution: From deference to defiance, 1985–1995*. Toronto: Viking.

Nie, N.H., & Anderson, K. (1974). Mass belief systems revisited: Political change and attitude structure. *Journal of Politics, 36*(August), 541–591.

Nimmo, D., & Bonjean, C. (1972). *Political attitudes and public opinion*. New York: McKay.

Nye, I., & Berardo, F.M. (1973). *The family: Its structure and interaction*. New York: Macmillan.

Oskamp, S. (1977). *Attitudes and opinions*. Englewood Cliffs, NJ: Prentice-Hall.

Page, B.I., & Shapiro, R.Y. (1983). Effects of public opinion on policy. *American Political Science Review, 77*, 175-90.

Page, B.I., & Shapiro, R.Y. (1989). Educating and manipulating the public. In M. Margolis & G. Mauser (Eds.), *Manipulating public opinion: Essays on public opinion as a dependent variable* (pp. 294–320). Pacific Grove, CA: Brooks/Cole.

Page, B.I., & Shapiro, R.Y. (1992). *The rational public: Fifty years of trends in America's policy preferences*. Chicago: University of Chicago Press.

Palmer, H. (1993). Mosaic versus melting pot? Immigration and ethnicity in Canada and the United States. In D. Taras, B. Rasporich & E. Mandel (Eds.), *A passion for identity: An introduction to Canadian studies*. Scarborough, ON: Nelson.

Pammett, J.H., & Dornan, C. (2004). Election night in Canada. In J.H. Pammett and C. Dornan (Eds.), *The Canadian general election of 2004*. Toronto: Dundurn.

Parsons, T. (1964/1951). *The social system*. New York: Free Press.

Parsons, T. (1968). *The structure of social action*. New York: Free Press.

Perlin, G. (Ed.). (1988). *Party democracy in Canada: The politics of national party conventions*. Scarborough, ON: Prentice-Hall.

Petry, F. (1999). The opinion-policy relationship in Canada. *Journal of Politics, 61*(2), 540–50.

Pinard, M., Breton, A., & Breton, R. (1960). *Quebec provincial election study*. Montreal: Groupe de Recherches Sociale / Social Research Group.

Pollara. (2005). *Health care in Canada: Survey and roundtable*. Ottawa: Author.

Porter, J. (1967). *The vertical mosaic*. Toronto: University of Toronto Press.

Pross, A.P. (1992). *Group politics and public policy* (2nd ed.). Don Mills, ON: Oxford University Press.

Public Works and Government Services Canada. (2004). *POR Annual Report 2003–2004. The Public Opinion Research Directorate at Work*. Retrieved 1 November 2004 from http://www.communication.gc.ca/reports_rapports/por_rop/2003-2004/03-04_04_e.html

Ragin, C.C. (1994). *Constructing social research*. Thousand Oaks, CA: Pine Forge Press.

Rao, P.V.L.N. (2002, 12 February). Should opinion polls be banned? *The Hindu*. Retrieved 1 June 2006 from http://www.hinduonnet.com/thehindu/op/2002/02/12/stories/2002021200020100.htm.

Reichert, T., & Lambiase, J. (Eds.). (2003). *Sex in advertising: Perspectives on the erotic appeal*. Mahwah, NJ: Erlbaum.

Riesman, D. (1965). *The lonely crowd: A study of the changing American character*. New Haven, CT: Yale University Press.

Rinehart, J.W. (1991). *The tyranny of work* (4th ed.). Toronto: Harcourt, Brace.

Robertson, R. (1992). *Globalization: Social theory and global culture*. London: Sage.

Romanow, R.J. (Commissioner). (2002). *Building on values: The future of health care in Canada – final report*. Commission on the Future of Health Care in Canada.

Ross, K., & Nightingale, V. (2003). *Media and audiences: New perspectives*. Berkshire: Open University Press.

Sabato, L.J. (1981). *The rise of political consultants: New ways of winning elections.* New York: Basic Books.

Sawatsky, J. (1987). *The insiders: Government, business, and the lobbyists.* Toronto: McClelland and Stewart.

Schaefer, D.R., & Dillman, D.A. (1998). Development of a standard e-mail methodology: Results of an experiment. *Public Opinion Quarterly, 62*(3), 378–97.

Seely, P. (1994). The mirror and the window on the man of the nineties: Portrayals of males in television advertising. In L. Manca (Ed.), *Gender & utopia in advertising.* Lisle, IL: Procopian.

Shapiro, R.Y., & Jacobs, L. (1999). Public opinion and policy making. In C. Glynn, S. Herbst, G. O'Keefe & R. Shapiro (Eds.), *Public opinion.* Boulder, CO: Westview.

Shiraev, E., & Sobel, R. (2006). *People and their opinions: Thinking critically about public opinion.* New York: Pearson Longman.

Siegel, A. (1983). *Politics and the media in Canada* (2nd ed.). Toronto: McGraw-Hill Ryerson.

Siegel, A. (1996). *Politics and the media in Canada.* Toronto: McGraw Hill Ryerson.

Singer, B.D. (1970). Violence, protest and war in television news: The US and Canada compared. *Public Opinion Quarterly, 34*(4), 611–16.

Singer, B.D. (1986). *Advertising & society.* Don Mills, ON: Addison-Wesley.

Singer, B.D. (1995). *Communications in Canadian Society.* Don Mills, ON: Addison-Wesley.

Smith, T.W. (1990). The first straw: A study of the origins of election polls. *Public Opinion Quarterly, 54*(Spring), 21–36.

Soroka, S. (2002). *Agenda-setting dynamics in Canada.* Vancouver: UBC Press.

Stacey, J. & Biblarz, T.J. (2001). (How) Does sexual orientation of parents matter? *American Sociological Review, 65,* 159–183.

Statistics Canada. (2002). *The Daily.* 26 September. Retrieved September 26, 2002 from http://www.statcan.ca/Daily/English/020926/d020926d.htm

Stouffer, S.A., et al. (1949). *The American soldier: Combat and its aftermath.* Princeton, NJ: Princeton University Press.

Strategic Counsel. (2005). Immigration, terrorism and national security. August survey for *The Globe and Mail* and CTV. 7 August.

Taras, D. (1990). *The newsmakers: The media's influence on Canadian politics.* Scarborough, Ontario: Nelson Canada.

Taylor, H. (1995). Horses for courses: How different countries measure public opinion in different ways. *Public Perspective, 6*(2), 3–7.

Taylor, H. (2000a). Does internet research work? Comparing online survey results with telephone survey. *International Journal of Market Research*, 42(1).

Taylor, H. (2000b). Public opinion polls. In C. Chakrapani (Ed.), *Marketing research: State of the art perspective* (pp. 431–453). American Marketing Association.

Taylor, H., Brenner, J, Overmeyer, C., Siegel, J.W., & Terhanian, G. (2001). Touchdown! Online polling scores big in November 2000. *Public Perspective*, 12(March/April), 38–39.

Tepperman, L. & Blaine, J. (1999). *Think twice: Sociology looks at current social issues*. Upper Saddle River, NJ: Prentice Hall.

Thompson, K. (1998). *Moral panics*. London: Routledge.

Thorburn, H.G., & Whitehorn, A. (Eds.). (2001). *Party politics in Canada*. Toronto: Pearson Education.

Tomlinson, J. (1999). *Globalization and culture*. Chicago: University of Chicago Press.

Turcotte, A. (2005). Different strokes: Why young Canadians don't vote. *Electoral Insight*, 7(1), 12–16.

Twitchell, J.B. (2003). Adult and gender. In T. Reichert & J. Lambaise (Eds.), *Sex in advertising*. New York: Erlbaum.

Weinreb, A. (2002, 5 August). Media polls. *Canada Free Press*. Retrieved 1 June 2006 from http://www.canadafreepress.com/2002/media80502.htm

Weissberg, R. (1976). *Public opinion and popular government*. Englewood Cliffs, NJ: Prentice-Hall.

Whitaker, R., & Marcuse, G. (1994). *Cold War Canada: The making of a national insecurity state – 1945-1957*. Toronto: University of Toronto Press.

Wilson-Smith, A. (2004, 25 October). Hey we're not stupid. *Maclean's*, 4.

Winter, J. & Goldman, I. (1995). Mass media and Canadian identity. In B.D. Singer (Ed.), *Communications in Canadian society* (4th ed.). Scarborough, ON: Nelson Canada.

Worcester, R.M. (1980). Pollsters, the press, and political polling in Britain. *Public Opinion Quarterly*, 44, 548-566.

Zaller, J. (1992). *The nature and origins of mass opinion*. Cambridge: Cambridge University Press.

Zetterberg, H. (2004). *U.S. election 1948: The first great controversy about polls, media and social science*. Paper presented at the WAPOR regional conference on Elections, News Media and Public Opinion in Pamplona, Spain, 24–26 November.

# Index